FREE Test Taking Tips Video/DVD Offer

To better serve you, we created videos covering test taking tips that we want to give you for FREE. **These videos cover world-class tips that will help you succeed on your test.**

We just ask that you send us feedback about this product. Please let us know what you thought about it—whether good, bad, or indifferent.

To get your **FREE videos**, you can use the QR code below or email freevideos@studyguideteam.com with "Free Videos" in the subject line and the following information in the body of the email:

>   a. The title of your product
>
>   b. Your product rating on a scale of 1-5, with 5 being the highest
>
>   c. Your feedback about the product

If you have any questions or concerns, please don't hesitate to contact us at info@studyguideteam.com.

Thank you!

CDL Study Guide 2023-2024

CDL Book with 3 Practice Tests
(Questions and Answers)
[5th Edition]

Joshua Rueda

Interested in buying more than 10 copies of our product? Contact us about bulk discounts:
bulkorders@studyguideteam.com

ISBN 13: 9781637754863
ISBN 10: 1637754868

Table of Contents

Welcome

Dear Reader,

Welcome to your new Test Prep Books study guide! We are pleased that you chose us to help you prepare for your exam. There are many study options to choose from, and we appreciate you choosing us. Studying can be a daunting task, but we have designed a smart, effective study guide to help prepare you for what lies ahead.

Whether you're a parent helping your child learn and grow, a high school student working hard to get into your dream college, or a nursing student studying for a complex exam, we want to help give you the tools you need to succeed. We hope this study guide gives you the skills and the confidence to thrive, and we can't thank you enough for allowing us to be part of your journey.

In an effort to continue to improve our products, we welcome feedback from our customers. We look forward to hearing from you. Suggestions, success stories, and criticisms can all be communicated by emailing us at info@studyguideteam.com.

Sincerely,
Test Prep Books Team

FREE Videos/DVD OFFER

Doing well on your exam requires both knowing the test content and understanding how to use that knowledge to do well on the test. We offer completely FREE test taking tip videos. **These videos cover world-class tips that you can use to succeed on your test.**

To get your **FREE videos**, you can use the QR code below or email freevideos@studyguideteam.com with "Free Videos" in the subject line and the following information in the body of the email:

    a. The title of your product
    b. Your product rating on a scale of 1-5, with 5 being the highest
    c. Your feedback about the product

If you have any questions or concerns, please don't hesitate to contact us at info@studyguideteam.com.

1

Quick Overview

As you draw closer to taking your exam, effective preparation becomes more and more important. Thankfully, you have this study guide to help you get ready. Use this guide to help keep your studying on track and refer to it often.

This study guide contains several key sections that will help you be successful on your exam. The guide contains tips for what you should do the night before and the day of the test. Also included are test-taking tips. Knowing the right information is not always enough. Many well-prepared test takers struggle with exams. These tips will help equip you to accurately read, assess, and answer test questions.

A large part of the guide is devoted to showing you what content to expect on the exam and to helping you better understand that content. In this guide are practice test questions so that you can see how well you have grasped the content. Then, answer explanations are provided so that you can understand why you missed certain questions.

Don't try to cram the night before you take your exam. This is not a wise strategy for a few reasons. First, your retention of the information will be low. Your time would be better used by reviewing information you already know rather than trying to learn a lot of new information. Second, you will likely become stressed as you try to gain a large amount of knowledge in a short amount of time. Third, you will be depriving yourself of sleep. So be sure to go to bed at a reasonable time the night before. Being well-rested helps you focus and remain calm.

Be sure to eat a substantial breakfast the morning of the exam. If you are taking the exam in the afternoon, be sure to have a good lunch as well. Being hungry is distracting and can make it difficult to focus. You have hopefully spent lots of time preparing for the exam. Don't let an empty stomach get in the way of success!

When travelling to the testing center, leave earlier than needed. That way, you have a buffer in case you experience any delays. This will help you remain calm and will keep you from missing your appointment time at the testing center.

Be sure to pace yourself during the exam. Don't try to rush through the exam. There is no need to risk performing poorly on the exam just so you can leave the testing center early. Allow yourself to use all of the allotted time if needed.

Remain positive while taking the exam even if you feel like you are performing poorly. Thinking about the content you should have mastered will not help you perform better on the exam.

Once the exam is complete, take some time to relax. Even if you feel that you need to take the exam again, you will be well served by some down time before you begin studying again. It's often easier to convince yourself to study if you know that it will come with a reward!

Test-Taking Strategies

1. Predicting the Answer

When you feel confident in your preparation for a multiple-choice test, try predicting the answer before reading the answer choices. This is especially useful on questions that test objective factual knowledge. By predicting the answer before reading the available choices, you eliminate the possibility that you will be distracted or led astray by an incorrect answer choice. You will feel more confident in your selection if you read the question, predict the answer, and then find your prediction among the answer choices. After using this strategy, be sure to still read all of the answer choices carefully and completely. If you feel unprepared, you should not attempt to predict the answers. This would be a waste of time and an opportunity for your mind to wander in the wrong direction.

2. Reading the Whole Question

Too often, test takers scan a multiple-choice question, recognize a few familiar words, and immediately jump to the answer choices. Test authors are aware of this common impatience, and they will sometimes prey upon it. For instance, a test author might subtly turn the question into a negative, or he or she might redirect the focus of the question right at the end. The only way to avoid falling into these traps is to read the entirety of the question carefully before reading the answer choices.

3. Looking for Wrong Answers

Long and complicated multiple-choice questions can be intimidating. One way to simplify a difficult multiple-choice question is to eliminate all of the answer choices that are clearly wrong. In most sets of answers, there will be at least one selection that can be dismissed right away. If the test is administered on paper, the test taker could draw a line through it to indicate that it may be ignored; otherwise, the test taker will have to perform this operation mentally or on scratch paper. In either case, once the obviously incorrect answers have been eliminated, the remaining choices may be considered. Sometimes identifying the clearly wrong answers will give the test taker some information about the correct answer. For instance, if one of the remaining answer choices is a direct opposite of one of the eliminated answer choices, it may well be the correct answer. The opposite of obviously wrong is obviously right! Of course, this is not always the case. Some answers are obviously incorrect simply because they are irrelevant to the question being asked. Still, identifying and eliminating some incorrect answer choices is a good way to simplify a multiple-choice question.

4. Don't Overanalyze

Anxious test takers often overanalyze questions. When you are nervous, your brain will often run wild, causing you to make associations and discover clues that don't actually exist. If you feel that this may be a problem for you, do whatever you can to slow down during the test. Try taking a deep breath or counting to ten. As you read and consider the question, restrict yourself to the particular words used by the author. Avoid thought tangents about what the author *really* meant, or what he or she was *trying* to say. The only things that matter on a multiple-choice test are the words that are actually in the question. You must avoid reading too much into a multiple-choice question, or supposing that the writer meant something other than what he or she wrote.

3

5. No Need for Panic

It is wise to learn as many strategies as possible before taking a multiple-choice test, but it is likely that you will come across a few questions for which you simply don't know the answer. In this situation, avoid panicking. Because most multiple-choice tests include dozens of questions, the relative value of a single wrong answer is small. As much as possible, you should compartmentalize each question on a multiple-choice test. In other words, you should not allow your feelings about one question to affect your success on the others. When you find a question that you either don't understand or don't know how to answer, just take a deep breath and do your best. Read the entire question slowly and carefully. Try rephrasing the question a couple of different ways. Then, read all of the answer choices carefully. After eliminating obviously wrong answers, make a selection and move on to the next question.

6. Confusing Answer Choices

When working on a difficult multiple-choice question, there may be a tendency to focus on the answer choices that are the easiest to understand. Many people, whether consciously or not, gravitate to the answer choices that require the least concentration, knowledge, and memory. This is a mistake. When you come across an answer choice that is confusing, you should give it extra attention. A question might be confusing because you do not know the subject matter to which it refers. If this is the case, don't eliminate the answer before you have affirmatively settled on another. When you come across an answer choice of this type, set it aside as you look at the remaining choices. If you can confidently assert that one of the other choices is correct, you can leave the confusing answer aside. Otherwise, you will need to take a moment to try to better understand the confusing answer choice. Rephrasing is one way to tease out the sense of a confusing answer choice.

7. Your First Instinct

Many people struggle with multiple-choice tests because they overthink the questions. If you have studied sufficiently for the test, you should be prepared to trust your first instinct once you have carefully and completely read the question and all of the answer choices. There is a great deal of research suggesting that the mind can come to the correct conclusion very quickly once it has obtained all of the relevant information. At times, it may seem to you as if your intuition is working faster even than your reasoning mind. This may in fact be true. The knowledge you obtain while studying may be retrieved from your subconscious before you have a chance to work out the associations that support it. Verify your instinct by working out the reasons that it should be trusted.

8. Key Words

Many test takers struggle with multiple-choice questions because they have poor reading comprehension skills. Quickly reading and understanding a multiple-choice question requires a mixture of skill and experience. To help with this, try jotting down a few key words and phrases on a piece of scrap paper. Doing this concentrates the process of reading and forces the mind to weigh the relative importance of the question's parts. In selecting words and phrases to write down, the test taker thinks about the question more deeply and carefully. This is especially true for multiple-choice questions that are preceded by a long prompt.

9. Subtle Negatives

One of the oldest tricks in the multiple-choice test writer's book is to subtly reverse the meaning of a question with a word like *not* or *except*. If you are not paying attention to each word in the question, you can easily be led astray by this trick. For instance, a common question format is, "Which of the following is…?" Obviously, if the question instead is, "Which of the following is not…?," then the answer will be quite different. Even worse, the test makers are aware of the potential for this mistake and will include one answer choice that would be correct if the question were not negated or reversed. A test taker who misses the reversal will find what he or she believes to be a correct answer and will be so confident that he or she will fail to reread the question and discover the original error. The only way to avoid this is to practice a wide variety of multiple-choice questions and to pay close attention to each and every word.

10. Reading Every Answer Choice

It may seem obvious, but you should always read every one of the answer choices! Too many test takers fall into the habit of scanning the question and assuming that they understand the question because they recognize a few key words. From there, they pick the first answer choice that answers the question they believe they have read. Test takers who read all of the answer choices might discover that one of the latter answer choices is actually *more* correct. Moreover, reading all of the answer choices can remind you of facts related to the question that can help you arrive at the correct answer. Sometimes, a misstatement or incorrect detail in one of the latter answer choices will trigger your memory of the subject and will enable you to find the right answer. Failing to read all of the answer choices is like not reading all of the items on a restaurant menu: you might miss out on the perfect choice.

11. Spot the Hedges

One of the keys to success on multiple-choice tests is paying close attention to every word. This is never truer than with words like almost, most, some, and sometimes. These words are called "hedges" because they indicate that a statement is not totally true or not true in every place and time. An absolute statement will contain no hedges, but in many subjects, the answers are not always straightforward or absolute. There are always exceptions to the rules in these subjects. For this reason, you should favor those multiple-choice questions that contain hedging language. The presence of qualifying words indicates that the author is taking special care with their words, which is certainly important when composing the right answer. After all, there are many ways to be wrong, but there is only one way to be right! For this reason, it is wise to avoid answers that are absolute when taking a multiple-choice test. An absolute answer is one that says things are either all one way or all another. They often include words like *every*, *always*, *best*, and *never*. If you are taking a multiple-choice test in a subject that doesn't lend itself to absolute answers, be on your guard if you see any of these words.

12. Long Answers

In many subject areas, the answers are not simple. As already mentioned, the right answer often requires hedges. Another common feature of the answers to a complex or subjective question are qualifying clauses, which are groups of words that subtly modify the meaning of the sentence. If the question or answer choice describes a rule to which there are exceptions or the subject matter is complicated, ambiguous, or confusing, the correct answer will require many words in order to be expressed clearly and accurately. In essence, you should not be deterred by answer choices that seem

5

excessively long. Oftentimes, the author of the text will not be able to write the correct answer without offering some qualifications and modifications. Your job is to read the answer choices thoroughly and completely and to select the one that most accurately and precisely answers the question.

13. Restating to Understand

Sometimes, a question on a multiple-choice test is difficult not because of what it asks but because of how it is written. If this is the case, restate the question or answer choice in different words. This process serves a couple of important purposes. First, it forces you to concentrate on the core of the question. In order to rephrase the question accurately, you have to understand it well. Rephrasing the question will concentrate your mind on the key words and ideas. Second, it will present the information to your mind in a fresh way. This process may trigger your memory and render some useful scrap of information picked up while studying.

14. True Statements

Sometimes an answer choice will be true in itself, but it does not answer the question. This is one of the main reasons why it is essential to read the question carefully and completely before proceeding to the answer choices. Too often, test takers skip ahead to the answer choices and look for true statements. Having found one of these, they are content to select it without reference to the question above. Obviously, this provides an easy way for test makers to play tricks. The savvy test taker will always read the entire question before turning to the answer choices. Then, having settled on a correct answer choice, he or she will refer to the original question and ensure that the selected answer is relevant. The mistake of choosing a correct-but-irrelevant answer choice is especially common on questions related to specific pieces of objective knowledge. A prepared test taker will have a wealth of factual knowledge at their disposal, and should not be careless in its application.

15. No Patterns

One of the more dangerous ideas that circulates about multiple-choice tests is that the correct answers tend to fall into patterns. These erroneous ideas range from a belief that B and C are the most common right answers, to the idea that an unprepared test-taker should answer "A-B-A-C-A-D-A-B-A." It cannot be emphasized enough that pattern-seeking of this type is exactly the WRONG way to approach a multiple-choice test. To begin with, it is highly unlikely that the test maker will plot the correct answers according to some predetermined pattern. The questions are scrambled and delivered in a random order. Furthermore, even if the test maker was following a pattern in the assignation of correct answers, there is no reason why the test taker would know which pattern he or she was using. Any attempt to discern a pattern in the answer choices is a waste of time and a distraction from the real work of taking the test. A test taker would be much better served by extra preparation before the test than by reliance on a pattern in the answers.

Bonus Content

We host multiple bonus items online, including all three practice tests in digital format. Scan the QR code or go to this link to access this content:

testprepbooks.com/bonus/cdl

The first time you access the page, you will need to register as a "new user" and verify your email address.

If you have any issues, please email support@testprepbooks.com

Introduction to the CDL Test

Each state is federally mandated to have certain minimum requirements for issuing commercial driver's licenses (CDLs).

This document is designed to serve as an informational guide to the various sections of the CDL test. It does not outline all the federal and state requirements that are necessary to operate a commercial motor vehicle (CMV). Information on specific CMV operation requirements may be obtained from your state Division of Motor Vehicles (DMV), or the Federal Motor Carrier Safety Administration (FMCSA).

There are three different types of CDLs:

- **Class A**: A driver qualifies for this license if the vehicles' they are driving have gross combination weight rating of 26,001 pounds or more as a result of the vehicle(s) in tow having a gross vehicle weight rating (GVWR) of more than 10,000 pounds.

- **Class B**: A driver qualifies for this license if the single vehicle they drive has a GVWR of 26,001 pounds or more; they can also qualify if their vehicle is towing another vehicle with a GVWR not exceeding 10,000 pounds.

- **Class C**: A driver qualifies for this license if their vehicle is intended to carry multiple passengers including the driver; they also qualify if their vehicle is used to transport hazardous materials, select agents, toxins and if it necessitates federal placarding. Rules for hazardous materials may vary by state, so check with your state DMV for specifics.

Commercial Driver License Tests

Obtaining a commercial driver license (CDL) is a two-part process involving a knowledge (written) portion and a skills (driving) portion.

Knowledge Tests

The knowledge portion consists of one or more knowledge tests. The one(s) you will need to take will depend on the license class and endorsements you are seeking to acquire. The CDL knowledge tests include:

- The general knowledge test, required for everyone taking the CDL exam

- The passenger transport test, required for all bus drivers

- The air brakes test, required for operation of vehicles with air brakes; this includes air over hydraulic brakes.

- The combination vehicles test, necessary for those who wish to operate combination vehicles

- The hazardous materials test, required for drivers hauling hazardous materials; a Transportation Security Administration (TSA) background check is also required for this endorsement.

- The tank vehicle test, necessary for drivers hauling liquid or gaseous substances in one or more tanks; check with your state DMV for the specific individual rated capacity for your vehicle.

- The doubles/triples test, necessary for those operating double or triple trailers

- The school bus test, necessary for school bus drivers

Skills Tests

Once you obtain a passing score on the required knowledge test(s), you will need to take the CDL skills tests, using the type of vehicle for which you seek to be licensed. You will be tested on three types of skills: pre-trip inspection, basic vehicle control, and on-road driving. When taking the Pre-Trip Inspection Test, you cannot use a vehicle with mechanisms that are marked or labeled in any way.

Pre-Trip Vehicle Inspection
This test will determine your knowledge of all the checks necessary prior to safe operation of your vehicle. You will need to perform a pre-trip inspection, specifying the vehicle components you would check and the reasoning behind each.

Basic Vehicle Control
This test determines how well you operate the vehicle. You will need to drive your vehicle forward and backward, and turn it within a designated space indicated by traffic lanes, cones, barriers, etc. The examiner will explain the specifics of each test segment.

On-Road Test
This test determines how well you safely operate your vehicle in various traffic conditions. After the examiner explains the route to you, you may be required to perform left and right turns, navigate intersections, railroad crossings, curves, hills, single or multi-lane roads, streets, or highways.

Medical Documentation Requirements

As of January 30, 2014, if you apply for a CDL Permit or if you apply to renew, upgrade, add endorsements to or transfer a CDL from another state, it is mandated that you provide the necessary information to your State or Tax Collector Driver's License Agency (STDLA) regarding the type of commercial motor vehicle you drive or plan to drive. Your STDLA may require a "certified" medical status as part of your driving record. If so, you will need to send in your current medical examiner's certificate and any pertinent medical adjustments. Your STDLA will be able to tell you the procedure for submitting this documentation.

If you are given a "certified" medical status classification but you do not send in or keep your certification current, you will be deemed "noncertified" and may have your CDL taken away. The following explanations help clarify this updated self-certification process:

Interstate vs. Intrastate Commerce

There are two types of commerce classifications for drivers who operate a CMV requiring a CDL. You will need to determine which pertains to you.

Interstate commerce involves operating a CMV:

- Across state lines or to a foreign country;

- Intrastate travel, but the vehicle must cross state or country lines at some point during the trip

- Intrastate travel, but the cargo or passengers in transit are will terminate in a different state or foreign country

Intrastate commerce involves operating a CMV within state boundaries only.

If your routes include both types of commerce classifications, you must choose interstate commerce.

Inter/Intrastate Commerce: Status Non-excepted or Excepted?

There are four types of commerce that require self-certification:

- Interstate non-excepted
- Interstate excepted
- Intrastate non-excepted
- Intrastate excepted

After identifying your inter/intrastate commerce classification, you must determine if your driving status will be non-excepted or excepted.

Interstate Commerce

Excepted interstate commerce involves driving a vehicle in interstate commerce *only* for any of these activities:

- The transportation of children or staff between their home and school

- The transportation of any form of government employee

- The transportation of human cadavers or people who are sick or injured

- Any form of emergency response personnel responding to an event

- The transportation of propane response to a damaged propane gas system that requires immediate attention

- When responding to a pipeline emergency that needs urgent attention such as a leak or rupture

- The transportation of farm machinery and materials as well as for a harvesting operation; the transportation of crops to a storage or market location

- The seasonal transportation of bees by a beekeeper

- Farmer controlled and operated vehicles that are not comprised of power and towed units; these vehicles must be used for the purpose of transporting farming related materials (with the exception of hazardous materials) between farms, not exceeding a 150 air-miles radius

- The transportation of passengers for leisure (not business related) by a private motor

- The transportation of migrant workers

If your main driving activity aligns with one or more of the aforementioned exceptions, then your status is considered to be "**excepted interstate commerce**". This means that you DO NOT require a Federal medical examiner's certificate.

If your answer is no to all of the above situations, your operating status is **non-excepted interstate commerce**—you need to submit a current **medical examiner's certificate** (also known as a medical certificate or DOT card), to your **State Driver Licensing Agency (SDLA)**.

In most cases, people with CDLs who drive CMVs in interstate commerce have non-excepted interstate commerce status. In the instance of a driver operating in both excepted and non-excepted interstate commerce, it is expected that the driver opt for non-excepted status so that they may drive within both types of interstate commerce.

Intrastate Commerce
Excepted intrastate commerce involves driving a CMV in intrastate commerce situations that are not deemed necessary to require medical certification by the state that issued your CDL. Since these vary by state, contact your SDLA for specifics.

Non-excepted intrastate commerce involves operating a CMV in intrastate commerce situations that do require medical certification by the state that issued your CDL. Since these vary by state, contact your SDLA for specifics.

Drivers who operate in both excepted and non-excepted intrastate commerce are required to have non-excepted intrastate commerce.

Self-Certification Statements

You will need to indicate your self-certification status on your CDL application. The exact wording may vary from state to state, but the following examples will give you an idea of the type of statements to expect:

- Interstate non-excepted: I verify that I currently (or anticipate to) operate in interstate commerce. I am aware of and meet Federal DOT medical card requirements, and I am required to carry my medical examiner's certificate.

- Interstate excepted: I verify that I operate (or anticipate to) operate in interstate commerce. I am aware that because my operations are considered excepted, there is no need for me to obtain a medical examiner's certificate.

11

- Intrastate non-excepted: I verify that I currently (or anticipate to) operate exclusively in intrastate commerce. I am aware of and meet my state's medical regulations; I understand that I am required to carry my medical examiner's certificate.

- Intrastate excepted: I verify that I currently (or anticipate to) operate exclusively in intrastate commerce. I am aware that I am not held to my state's medical requirements; I understand that it is not required that I obtain a medical examiner's certificate.

Disqualifications

General

If you are disqualified for any reason, you will not be permitted to operate a CMV. This includes any violations you commit driving either a CMV or your own vehicle that result in the withdrawal of your driver's license.

The following are examples of the types of violations that may disqualify you from being able to legally drive a CMV. Again, since there are variations from state to state, it is best to check with your DMV to find out the specific laws for the state issuing your CDL.

Alcohol, Leaving the Scene of an Accident, and Commission of a Felony

The following offenses will result in a one-year disqualification:

- If your **BAC** (blood alcohol content) is .04% or higher
- Operating a vehicle while influenced by alcohol or a controlled substance
- Refusing blood and/or breath testing
- Abandoning the scene of an accident you are involved in
- Committing a felony that involves the use of CMV
- Driving with a suspended CDL
- If your negligent activity while operating a CMV results in a fatality

You stand to lose your CDL for a minimum of three years if a violation occurs while operating a CMV labeled for hazardous materials.

You stand to lose your CDL indefinitely should a second violation occur.

You also stand to lose your CDL indefinitely if you utilize a CMV to commit a felony involving controlled substances.

While having a BAC of .04% or more will result in the one-year disqualification of your CDL, you will be put out-of-service for 24 hours if a BAC of less than .04% is found in your system.

Traffic Violations

Serious traffic violations while driving a CMV include:

- Unnecessary speeding (going 15 mph or higher above the limit)
- Reckless driving

- Improper or inconsistent lane changes
- Tailgating (travelling too closely behind a vehicle)
- Traffic violations resulting in accident fatalities
- Not having a CDL or failure to have one in the vehicle
- Failure to have the proper CDL classification and/or endorsements
- Texting while driving
- Using a handheld mobile device

Your CDL will be revoked:

- For at least sixty days if you commit two serious traffic violations within the time of three years.
- For at least 120 days if you commit three or more serious traffic violations within the time of three years.

Violation of Out-of-Service Orders

Upon violation of an out-of-serviced order, your CDL will revoked:

- For at least ninety days for a first violation
- For at least one year after two violations within ten years
- For at least three years after three or more violations within ten years

Railroad-Highway Grade Crossing Violations

You will lose your CDL:

- For at least sixty days for a first-time violation
- For at least 120 days after a second violation within three years
- For at least one year after a third violation within three years

These violations involve breaking federal, state or local laws related to the following offenses:

- For drivers not required to always yield
- Failure to stop if the tracks are not clear
- Failure to slow down to check if a train is approaching
- Failure to stop before driving through a crossing
- Not having enough space to drive through a crossing without stopping
- Failure to follow traffic control directions at a crossing
- Not driving through a crossing because of low undercarriage clearance

Hazardous Materials Endorsement Background Check and Disqualifications

You must have your fingerprints and background check fully processed if you anticipate operating a vehicle with a hazardous materials endorsement

Your hazardous materials endorsement will be refused or confiscated if you:

- Are not a legal permanent U.S. resident
- Renounce your U.S. citizenship

- Are sought out or indicted for qualifying felonies
- Have been convicted in for qualifying felonies
- Have been judged mentally defective or spent time in a mental institution.
- Are considered a security threat by the Transportation Security Administration

Hazardous materials endorsement regulations differ from state to state, so check with your DMV for specifics.

Traffic Violations in Your Personal Vehicle

CDL holders who violate particular traffic laws while driving a personal vehicle may be subject to CMV operation disqualifications, as per the **Motor Carrier Safety Improvement Act (MCSIA) of 1999**. These include:

- Loss of your CDL: Your personal driver's license is revoked, cancelled, or suspended due to traffic violations (parking violations do not apply)

- Loss of your CDL for one year: Your personal driver's license is revoked, cancelled, or suspended due to alcohol, controlled substances, or felony violations

- Loss of your CDL for life: You receive a second violation while driving either your personal vehicle or a CMV

Other CDL Rules

The following federal and state rules pertain to all CMV drivers:

- CDL holders are not permitted to obtain licenses from more than one state. Violators may be subject up to $5,000 fine or time in prison. The court may also take the CDL issued by your resident state and send any others back.

- Traffic violation convictions (except parking) committed while driving your personal vehicle or a CMV must be reported to your employer within thirty days.

- Traffic violation convictions (except parking) committed while driving your personal vehicle or a CMV in another jurisdiction must be reported to your Department of Highway Safety and Motor Vehicles within thirty days.

- If your driving privileges are suspended, withdrawn, canceled or disqualified, you need to inform your employer within two business days.

- When seeking commercial driving employment, you are required to give your prospective employer a list of driving positions going back ten years.

- It is illegal to operate a CMV without a valid CDL. Violation of this regulation is subject to a $5,000 fine or time in jail.

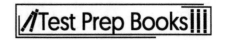
- You must alert your certifying state and relinquish your hazardous materials endorsement within 24 hours should the following situations become relevant for your:

    o If you are convicted or indicted in any jurisdiction, or if you are deemed not responsible due to insanity of a disqualifying violation listed in 49 CFR 1572.103

    o If you are determined to be mentally defective, or if you require commitment to a mental institution as specified in 49 CFR 1572.109

    o Renouncement of U.S. citizenship

- If you possess multiple CDLs, or if yours is revoked or rescinded, your employer may be subject to a $5,000 fine or time in prison.

- States can track CDL driver data through a singular computer system. Investigations on accident records can pinpoint holders of multiple CDLs.

- You are prohibited from talking on or pressing multiple buttons on a mobile device while operating your vehicle.

- Sending or reading text messages while driving is forbidden.

- You are required to always wear a seat belt, for both your own safety and that of others. In the event of an accident, it will help keep you restrained and in control of the vehicle, decreasing the possibility of serious injury or death. Drivers failing to wear a seat belt are four times more likely to suffer fatal injuries if thrown from the vehicle.

- You may not be receive a "hardship" license to operate a CMV should your personal driver's license be revoked in any way.

Other CDL rules and/or regulations may pertain specifically to the state issuing your CDL. Contact your DMV for specifics.

International Registration Plan International Fuel Tax Agreement

Most CMVs used for interstate commerce need to be registered as part of the **International Registration Plan (IRP)** and the **International Fuel Tax Agreement (IFTA)**. This is to ensure that vehicles operating within the forty-eight adjoining U.S. states and ten Canadian provinces are equally taxed.

It is the responsibility of each jurisdiction to register applicable vehicles. The process entails the following:

- Issuing license plates and cab cards or proper credentials
- Calculating, collecting and distributing fees
- Performing audits to guarantee distance and fees are properly reported
- Enforcing IRP requirements

Each licensee (motor carrier) is given an assigned base jurisdiction for IRP tax reporting and payment and identification that permits operation throughout all IFTA member areas.

Requirements for registration include:

- Applying for registration
- Providing proper documentation
- Paying fees
- Showing credentials
- Keeping correct distance records
- Having records available for review

IRP registrants and IFTA licensees may be either vehicle owners or operators.

IFTA fuel tax is determined by the distance traveled and the number of gallons (liters) used within member jurisdictions. Licensees report activities through IFTA member jurisdictions via filing a quarterly tax return with the base jurisdiction. The base jurisdiction is then responsible for submitting the taxes and representing the other jurisdictions throughout the tax collection process, including performing audits. Licensees are required to keep any documentation backing the tax return data.

Requirements for IRP vehicle plates and IFTA motor carrier licenses are defined by the IRP Plan and the IFTA for Qualified Vehicle and Qualified Motor Vehicle:

As per the IRP:

A **Qualified Vehicle** (with the exception of those below) is one which intended to operate within multiple Member Jurisdictions. It should be used for the purposes of transporting either people for hire or for the transportations of goods. Additionally a Qualified Vehicle:

- Has two axles and a GVWR or registered GVWR greater than 26,000 pounds (11,793.401 kilograms)

- Possesses three or more axles, despite its weight

- Is used in combination, when the combined GVWR is more than 26,000 pounds (11,793.401 kilograms)

As per the IFTA:

A **Qualified Motor Vehicle** is a vehicle (except recreational vehicles) that is utilized, intended, or maintained to transport people or goods and:

- Has two axles and a GVWR or registered GVWR greater than 26,000 pounds or 11,797 kilograms; or

- Is used when the combined GVWR is greater than 26,000 pounds or 11,797 kilograms.

IFTA-licensed carriers operating IRP-registered vehicles must record the amount of fuel used and distance traveled for each trip. Many drivers use an Individual **Vehicle Distance Record (IVDR)**, (also

16

known as a **Driver Trip Report**) to fulfill this requirement. IVDR forms may differ, but the necessary data is the same across the board and must include:

Distance
(According to Article IV of the IRP Plan)

- Beginning and end dates for the trip
- City and State or Province for the trip's source and endpoint
- Travel route(s)
- Odometer or hubodometer reading for start and conclusion of trip
- Total distance traveled
- Distance traveled within the jurisdiction
- Power unit or vehicle identification number

Fuel
(According to Section P560 of the IFTA Procedures Manual)

Receipts/invoices must show (but are not limited to):

- Purchase date
- Name and address of seller
- Gallons/liters purchased
- Type of fuel
- Cost per gallon/liter or total sale price
- Vehicle unit number or other unique identifier
- Name of buyer

Include data for just one vehicle on each IVDR. To keep on track, record odometer readings as per the following schedule:

- When the day begins
- When leaving the state or province
- At the end of the trip/day

Log all trip data in descending order. This includes dates, routes, odometer readings, and fuel purchases. Every state/province included on your route must be recorded on the IVDR. Make sure you retain all fuel receipts and submit them with your completed IVDR.

All logs and documentation must be properly recorded in order to ensure drivers and their carriers meet IRP and IFTA regulations. Keep IVDRs for four years for tax audit purposes. Failure to do so may result in fines or penalties or IRP/IFTA registration or license suspension or withdrawal.

Further questions about the IRP and its requirements can be directed toward your base jurisdiction DMV or IRP, Inc. (www.irponline.org). The IRP website has English, Spanish, and French training videos on its home page. Further questions about IFTA and its requirements can be directed to your base jurisdiction agency or IFTA (http://www.iftach.org/index.php).

Study Prep Plan for the CDL Test

1   **Schedule -** Use one of our study schedules below or come up with one of your own.

2   **Relax -** Test anxiety can hurt even the best students. There are many ways to reduce stress. Find the one that works best for you.

3   **Execute -** Once you have a good plan in place, be sure to stick to it.

One Week Study Schedule

Day 1	Driving Safely
Day 2	Transporting Cargo Safely
Day 3	Hazardous Materials
Day 4	School Buses
Day 5	CDL Practice Tests #1 & #2
Day 6	CDL Practice Test #3
Day 7	Take Your Exam!

Two Week Study Schedule

Day 1	Driving Safely	Day 8	Bulk Packaging Marking, Loading, and Unloading
Day 2	Managing Space	Day 9	School Buses
Day 3	Railroad-Highway Crossings	Day 10	Pre-Trip Vehicle Inspection Test
Day 4	Transporting Cargo Safely	Day 11	CDL Practice Test #1
Day 5	Combination Vehicles	Day 12	CDL Practice Test #2
Day 6	Doubles and Triples	Day 13	CDL Practice Test #3
Day 7	Hazardous Materials	Day 14	Take Your Exam!

18

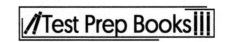

One Month Study Schedule					
Day 1	Driving Safely	Day 11	Transporting Passengers Safely	Day 21	Pre-Trip Vehicle Inspection Test
Day 2	Basic Control of Your Vehicle	Day 12	Air Brakes	Day 22	Trailer
Day 3	Communicating	Day 13	Combination Vehicles	Day 23	On-Road Driving
Day 4	Managing Space	Day 14	Coupling and Uncoupling	Day 24	CDL Practice Test #1
Day 5	Distracted Driving	Day 15	Doubles and Triples	Day 25	Answer Explanations #1
Day 6	Driving in Fog	Day 16	Hazardous Materials	Day 26	CDL Practice Test #2
Day 7	Railroad-Highway Crossings	Day 17	Loading and Unloading	Day 27	Answer Explanations #2
Day 8	Antilock Braking Systems (ABS)	Day 18	Hazardous Materials: Emergencies	Day 28	CDL Practice Test #3
Day 9	Alcohol, Other Drugs, and Driving	Day 19	School Buses	Day 29	Answer Explanations #3
Day 10	Transporting Cargo Safely	Day 20	Emergency Exit and Evacuation	Day 30	Take Your Exam!

Build your own prep plan by visiting:
testprepbooks.com/prep

Driving Safely

Information specific to CMV operation and safe driving practices are included in this section and will be featured on the CDL exam.

Inspection of Vehicle

Federal and state laws require commercial drivers to inspect their vehicles to ensure their safety and the safety of other drivers on the road. Inspections can detect problems that could end up causing a vehicle to dysfunction or even crash. Your vehicle may also undergo inspection spot checks by federal and state inspectors. If your vehicle is deemed unsafe, it will be placed "out of service" until it is repaired.

Three Types of Vehicle Inspections

- Pre-Trip Inspection: This helps discover problems that could cause a service malfunction or accident.

- During a Trip: For safety reasons you should check gauges frequently for signs of trouble and use your senses (sight, hearing, smell, and touch) to check for possible issues. Critical items to examine when you stop:

  - Tires, wheels and rims
  - Brakes
  - Lights and reflectors
  - Brake and electrical connections to trailer
  - Trailer coupling devices
  - Cargo securement devices

- After-Trip Inspection and Report: An after-trip inspection should be performed at the end of your trip, day, or driving time period. You may need to fill out a vehicle condition report listing any detectable defects—this alerts the motor carrier that the vehicle needs repairs.

What to Look For

<u>Tire Problems</u>
- Tread separation
- Cuts or other damage
- Tires that are not the same size
- Imbalanced air pressure (excessive or lacking)
- Using radial and bias-ply tires simultaneously
- Valve stems that are cut or cracked
- Dually situated tires interacting with each other or the vehicle
- Uneven wear; front tires should have 4/32-inch tread depth and back tires need at least 2/32 inch; fabric should not be visible through the tread or sidewall.
- The front wheels of a bus which have been regrooved, recapped, or retreaded; arising problems with the wheels and rims

- Damaged rims
- Mismatched, bent, or cracked lock rings are hazardous
- Wheels or rims with prior welding repairs are not safe
- Missing clamps, spacers, studs, or lugs indicates a danger warning
- Rust around the wheel nuts; You should check the tightness as this could indicate the nuts are loose. Once you have changed out a tire, it is important to stop after a while of driving and confirm that the nuts are still secure.

Bad Brake Drums or Shoes
- Drums that are cracked
- Oil, grease, or brake fluid stains on the shoes or pads
- Shoes that are worn, thin, missing, or broken

Steering System
- Misplaced or undetectable nuts, bolts, cotter keys, or other parts
- Bent, loose, or broken parts (e.g. the steering column, steering gear box, or tie rods)
- In the instance of a vehicle with power steering, you should check the hoses, pumps, and fluid level. You should be checking for leaks in any of these areas.
- If your steering wheel movement is exceeding 10 degrees (about 2 inches at the rim of a 20-inch steering wheel), this can pose a challenge when trying to steer the vehicle.

Suspension System
The **suspension system** holds the axles in place while supporting the vehicle and its cargo, making any broken parts within the system very hazardous. Refer to diagrams below for specifics.

Look for the following:

- Spring hangers that allow the axle to move from its proper position
- Spring hangs that appear to be broken or have cracks in them
- Leaves which are broken off of a leaf spring; If the vehicle is missing at least a quarter of the leaves, the vehicle will be deemed "out of service." It's important to note that any defect can be dangerous and should be checked.
- Leaves which are broken or coming out of place in a multi-leaf spring have the potential to interfere with a tire or other part of the vehicle.
- Leaking shock absorbers
- Any axle positioning parts that are cracked, damaged, or missing (e.g. torque rod or arm, u-bolts, or spring hangers)
- Damaged and/or leaking air suspension systems
- Loose, damaged, or missing frame members

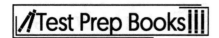
Be mindful of these key suspension parts:

Key Suspension Parts

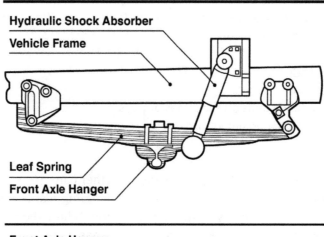

Hydraulic Shock Absorber
Vehicle Frame
Leaf Spring
Front Axle Hanger

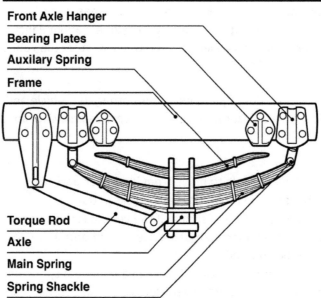

Front Axle Hanger
Bearing Plates
Auxilary Spring
Frame
Torque Rod
Axle
Main Spring
Spring Shackle

Exhaust System

If an exhaust system is broken, toxic fumes could seep into the cab of the vehicle.

Inspect the vehicle for the following to avoid exhaust toxicity:

- Exhaust pipes, mufflers, tailpipes, or vertical stacks which are not secured, damaged, or appear to be lost
- Mounting brackets, clamps, bolts, or nuts which are not secured, damaged, or appear to be lost

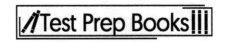

- Any parts from the exhaust system that are interacting with the fuel system, tires, or other moving parts of vehicle in abnormal ways
- Leaking exhaust system components

Emergency Equipment
Emergency equipment must be present on your vehicle.

Look for the following:

- Properly charged and mounted fire extinguisher(s) in working order
- Spare electrical fuses (unless the vehicle has circuit breakers)
- Emergency warning devices (e.g. three reflective warning triangles, six fuses or three liquid burning flares)

Cargo (Trucks)
Prior to each trip, make sure your vehicle is not overloaded and the cargo is stable and secure. If you are hauling hazardous materials, make sure you have the necessary documentation and placarding.

CDL Pre-Trip Vehicle Inspection Test

You will be asked to inspect your vehicle as you would prior to a trip to determine whether it is safe to drive. During this pre-trip inspection, you will need to describe the components you would check and why.

In order to understand and remember all the steps in the pre-trip inspection process, it should be performed the exact same way every time. Take note of the vehicle's overall condition. Check for damaged areas and whether the vehicle appears to be leaning to one side. Inspect the underside of the vehicle for traces of fresh oil, coolant, grease, or fuel leaks. Check the area around the vehicle for possible obstructions.

This seven-step inspection method is a good guide to follow:

Step 1: Vehicle Overview
Review Last Vehicle Inspection Report. Drivers may need to generate a daily vehicle inspection report. Any items flagged as safety hazards must be directed to the motor carrier to make repairs and confirm these issues were fixed or not needed. Sign the report only after receiving validation from the carrier.

Step 2: Check Engine Compartment
Make sure the parking brakes are on and wheel chocks are in place.

It might be necessary to open the hood of the vehicle, to tilt the cab after securing the loose items or to open the engine compartment. You may need to open the hood, tilt the cab after securing loose items, or open the engine compartment door.

Check the following:

- Engine oil level
- Radiator coolant level and condition of hoses
- Power steering fluid level and hose condition (if so equipped)

23

- Windshield washer fluid level
- Battery fluid level, connections and tie downs (battery may be situated somewhere else in the vehicle)
- Automatic transmission fluid level (the engine may need to be running)
- Inspect the alternator, water pump, and air compressor belts for proper tightness, wear, and "give"
- Engine compartment leaks (fuel, coolant, oil, power steering fluid, hydraulic fluid, battery fluid)
- Inspect the electrical wiring insulation to make sure it is not damaged or too worn down
- Release and secure the engine compartment door or area in which you were working

Step 3: Start Engine and Inspect Inside the Cab
Get in the vehicle and start the engine.

- Make sure the parking brake is on.

- Put the gearshift in neutral (or "park" if automatic).

- Start the engine; listen for unusual noises.

- Check the **Anti-lock Braking System (ABS)** indicator lights if the vehicle is equipped with this feature. The dashboard light should briefly go on and then turn off. If it does not, there is a problem with the ABS. There is also a problem with the ABS if the vehicle has a trailer and the yellow light on the left rear does not turn off.

Look at the gauges.

- Oil pressure: Once the engine is started, it should show a normal reading within seconds.

- Air pressure: This should rise from 50 to 90 psi in the time of three minutes. Build air pressure to governor cut-out (usually around 120–140 psi). Make sure you know your vehicle's requirements.

- Ammeter and voltmeter should be within normal ranges.

- Coolant temperature is expected to slowly increase to normal operating range as vehicle is started.

- Engine oil temperature is expect to slowly increase to normal operating range as vehicle is started.

- All warning lights and buzzers should turn off after initially turning the vehicle on. If one (or more) remain, it could indicate a problem with the vehicle.

Inspect the condition of the controls. Check the following to make sure they are not too loose, stuck, damaged, or inadequately positioned:

- Steering wheel
- Clutch
- Accelerator ("gas pedal")

24

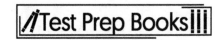

- Brake controls
- Foot brake
- Trailer brake (if vehicle so equipped)
- Parking brake
- Retarder controls (if vehicle so equipped)
- Transmission controls
- Interaxle differential lock (if vehicle so equipped)
- Horns
- Windshield wiper and washer
- Lights
- Headlights
- Dimmer switch
- Turn signal
- Four-way flashers
- Parking, clearance, identification, marker switches

Check the mirrors and windshield of the vehicle for any damage, vandalism, or items that could potentially obstruct your view while operating the vehicle. Clean and adjust as needed.

Check emergency equipment. Make sure safety supplies include:

- Extra electrical fuses, though these will not be necessary if the vehicle contains circuit breakers
- Three reflective triangles, six fuses, or three liquid burning flares
- Properly charged and safety rated fire extinguisher

Check for optional items such as:

- Chains (when required due to winter conditions)
- Tire changing equipment
- Emergency phone number list
- Accident reporting kit (packet)

Check safety belt. Make sure the safety belt is not ripped or frayed and that it is adjustable, securely mounted, and fastens properly.

Step 4: Turn Off Engine and Check Lights
Once the parking break is set, shut off the engine and take out the key. The headlights and emergency flashers should be turned on before stepping out of the vehicle.

Step 5: Do Walking Inspection
- Walk to the front of the vehicle and make sure the low beams are illuminated and the four-way flashers are both functioning correctly.
- Flick the dimmer switch to make sure the high beams go on.
- Shut off the headlights and emergency flashers.
- Check that the parking, clearance, side-marker, and identification lights work properly.
- Turn on the right side turn signal, and begin your walk-around inspection.

General
- Walk around and inspect the outside of the vehicle.
- Clean all exterior lights, reflectors, and glass components.

Left Front Side
- Make sure the window glass on the driver's side door is clean.
- Check to see if door latches or locks are in working order.
- Left front wheel
- Check the alignment and for any loose or missing parts of the wheel and rim.
- Check to make sure the tires have enough air and that all parts of the system work properly and are without damage.
- Use a wrench to test any lug nuts with rust streaks, which can signify loosening.
- Make sure the hub oil level shows a correct reading, with no visible leaking.
- Left front suspension
- Check the condition of the spring, spring hangers, shackles, and U-bolts.
- Check the condition of the shock absorbers.
- Left front brake
- Check the condition of the brake drum or disc.
- Check the condition of the hoses.

Front
- Inspect the condition of the front axle.
- Inspect the condition of the steering system.
- Parts should not be loose, out-of-date, damaged, lost, or in any sort of poor condition.
- Grab the steering mechanism to check for looseness.
- Inspect the condition of the windshield.
- Inspect for signs of damage and maintain cleanliness.
- Inspect windshield wiper arms for appropriate spring tension.
- Inspect the wiper blades for any damage or signs of wear; ensure they are attached correctly.
- Lights and reflectors
- Parking, clearance, and identification lights should be clean, operational, and the proper color (amber in the front).
- Reflectors should be clean and the proper color (amber in the front).
- Right front turn signal light should be clean, operational, and the proper color (amber or white on the forward facing signals).

Right Side
- Right front: Inspect all items as per the left front procedure.
- Ensure the primary and secondary safety cab locks are engaged (if vehicle has a cab-over-engine design).
- Right fuel tank(s)
- Make sure it is securely mounted and not damaged or leaking.
- Secure the the fuel crossover line.
- Make sure the tank(s) contain enough fuel.
- Make sure the caps are on and secure.

- Condition of visible parts
- Check the rear of engine and make sure it is free of leaks.
- Check the transmission and make sure it is free of leaks.
- Check that the exhaust system is secure, not leaking, and not touching any wires, fuel, or air lines.
- Check the frame and cross members to ensure there are no bends or cracks.
- Check that the air lines and electrical wiring are properly secured against any snagging, rubbing, or wearing.
- Make sure that the spare tire carrier or rack is not damaged.
- Make sure the spare tire and wheel is securely mounted in the rack.
- Make sure the spare tire and wheel are the correct size and properly inflated.
- Cargo securement (trucks)
- Make sure the cargo is properly secured (blocked, braced, tied, chained, etc.)
- Make sure the header board is adequate and secure (if required).
- Make sure the sideboards and stakes are strong, undamaged, and properly secured (if the vehicle has them).
- If the cargo needs a canvas or tarp, make sure it is correctly in place so it does not tear, flap, or block mirrors.
- In the event of an oversized vehicle, it is imperative that all safety signals are properly and securely mounted and that all of the necessary permits are present.
- Confirm that the curbside compartment doors are in ideal condition, are secure, and are equipped with the correct seals.

Right Rear
- Check the wheels and rims to make sure that nothing is out of place or damaged.
- Check to make sure the tires have enough air and that all parts of the system work properly and are without damage
- Make sure the tires are matches for one another as opposed to being different types.
- Make sure the tires are evenly matched sizes.
- Make sure the wheel bearing/seals are not leaking.
- Suspension
- Inspect the spring(s), spring hangers, shackles, and U-bolts and make sure they are functioning properly.
- Make sure the axle is secure.
- Make sure no lube (gear oil) is leaking from the powered axle(s).
- Check the condition of the torque rod arms and bushings.
- Check the condition of the shock absorber(s).
- In the event that the vehicle is retractable axle equipped, you need to inspect the condition of its lift mechanism.
- If the vehicle is air powered, check for leaks.
- Check the condition of the air ride components.
- Brakes
- Inspect the brake adjustment.
- Inspect the condition of the brake drum(s) or discs.
- Inspect the hoses for any wear due to rubbing.

- Lights and reflectors
- Check that the side-marker lights are clean, operational, and the proper color (red in the rear, amber in other areas).
- Check that the side-marker reflectors are clean and the proper color (red in the rear, amber in other areas).

Rear
- Lights and reflectors
- Check that the rear clearance and identification lights are clean, operational, and the proper color (red in the rear).
- Check that the reflectors are clean and the proper color (red in the rear).
- Make sure the taillights are clean, operational, and the proper color (red in the rear).
- Make sure the right rear turn signal is operational, and the proper color (red, yellow, or amber in the rear).
- Make sure the license plate(s) are present, clean, and secured.
- Make sure the vehicle has correctly fastened splashguards, and they are not dragging on ground or rubbing against the tires.
- Make sure the cargo is secure (trucks).
- Make sure the cargo is properly secured (blocked, braced, tied, chained, etc.)
- Make sure the tailboards are up and properly secured.
- Make sure the end gates are undamaged and properly secured in the stake sockets.
- Be sure to correctly secure a canvas or tarp if it is required for your vehicle. It must be secured in a way that prevents it from tearing, flapping around, or blocking your vehicle's rearview mirror and lights; additionally, it should not pose as a driving hazard to those around you.
- In the event of an oversized vehicle, it is imperative that all safety signals are properly and securely mounted and that all of the necessary permits are present.
- Make sure the rear doors are securely closed, latched/locked.

Left Side
- Follow the checklist that was performed on the right side, and carry out these tasks additionally:
- Battery(ies) (if not mounted in engine compartment)
- Battery boxes—securely mounted to vehicle.
- Battery box cover is securely in place
- Battery secured against movement
- Battery not broken or leaking
- Fluid in battery at proper level (except those that are maintenance-free)
- Cell caps in place and securely tightened (except those that are maintenance-free)
- Vents in cell caps are free of foreign material (except those that are maintenance-free)

Step 6: Check Signal Lights
Get into the vehicle and turn off the lights:

- Switch all of the lights to "off".
- Turn on the brake lights.
- Turn on left turn-signal lights.

Get out of the vehicle and check the lights:

- Make sure that the left front turn-signal light is functioning properly, easily visible, and is the correct color (amber or white).
- Make sure that the left rear turn-signal light and brake lights are functioning properly, easily visible, and are the correct colors (red, yellow, or amber).

Get In Vehicle

- Turn off lights not required for driving.
- Make sure all necessary papers, trip manifests, permits, etc. are present.
- Make sure there are no loose articles in the cab that could impede driving or even strike you in the event of an accident.
- Start the engine.

Step 7: Start the Engine and Check Test for Hydraulic Leaks

For a vehicle with hydraulic brakes, you need to pump the brake pedal three times, then firmly press and hold for five seconds. The pedal should stay firm. Any movement could indicate a leak or other problem that you will need to repair before driving the vehicle. For a vehicle with air brakes, refer to the "Air Brake" section and perform the checks described there.

Brake System

- Test Parking Brake(s)
- Fasten safety belt.
- Set the parking brake (power unit only).
- Release the trailer parking brake (if applicable).
- Place vehicle in low gear.
- Gradually pull against the parking brake to check its stability.
- If there is a trailer for the vehicle, follow the same steps with the trailer parking brake set and make sure the vehicle parking brake is off.
- If the parking brake does not hold the vehicle, it is faulty and needs to be fixed.
- Test Service Brake Stopping Action
- Drive slowly forward (about five miles per hour).
- Firmly depress the brake pedal.
- If the vehicle "pulls" to one side or the other, it could indicate brake trouble.
- If the pedal feels "off" or is delayed, it might indicate faulty brakes

Federal and state regulations prohibit the operation of any CMV deemed a safety hazard. If you detect any safety issues during the pre-trip inspection, you must get them repaired.

Inspection During a Trip

Check the vehicle operation often. The following is a list of items you should check:

- Instruments
- Air pressure gauge (if the vehicle is equipped with air brakes)
- Temperature gauges

- Pressure gauges
- Ammeter/voltmeter
- Mirrors
- Tires
- Cargo, cargo covers
- Lights

Use your senses. Inspect anything that looks, sounds, smells, or feels unsafe.

<u>Safety Inspection</u>
Drivers of trucks and truck tractors transporting cargo must check that the cargo is securely in place within the first 50 miles of a trip and every 150 miles or every three hours during the trip (whichever comes first).

After-Trip Inspection and Report

You may need to log a daily report regarding the condition of the vehicle(s) you operated. Report anything that could affect vehicle safety or cause a possible mechanical failure.

Basic Control of Your Vehicle

In order to operate a CMV safely, you will need to be able to manipulate its speed and direction, which requires the following skills:

- Accelerating
- Steering
- Stopping
- Backing up safely
- Shifting gears

Your seatbelt needs to be secured at all times when driving. When leaving your vehicle, make sure the parking brake is on.

Accelerating

When you start up your vehicle, make sure it doesn't roll back, as you may hit someone. To prevent rollback, use the parking brake whenever needed. When using a manual transmission vehicle, partly engage the clutch before removing your right foot from the brake. You can also prevent rollback by disengaging the parking brake only after you have given the engine enough power. If a trailer brake hand valve is attached to the vehicle, it can be used to prevent rollback.

Accelerate slowly and smoothly to prevent jerking motions. If you accelerate roughly, it can damage the vehicle's mechanical system or the coupling in vehicles hauling a trailer.

Accelerate slowly in rain or snow conditions, or anytime there is poor traction. Applying excessive power can make the drive wheels spin, resulting in the loss of control of the vehicle. Lift your foot from the gas pedal in the event that the wheels begin to spin.

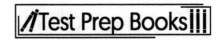

Steering

Make sure you have a firm grip on the steering wheel with each hand on an opposite side of the wheel. If you do not have a firm grasp on the wheel, it could slip out of your hands if you hit a curb or a pothole.

Stopping

When you need to stop, depress the brake pedal with a gradual motion so that the vehicle comes to a smooth, safe stop. The weight and speed of the vehicle determines how much brake pressure is needed to bring the vehicle to a complete stop. The amount of brake pressure needed can also be impacted by the reaction time of the driver. For a vehicle with manual transmission, press the clutch when the engine is near the idling stage.

Backing Safely

You should avoid having to back up in a CMV as much as possible due to the hazards of not being able to see everything behind the vehicle. You can prevent this by parking the vehicle so that you can drive forward when leaving.

Follow these safety rules if it is necessary for your to back up in a CMV:

- While in the proper position, determine the type of backing you will need to do and position the vehicle in the best way to permit backing up safely.

- Analyze the path you will need to take before you begin backing up. This may need to involve getting out of the vehicle and checking any possible obstructions to the sides, overhead, and in the route of the vehicle.

- All mirrors should be utilized when backing up a CMV. Frequently check the outside mirrors on both sides of the vehicle. If you are unsure, get out and check your path.

- Back up slowly. Always back up slowly and use the lowest gear setting. This makes it easier to fix any steering errors and stop quickly if needed.

- You should back up and turn toward the left side. It is more difficult to see clearly when you back to the right side. Backing up toward the left side allows you to view the rear of your vehicle and to check your view through the side window. The added degree of safety is worth it.

- Use a helper. Use a helper whenever possible to help observe blind spots you cannot detect. Have a helper should stand toward the back of your vehicle; make sure they are in clear sight. Before starting to back up, make sure there is a set of hand signals that you both understand, including a signal for "stop."

Shifting Gears

It is very important to shift gears correctly. You will not be able to accurately control your vehicle if you cannot shift into the proper gear while driving.

Manual Transmissions

It is common for CMVs with manual transmissions to require double clutching in order to shift into different gears. Here is the method to follow:

- Release the accelerator, push in the clutch, and shift into neutral at the same time.
- Release the clutch.
- Let the engine and gears slow down to the rpm required for the next gear (this takes practice).
- Push in the clutch and shift to the higher gear simultaneously.
- Release the clutch and press the accelerator simultaneously.

It takes practice to shift gears using the double clutch method. Remaining in neutral longer than necessary, may make shifting into the next gear more difficult. Instead of forcing this step, return to neutral position, release the clutch, increase engine speed to match the posted speed, and keep trying.

Knowing When to Shift Up
Keep these speeds in mind for help with knowing when to shift:

Use Engine Speed (rpm)
Before anything, you will need to consult your vehicle's manual to determine the vehicle's rpm range while operating. Keep this in mind, and when the engine reaches the high end of that range, shift up. Some vehicles utilize "progressive" shifting: the **shifting rpm rate** is determined as you get into the higher gears. Make sure you know the correct method for the vehicle you will operate.

Use Road Speed (mph)
Learn the optimum speeds for each gear so you will know when to shift up by checking the speedometer. With either method, engine sounds may also help you determine when to shift.

Basic Procedures for Shifting Down
- Release the accelerator, push in the clutch, and shift into neutral at the same time.

- Release the clutch.

- Press down on the accelerator; increase the engine and gear speed to the correct rpm for the lower gear. Simultaneously depress the clutch and shift to the lower gear.

- Simultaneously release the clutch and press down on the accelerator.

- To downshifting properly, you should the tachometer or the speedometer and shift at the correct rpm or road speed.

Situations where you should downshift:

Before Starting Down a Hill
When you are coming up on a hill, begin slowing the vehicle to a speed you can comfortably control without heavy use of your brakes. Downshift before you start driving down the hill. You will need to be in a low enough gear; usually, this is a lower gear than what is typically needed to climb the same hill.

Before Entering a Curve

Slow to a safe speed and downshift to the correct gear. The goal is to maintain power through the curve in order to keep the vehicle stable.

Multi-Speed Rear Axles and Auxiliary Transmissions

Many vehicles feature extra gears through the use of multi-speed rear axles and auxiliary transmissions. They are typically controlled via a switch on the gearshift lever of the main transmission. You will need to learn how to correctly shift gears for each vehicle you will be expected to operate. Different vehicles often have varying shift patterns.

Automatic Transmissions

If your vehicle has an automatic transmission, it is important to select a low range when going down graded roads. This will allow you to better control engine braking and help prevent the transmission from upshifting beyond the selected gear (unless the governor rpm is exceeded).

Retarders

Retarders on a vehicle help slow it down, reducing brake wear and providing another alternative to decreasing speed. The basic types of retarders include: exhaust, engine, hydraulic, and electric. All can be switched on or off by the driver and some allow the power to be adjusted. When powered "on," retarders enforce their braking power to the drive wheels as the accelerator is also fully released. Because these devices can be noisy, some areas restrict usage. Make sure you know if their use is permitted on your route.

Use caution. The retarder can cause the wheels to skid if the proper traction is lacking. It is important to shut off the retarder if the road conditions are wet, icy, or covered in snow.

Seeing

Many accidents are the result of distracted driving. It is essential that you are aware of your vehicle's surroundings at all times.

Seeing Ahead

Looking Far Enough Ahead

Be aware of the traffic around the perimeter of your vehicle. It may require a great deal of space to stop or switch lanes. It is important to look ahead as much as possible and to anticipate anything that may obstruct your view or chances of safely maneuvering your vehicle.

How Far Ahead to Look

While on the road, you should anticipate approximately how far you would drive in 12 to 15 seconds. That's driving about one block at a low speed (city driving) and a quarter of a mile at a higher speed (highway driving). Failing to anticipate ahead may require fast braking or hasty lane changes. However, items in closer range should not be ignored. You should strike a balance between near and far views.

Look for Traffic

Be aware of the vehicles around you. This includes those merging onto the highway, moving into your lane, turning, and braking. Looking far enough ahead gives you the ability to predict and compensate by altering your speed or switching lanes to prevent an issue. If you are approaching a green traffic light, it is best practice to begin slowing down, as there is a chance it will turn red before you reach it. It is better to anticipate the traffic light change than to be caught last minute.

Seeing to the Sides and Rear

It is crucial to have an awareness of what's behind you and on both sides of your vehicle. This requires frequently inspecting your mirrors, particularly in special circumstances.

Mirror Adjustment

You should adjust your vehicle's mirrors before each trip when the trailer is parked straight. Position each to see various views of the vehicle in order to have a point of reference.

Regular Checks

Frequently inspect your mirrors to ensure you can correctly see your vehicle and the vehicles around you.

Traffic

Use your mirrors to check for passing vehicles and those beside and behind you in case you need to change lanes quickly. Be aware of "blind spots" your mirrors cannot reach. Vehicles traveling around you may move into these blind spots. Frequently check your mirrors to ascertain their location.

Check Your Vehicle

Mirrors should also be used to watch for tire fires and help keep an eye on any open cargo you may be carrying. Be on the lookout for loose fastenings or a tarp that is fluttering or ballooning.

Special Situations

Certain circumstances such as lane changes, turns, merges, and tight maneuvers necessitate heightened mirror checks.

Lane Changes

Check your mirrors to avoid collision with other vehicles:

- Prior to changing lanes to ensure there is enough room.
- After switching on your turn signal, to ensure a vehicle has not migrated into your blind spot.
- Right after you start changing lanes, to ensure the road is clear.
- Once the lane change is completed.

Turns

Your mirrors should be used when you are making turns. They can be useful in making sure your vehicle will not hit anything during the turn.

Merges

Check your mirrors when merging to ensure there is enough space between vehicles to safely enter traffic.

Tight Maneuvers

Check your mirrors frequently whenever you are in a situation where you don't have much clearance around your vehicle.

How to Use Mirrors

Accurate use of your mirrors requires inspecting them quickly while recognizing what you are viewing.

Switch your view between the mirrors and the road ahead but don't concentrate too long on the mirrors or you may drive quite a distance without an awareness of what's ahead.

Larger vehicles are sometimes equipped with curved mirrors. These reflect a wider viewing range than traditional flat mirrors, causing objects in the curved mirrors to appear smaller and farther away than in actuality. Keep this in mind when checking your curved mirrors.

Communicating

Signaling

It is essential to use your turn signals to alert other drivers of your intentions. Here are some general rules for safe signaling:

Turns

Follow these three rules for using turn signals:

- Signal early. Signal before turning to prevent other vehicles from trying to pass.
- Signal continuously. In order to turn safely, keep both hands on the wheel. Complete the turn before cancelling the signal.
- Cancel your signal. Switch your turn signal off after you've turned (if not self-canceling).

Lane Changes

Lane changes should be slow and smooth. Switch your turn signal on first to alert any driver that may be in your blind spot.

Slowing Down

If you plan to slow down or stop, you can signal to the people behind you by using your vehicle's four-way emergency flashers. Send a warning to other drivers if experiencing any of these situations:

Trouble Ahead

If you see a problem that requires other vehicles to slow down, use your emergency flashers to alert drivers behind you. Your vehicle's size may obstruct their view in seeing danger up ahead.

Stopping on the Road

If you need to unload passengers or make a stop at a railroad crossing, alert drivers behind you by using your four-way emergency flashers. Do not make any sudden stops.

Driving Slowly

If you need to drive at a consistent slow speed, warn drivers behind you by using your emergency flashers. Flasher regulations vary from state to state. Be aware of and follow the states' laws where you will be driving.

Don't Direct Traffic

Some drivers try to be helpful by alerting other vehicles when it is safe to pass. Do not attempt to do this, as it could cause an accident, putting you at fault.

Communicating Your Presence

You should make other drivers aware of your presence in order to prevent accidents. Even when your vehicle is in clear view, others may not see it.

When Passing

Other vehicles, pedestrians, or bicyclists can move into your path at any time. To make sure they are aware of your presence, gently honk your horn or flash your lights. Careful operation of your vehicle will help prevent an accident if they don't see or hear you.

When It's Hard to See

You need to make your presence known at dawn or dusk, or in inclement weather such as rain, snow, or fog. If you have difficulties seeing other vehicles, assume they also have difficulty seeing you. Turn on your headlights to the low setting. High beams can irritate other drivers.

When Parked on the Side of the Road

Make sure you use your four-way emergency flashers if you need to pull over to the side of the road, particularly at night. Your taillights are not a warning signal. Emergency warning devices should be set up within ten minutes of pulling over or stopping. Adhere to the following procedures:

- You should place warning signs 10, 100, and 200 feet ahead of traffic should you need to stop on or by a one-way highway.

- Should you need to stop on a two-lane highway, place warning signs at both 10 and 100 feet of the front and rear of your vehicle where you are parked.

- If a hill or curve is blocking the line of sight of where your vehicle is stopped, move the warning device beyond the hill or curve so drivers have enough warning.

- You will need to place warning signs in a way that helps other drivers to see you so as to avoid any further incidents.

Use Your Horn When Needed

Use your horn only when necessary. While it can help prevent an accident by notifying others around you of your presence, the noise can surprise and frighten others when used needlessly.

Controlling Speed

Many accidents are the result of speeding. It is imperative to modify your speed based on driving conditions such as traction, curves, visibility, traffic, and hills.

Stopping Distance

Perception Distance + Reaction Distance + Braking Distance = Total Stopping Distance

Perception Distance

Perception distance refers to a combination of the distance your vehicle travels, the time danger is perceived, and when this danger is actually acknowledged by your brain. It can be influenced by a variety of mental and physical factors, particularly the danger itself and visibility conditions. An observant driver has an average perception time of 1¾ seconds, which is about 142 feet when traveling 55 mph.

Reaction Distance

Reaction distance refers to the distance of road that can be traveled before having to brake in avoidance of danger. The average driver's reaction time is ¾ second to one second, about 61 feet when traveling 55 mph.

Braking Distance

This is the length of road your vehicle will travel in optimum conditions while you are braking, typically about 216 feet when traveling 55 mph on dry pavement with decent brakes.

Total Stopping Distance

This is the entire length of road traveled by your vehicle in ideal conditions taking into account all factors (perception, reaction, and braking distance) prior to completely stopping your vehicle. It is typically a minimum of 419 feet when traveling 55 mph.

The Effect of Speed on Stopping Distance

Speed is a major factor in the amount of time it takes to stop and the impact of your vehicle in the event of a crash. When driving at 40 mph, the braking distance is four times greater than if driving at 20 mph. When driving at 60 mph, the braking distance is then nine times greater; at this rate, your stopping distance would measure more than the length of a football field. If driving at 80 mph, the braking distance is then 16 times greater than when it was at initially travelling 20 mph. Maintaining higher speeds while driving drastically increases your stopping distances and ultimately the severity of potential crashes. By reducing speed, you can greatly decrease the distance you need to stop.

The Effect of Vehicle Weight on Stopping Distance

The brakes on heavier vehicles work harder and absorb more heat. However, the brakes, tires, springs, and shock absorbers on a CMV function best with a full payload; empty vehicles have less traction and require greater stopping distances.

Matching Speed to the Road Surface

Traction—the friction between the tires and the road—is essential to steering and stopping a vehicle. Certain road conditions lessen the effects of traction, requiring lower speeds.

Slippery Surfaces

When the road is slippery, it will be more difficult to turn without skidding and take longer to stop. Since wet roads can increase your stopping distance twice as much, you should travel at a lower speed in order to brake in the same length of time as on a dry road. When driving on a wet road, reduce your speed by a third (from 55 to about 35 mph). When driving on a snow-packed road, slow your speed in half or more. If you are driving on an icy road, you will need to cautiously reduce the speed of your vehicle and eventually come to a stop as soon as possible.

Identifying Slippery Surfaces

Sometimes it is difficult to determine whether the road is slippery. Warning signs include:

- **Shaded** Areas: Parts of the road stay icy and slippery much longer than other areas.

- **Bridges**: Surfaces will freeze prior to the road. Extra caution is required when outside temps dip near 32 degrees Fahrenheit.

- **Melting Ice**: These conditions cause the road to be excessively slippery.

- **Black Ice**: This is a transparent layer of very thin ice. Although the road may appear wet, black ice will make it very slick.

- **Vehicle Icing**: If you detect ice on your vehicle, the road surface is likely beginning to ice up as well.

- **Just After Rain**: In the event of rain, you will need to be aware that the rain will mix with oil on the road. This makes the road very slick at first; if it keeps raining, the mixture will get washed away.

- **Hydroplaning**: Water or slush can collect on the road in certain types of weather, causing your vehicle to hydroplane. Similar to water skiing, the tires skim along the surface of the water and lose traction, making it impossible to steer or stop. Try to regain control by taking your foot off the accelerator and pushing on the clutch, which will slow your vehicle and allow the wheels to turn more easily. Do not use the brakes—depress the clutch if the drive wheels start to skid.

  o Your vehicle is at risk for hydroplaning as long as there is water on the road. You will need to make sure your tires' grooves are in good condition and that your tires' pressures are at the appropriate level to avoid hydroplaning.

  o Vehicles are more likely to hydroplane when traveling over surfaces where water collects. Be on the lookout for clear reflections, tire splashes, and rain on the road.

Speed and Curves

Safely navigating curves requires modifying your speed. Driving too fast when approaching a curve can cause you to skid off the road or roll your vehicle, particularly if it has a high center of gravity. Prior to entering a curve, slow down and then lightly accelerate when needed. This will help you control the vehicle and retain traction in the tires.

Speed and Distance Ahead

While driving, it is important to maintain enough distance between your vehicle and the one in front of you that you can stop within that distance if needed. This parameter will vary depending on the situation. You will need to drive more slowly at night or in fog, rain, or other inclement weather.

Speed and Traffic Flow

Follow the flow of traffic, matching the speed of the other vehicles on the road as best you can without speeding. Many states have lower speed limits for CMVs than cars. Vehicles traveling in the same direction at similar speeds are less likely to have accidents. Driving faster than other vehicles requires frequent passing, which increases the possibilities of a crash. Use extra care when passing.

Speed on Downgrades

When traveling downhill, gravity will cause your vehicle's speed to build. It is essential to operate your vehicle at a speed that is not too fast for the:

- Weight of the vehicle and its cargo
- Length of the hill
- Steepness of the hill
- Road conditions
- Weather

Prior to driving down a hill, shift into a low gear and follow safe braking practices to control your speed. Heed to speed limit and grade postings specifying the hill's length and steepness. The brakes will have the most impact when your vehicle is in a lower gear and near the administered rpms. Use your brakes cautiously so you can safely slow or stop when conditions are hazardous. The section on "Mountain Driving" outlines how to carefully navigate down long, steep downgrades.

Roadway Work Zones

You will need to use extreme caution when driving through marked work zones on the roadways. The main cause of injury and death in these zones is speeding. Always heed posted speed limits, paying careful attention not to increase your speed as you pass through extensive areas of road construction. Slow down when road and weather conditions are unfavorable, decreasing your speed even more if you spot any workers near the highway.

Managing Space

Make sure there is enough space on all sides of your vehicle in order to give you enough time to safely react. Larger vehicles typically take up more space on the road and will require additional room to make stops and turns.

Space Ahead

It is essential to pay attention to and maintain the area in front of your vehicle.

The Need for Space Ahead

You must refrain from tailgating the vehicle in front of you in case you need to brake abruptly. Accident reports indicate these are vehicles CMVs crash into the most. It is important to remember that smaller vehicles can typically brake faster.

How Much Space?

Here's a good rule of thumb regarding the distance between vehicles:

If you are traveling at 40 mph, you should stay at least one second behind for each 10 feet of length of the vehicle in front of you. For example, allow 4 seconds for a 40-foot vehicle and 6 seconds for one that is 60-feet long. If you are traveling at speeds higher than 40 mph, it is a good idea to add an additional second for safety.

Use this method to determine the number of seconds: After the vehicle in front of you drives past a shadow or some other marking, slowly count "one thousand-and-one, one thousand-and-two" etc., until you get to the same place. Compare the number with the formula above. If you are driving too close, slow down a bit and don't forget you'll need quite a bit additional space if the road conditions are slick.

Space Behind

It's impossible to prevent other drivers from tailgating, but there are some steps you can follow to increase safety.

Stay to the Right

Stick to the right lane if you are carrying a heavy load. CMVs often have difficulties maintaining speed, particularly when traveling uphill. Do not try to pass a slower vehicle unless you are certain that you can pass them quickly and without posing a danger.

Dealing with Tailgaters Safely

The size of a CMV often makes it difficult to determine if a vehicle is driving closely behind you. Situations where you may be tailgated:

- If you are driving slowly, essentially trapping the vehicle in back of you.

- During inclement weather, which can make it tough for the driver behind you to clearly see the road ahead.

In the event that you are tailgated, you can decrease the possibilities of an accident by doing the following:

- Avoiding abrupt movements; Give other drivers enough warning by switching on your turn signal and decelerating if you need to slow down or turn.

- Increasing the space between you and other vehicles; This will help prevent the need to make any quick changes in your speed or direction and make it easier for the tailgater to pass you.

- Maintaining your speed; It's safer to be followed closely at a lower speed.

- Avoiding tricks; Do not flash your lights at others on the road.

Space to the Sides

Since CMVs are often wider and occupy a larger area than other vehicles on the road, you will need to wisely manage the space around you. The following two tips will help you keep on track:

Stay Centered in Your Lane
This allows for a safe amount of space on either side.

Strong winds can make it difficult to stay in your lane, and even more so for lighter vehicles, particularly when you are exiting a tunnel. If it is windy, try to avoid driving alongside other vehicles.

Avoid Traveling Next to Others
This is hazardous for two reasons:

1. Another driver could make a sudden lane change and crash into you.
2. You may find yourself hemmed in if you need to switch lanes. It's best to locate an opening in the flow of traffic, which may be difficult when traffic is heavy. If you cannot avoid driving alongside another vehicle, do your best to allow as much room as you can between the two vehicles. Slow down or pull ahead to make sure the other driver notices you.

Space Overhead

Driving a CMV requires an awareness of your vehicle's height. It is essential to keep the following in mind:

- Road maintenance or packed snow can decrease clearances on bridges and overpasses—don't presume that the posted figures are accurate.

- Hauling heavy cargo lowers the height of a CMV. You may not have the same clearance level when your vehicle is empty.

- Clearance signs are not always present on low structures such as bridges or tunnels. Proceed with caution if you are uncertain whether you can safely drive underneath. If it appears you cannot, then find an alternate route.

- Uneven surfaces can cause vehicles to sway, making it difficult to pass items located on the outside of the road such as signs, tree branches, or bridge supports. To prevent this issue, ease a little into the middle of the road.

- Prior to backing up your vehicle, get out and inspect for obstructions and other dangers that might not be easily spotted such as trees, branches, or electrical wires.

Space Below

CMVs often have low clearances underneath, which can be even less when you are carrying a full load of cargo. Road drainage channels, railroad tracks, and uneven or poorly paved surfaces can aggravate the issue. Proceed through these areas with caution.

Space for Turns

It is essential to consider the space required around a CMV when executing turns.

Right Turns
Tips to help prevent right-turn crashes:

- Proceed very slowly to allow your vehicle and others more time in the event of an issue.

- If your vehicle cannot turn right without crossing into another lane, prevent other drivers from overtaking you on the right by turning widely, making sure the back end of your vehicle is hugging the curb.

- As you begin to turn, make sure you do not turn wide to the left, or vehicles behind you may assume you are making a left turn and attempt to pass on your right causing you to collide.

- If you need to drive into the oncoming lane to make a turn, check for vehicles and allow them the space to pass or stop if needed. Do not back up or you could strike a vehicle in back of you.

Left Turns
Make sure you are in the middle of the intersection prior to making a left turn. If you turn too early, you risk the left side of your vehicle colliding with another. If the intersection has two left-turn lanes, always choose the one on the far right so you can easily see drivers to your left. Attempting the turn from the inside lane may require you to swerve to the right.

Space Needed to Cross or Enter Traffic

Because of their larger size and weight, CMVs require more room than a car to enter into traffic. If you are carrying a full load of cargo, it will take you longer to accelerate. Make sure you have enough space and time to make the turn and that you are able to drive all the way through before the approaching traffic.

Seeing Hazards

Importance of Recognizing Hazards

What is a Hazard?

A road condition or someone else using the road that seems to pose a risk or danger to others is considered a **hazard**. A good example of a hazardous situation: A car on the highway up ahead starts heading for an exit ramp but brakes hard all of the sudden. This could indicate that the driver is unsure about taking the exit and could re-enter the highway.

Spotting Hazards Allows You to be Prepared

Recognizing possible hazards in advance gives you more time to prevent them from turning into emergencies. If a driver cuts over in front of you, as in the scenario above, it would be smart to start slowing down or to switch lanes to avoid contact with the other driver. Being aware and prepared decreases the need to brake abruptly or make sudden lane changes.

Learning to See Hazards

Clues to help spot hazards in advance become more obvious and routine with time and experience. Many are outlined in the following section.

Hazardous Roads

Move-Over Laws

Move-over laws have been instituted to help reduce the increasing number of accidents involving individuals working on or near the highway, such as police officers, emergency medical personnel, fire department employees, and road construction workers. Participating states have signs posted along the highway. As per these regulations, drivers approaching a roadside incident must slow down and switch lanes. If you notice that an emergency vehicle is stopped near the road for whatever reason, you should begin slowing down and switch into another lane so as to give the emergency vehicle space possible. If you cannot safely switch lanes, slowly and carefully drive past the area as traffic conditions permit.

If you spot any of the following road hazards, slow down and proceed with caution:

Work Zones

Roadwork produces hazardous conditions such as narrower lanes, sharper curves, and uneven road surfaces. Construction workers and vehicles may obstruct your path and other drivers may become distracted. If you need to alert drivers behind you, you can use your flashers or brakes to send notice.

Drop Off

Sometimes the asphalt near the edge of the roadway has a sudden drop off. If your vehicle gets too close to the edge, it can sway to the side and clip objects such as signs and tree limbs. Crossing the drop off, pulling over to the side and re-entering the highway can also make it difficult to steer.

Foreign Objects

It is best to avoid any objects scattered on the road, as they can pose a hazard to your vehicle and potentially damage your tires, rims, or brake lights. It is often difficult to tell what the objects are from a

distance—boxes and bags may appear empty, but they could contain heavy items inside that could damage your vehicle. Spotting them in advance will help prevent you from having to swerve or brake.

Off Ramps/On Ramps

Use extra caution when exiting and merging onto highways and other major roadways, particularly when navigating a downgrade and curve simultaneously, as it may be difficult to slow your vehicle. The speeds posted for exits and on ramps often pertain to cars only. Make sure you are traveling at the proper speed prior to turning onto an on or off ramp.

Hazards

Always be aware of other vehicles or people along your route that may pose a hazard. Some examples are listed below:

Blocked Vision

Drivers with blocked or limited vision may not see you clearly. This includes:

- Vehicles with a blocked rear window.

- Rental trucks. Their drivers are often unaware that these vehicles have restricted side and rear views.

- Vehicles whose windows are covered with frost, ice, or snow.

- Vehicles partially concealed by blind intersections or alleys. If you cannot see the driver, he or she can't see you and could suddenly back out or swerve into your lane.

Delivery Trucks

Delivery drivers are often in a rush and may make sudden or erratic movements. Parcels or the vehicle door can also block their view.

Parked Vehicles

When you see a parked vehicle, check to see if there are any passengers or a driver inside and if you see any exhaust or brake/backup lights. This could indicate that someone will soon exit the vehicle or drive away. Be especially aware of buses dropping off passengers. They could walk in front of or behind the bus if they don't see you.

Pedestrians and Bicyclists

Walkers, joggers, and bicyclists traveling away from you will not be able to see or hear you approaching. Inclement weather days pose an additional danger since pedestrians may be wearing hats or carrying umbrellas that block their view and walking hastily with their head down to get to their destination.

Distractions

Distracted drivers will not be completely alert, even if they appear to be looking in your direction. They might assume that they have the right of way.

Children

Children playing in or near the road might not see you.

Talkers
Drivers or pedestrians might be so engaged in conversation that they fail to see you.

Workers
If you see people working alongside the road, beware of their movements, as they may not see you. Also, be on the lookout for distracted drivers, as the work itself interferes with traffic flow.

Ice Cream Trucks
Children often congregate near ice cream trucks, so be aware of sudden movements near the truck or stand.

Disabled Vehicles
Look out for vehicles pulled over on the side of the road. If you see a raised hood or jacked up wheels, this could indicate that a driver is trying to check an engine or change a tire and may be unaware of the traffic around them.

Accidents
Proceed with caution if approaching an accident scene—those at the scene may make sudden movements without regarding traffic. The accident itself also tends to cause rubbernecking, with other drivers abruptly slowing or braking.

Shoppers
Pedestrians and drivers near shopping areas are often distracted, as they are focused on window shopping or driving around looking for stores or parking.

Confused Drivers
Confused drivers often brake abruptly or make sudden movements, a common occurrence near highway and major junctions. Beware of drivers not local to the area, often signified by vehicles with car-top luggage carriers or out-of-state license plates, or drivers searching for house numbers or checking street signs or maps. They could be lost or unfamiliar with traffic patterns and drive hesitantly or erratically, therefore changing direction suddenly or stopping without warning.

Slow Drivers
Spotting a slow vehicle in the distance can help avoid an accident. Some vehicles (mopeds, farm and construction machinery, etc.) are naturally slow, so be on the lookout for them. Many are marked with a "slow moving vehicle" red/orange triangle symbol as a warning.

Drivers Signaling to Turn
Drivers who are turning typically drive more slowly, particularly if the turn is tight. They may have to wait for traffic to make the turn or stop traffic themselves. Sometimes they fail to use their signal. All these situations are hazardous.

Drivers in a Hurry
Some drivers become impatient and may cut you off in the process of trying to pass you. Other drivers may merge into traffic and cut you off as they are speeding up. It is important to be aware of these scenarios when driving, as either may cause you to need to brake suddenly. Use caution when doing so.

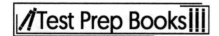

Impaired Drivers

Impaired drivers include those who are sleep-deprived, sick, or under the influence of drugs or alcohol. They may do any of the following:

- Weave or drift across the road.
- Drive off the road onto the shoulder or jump a curb while turning.
- Stop incorrectly, such as when a traffic light is green.
- Linger too long at a stop sign.
- Drive with the window open when it is cold outside.
- Abruptly increase or decrease speed.

Be especially watchful for drunk and sleepy drivers late in the evening.

Nonverbal Cues

The body language of other drivers can be a good indicator of their intentions, particularly if they fail to signal. Since drivers look in the direction they are turning, watch their head and body movements if they appear about to make a turn. Those looking back over their shoulder (especially those riding motorcycles and bicycles) may be getting ready to switch lanes.

Conflicts

Be alert for conflict conditions where you have to alter your speed and/or direction to stop from colliding with another vehicle. **High-risk situations** include intersections, on and off ramps, necessary lane changes/merges, slow/stopped traffic, and accidents. Conflicted drivers may react in a way that places them in conflict with you.

Always Have a Plan

Make sure you are always prepared for any type of hazardous situation. Stay alert at all times and think about how you will react based on your pre-planned strategy. A hazard can very quickly become an emergency. Using caution serves to protect both your own safety and the safety of other drivers.

Distracted Driving

Driving while distracted is extremely dangerous for yourself and others around you. Not paying attention can cause you to crash, leading to vehicle or property damage, injury, or even death. Distractions can come from either inside or outside your vehicle, including:

- Interacting with passengers
- Adjusting vehicle control knobs (e.g. radio, CD player, or temperature)
- Eating, drinking, or smoking
- Looking at maps or other reading material
- Reaching for an item that dropped
- Speaking on a cell phone or CB radio
- Reading or transmitting text messages
- Using an electronic device (such as a GPS, pager, tablet, computer, etc.)
- Being mentally preoccupied
- Traffic, other vehicles, or pedestrians

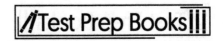
- Incidents such as police activity or an accident
- Sunlight/sunset
- Obstructions in the road
- Roadwork
- Billboards or other signs along the road

Distracted Driving and Accidents

Some significant statistics to keep in mind regarding the correlation between distracted driving and accidents involving large trucks:

- 8 percent of accidents each year involve CMV driver distractions outside the vehicle
- 2 percent of accidents each year are the result of distractions inside the vehicle (LTCCS Large Truck Crash Causation Study)
- About 5,500 people die each year in road accidents
- Distracted driving plays a part in about 448,000 motor vehicle accidents a year
- It has been found that using a cell phone (even if hands-free) uses up to 39 percent of brain energy that would otherwise be used for safe driving.
- A driver who uses a hand-held device is more likely to get into a serious accident resulting in injury
- (Source: NHTSA distracted driving website, www.distraction.gov).

Effects of Distracted Driving

Driving distracted can impair your awareness, causing you to see a potential danger too late or not at all. As a result, your reaction to the situation could be delayed or inadequate.

Types of Distractions

There are three types of distractions, all hazardous.

- **Physical distraction**: makes you take your hands off of the steering wheel or your eyes from the road

- **Mental distraction**: behavior that deflects your concentration from the road, such as talking with a passenger or being preoccupied about a previous occurrence

- **Combined physical and mental distraction**: uses both your mental and physical capacities, such as using your cell phone or even eating while driving

Use of Cell/Mobile Phones

According to **49 CFR Part 383, 384, 390, 391, and 392** of the **Federal Motor Carrier Safety Regulations (FMCSRs)** and the **Hazardous Materials Regulations (HMR)**, the use of hand-held mobile phones by CMV drivers must be limited and only used within these regulations. Drivers who do not abide by this Federal constraint or who have been charged several times for violating state or local regulations regarding cell phone usage are subject to ineligibility sanctions. Additionally, motor carriers may not force, encourage, or allow CMV drivers to use hand-held telephones.

47

Hand-held mobile phone usage is defined by any of the following:

- Having a voice conversation while holding a mobile telephone with at least one hand
- Pressing more than just one button when dialing a mobile phone
- Attempting to grab a phone while strapped into a seat belt

After two or more state violations of hand-held mobile phone regulations, your CDL will be revoked for 60 days for a second offense within three years and doubles for a total of 120 days in the event of three or more offenses within three years. After just the first violation (and each one after that) of this license ban, drivers may be fined up to $2,750 in civil penalties. Motor carriers may face fines of up to $11,000 for mandating a CMV driver to use a hand-held mobile device while operating their vehicle. The only circumstance where CMV drivers are permitted to use a hand-held mobile phone is to communicate with police officers or other emergency personnel in a crisis situation.

According to research, CMV drivers who use their phone while driving are six times more likely to cause a dangerous incident on the road as opposed to drivers who practice safer driving habits and abstain from phone use while driving. When dialing a phone, drivers take their eyes off the road for an average of 3.8 seconds, which is roughly 306 feet of roadway if traveling 55 mph (or 80.7 feet per second). A good deal could happen in that length of time. It is your responsibility as a CMV driver to pay attention to the road at all times.

It is important to keep in mind that hands-free devices are just as distracting as hand-held ones as they both reduce focus on driving. While using a phone while driving is dangerous, CMV drivers are allowed to use a hands-free mobile device (Bluetooth) if the device is already within close proximity to the driver's seat and if these actions are in compliance with the voice communication rules.

Texting

According to 49 CFR Part 383, 384, 390, 391, 392, the FMCSR, CMV drivers are not allowed to text while operating their vehicle for interstate commerce reasons. Drivers who are found noncompliant with this Federal regulation are subject to having their license(s) revoked for certain amounts of time. In addition, motor carriers cannot force or permit CMV drivers to text while driving.

Texting is defined as typing into or reading text from an electronic device. Things like traditional text messages, email, instant messaging, or accessing the internet, etc. are examples of texting that must be avoided when operating a vehicle.

Texting while driving is thought to be even more severe implications than talking on a phone because it distracts the driver both physically and mentally. To text, a driver must take their eyes off the road to look at a screen and hands off the wheel to type into the device.

According to research, CMV drivers who text while driving are 23.2 times more likely to cause a dangerous road incident than those who abstain from texting while driving. Texting causes drivers to take their eyes off the road for an estimated time of at least 4.6 seconds, which is roughly 371 feet of roadway if traveling 55 mph.

Don't Drive Distracted

You will need to clear all internal distractions prior to operating a CMV. Use these 4 steps to help:

- Look around the inside of your vehicle to pinpoint all possible distractions
- Map out a plan in advance to diminish/remove probable distractions
- Anticipate that distractions will happen
- Consider potential options prior to getting behind the wheel

Having a plan to prevent distractions is essential—statistics have shown that crashes can double if a driver's reaction time is a half-second slower. Follow these tips to avoid distractions:

- Switch off all electronic devices.
- If you need to use your mobile phone, make sure it is nearby so that you can operate it without having to unhook your seat belt. Utilize an earpiece, speakerphone, or voice activated/hands-free dialing. Reaching for your cell phone (even to use the hands-free function) is a violation of regulations.
- Do not engage with text messages in any way while driving.
- Make sure you are acquainted with your vehicle's features and mechanisms prior to getting behind the wheel.
- Before starting to drive, position all controls and mirrors to your preference.
- Make sure your music is set and programmed (radio stations, CDs, etc.).
- Secure cargo and make sure there are no superfluous items lying around.
- Plan your route prior to your trip by checking maps and setting your GPS coordinates.
- Don't try to read or write while driving.
- Do not smoke, eat, or drink while driving. Depart early so you have enough time to take a break to eat.
- Do not participate in complicated or in-depth discussions with passengers.
- Ask passengers to agree to act sensibly and minimize distractions.

Look Out for Other Distracted Drivers

Being able to identify drivers who are distracted can help you respond to and prevent an accident or other incident.

Look for the following:

- Drifting vehicles
- Vehicles driving at erratic speeds
- Preoccupied drivers
- Drivers talking to passengers and not paying attention to the road

If a driver appears distracted, stay clear of their vehicle and use caution if you need to pass.

Aggressive Drivers/Road Rage

What Is It?

Traffic gridlock coupled with today's stressful, fast-paced lifestyles has helped fuel aggressive driving and road rage. These drivers are often angry and hostile.

Don't Be an Aggressive Driver

Your state of mind prior to operating your vehicle directly correlates to the stress you feel while driving.

- Decrease your stress level before and while driving.

- Stay focused on the road and don't give in to distractions such as your mobile phone, eating, etc. Play mellow music to help ease stress.

- Expect that you will run into delays due to traffic, construction, or bad weather, and build in a travel time buffer for these unforeseen complications.

- Sometimes you can't help being late. If this is the case, just breathe deeply and acknowledge the delay.

- Have a sense of understanding for other drivers and why they may be driving a certain way. Do not take it personally.

- Lower your speed so you are not tailgating the vehicle ahead of you.

- Don't drive at a slow speed in the left lane.

- Keep your hands on the wheel at all times and do not make any motions that could irritate another driver, including shaking your head and signaling with your hands.

- Be thoughtful and considerate with your actions; for example, let other drivers in front of you.

If You Are Confronted by an Aggressive Driver

- Try your best to stay clear of them.

- Do not try to defy them by increasing your speed.

- Do not make eye contact.

- Pay no attention to their antagonistic actions and do not respond to them.

- Report the aggressive driver to law enforcement officials by describing their vehicle, license plate number, location of the incident, and details of where they were traveling.

- Call the police if you are able to safely make the call.

- If you notice that an aggressive driver has been involved in an accident down the road, park your vehicle a safe distance away and report to the police.

Driving at Night

It's More Dangerous

Driving at night is more dangerous than during the daytime—driver, road, and vehicle hazards are not as noticeable, which decreases your reaction time.

Driver Factors

Vision
In order to drive safely, it is essential for CMV drivers to maintain good vision. A driver can maintain their vision by getting frequent eye exams and wearing their appropriate eyewear. Regarding a driver's eyewear, it is important to remember to:

- Wear them at all times, even if only driving a short way. If your driver's license indicates that you must wear corrective lenses, it is illegal to drive without them.

- Make sure you always have an extra set of corrective lenses in your vehicle to use as a fallback in case your regular lenses are broken or lost.

- When driving at night, avoid tinted corrective lenses. Tinted lenses decrease the light you need in order to see clearly in the dark.

Glare
Bright lights can be very dangerous. Sometimes it takes several seconds for a driver to recover from this blinding glare.

Fatigue and Lack of Alertness
There are many reasons for a driver to become tired while driving, such a physical or mental strain, illness, or lack of sleep. It can hinder your vision and judgment, just like the effects of drugs and alcohol. Driving while tired will inhibit your reaction time and ability to recognize potential dangers on the road. If you fall asleep while driving, you could have an accident and end up hurting or killing yourself or others.

According to **the National Highway Traffic Safety Administration (NHTSA)**, fatigued or drowsy driving causes about 100,000 police-reported accidents per year. The **National Sleep Foundation (NSF)** conducted a study and found that about 60 percent of people in the United States have driven while feeling excessively tired, and more than a third (about 103 million people) admitted to actually having fallen asleep while operating their vehicles. This means that the drivers doze off for just a few seconds or even sincerely fell asleep for more than just a few seconds. Either scenario considerably increases the chances of an accident.

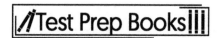

Those at Risk for Fatigue

Drowsiness is most common at night and in the mid-afternoon, which directly correlates to the times most crashes take place. People who drive at night are particularly at risk of falling asleep, especially after midnight and when driving for long periods of time. CMV drivers (particularly those considered to be long-haul drivers and those with sleep disorders or with short-term or chronic sleep deprivation) are of the higher at-risk groups for vehicle accidents caused by excessive tiredness. Others in this category include young men and shift workers. Drowsiness is a factor in at least 15 percent of all CMV crashes.

A study authorized by Congress that tracked 80 long-haul truck drivers in the United States and Canada found that each one got less than 5 hours of sleep per day on average (Federal Motor Carrier Safety Administration, 1996). Another report by the National Transportation Safety Board (NTSB) found that drowsy driving was the likely impetus for over half of the accidents involving the death of a truck driver (NTSB, 1990), and 3 or 4 additional individuals are killed for every truck driver casualty (NHTSA, 1994).

Warning Signs of Fatigue

Considering the NSF's "Sleep in America" poll, there are still many drivers who are unaware of the warning signs that they are in danger of falling asleep while driving. You should stop and rest if you experience any of the following:

- Finding it hard to focus, recurrent blinking, or heavy eyelids
- Repetitive yawning or eye rubbing
- Daydreaming; loss of concentration/confused thoughts
- Difficulty keeping track of exits or traffic signs
- Nodding your head
- Straying from your lane, tailgating or drifting onto the shoulder rumble strip
- Feeling edgy and short-tempered

Attempting to drive when you are fatigued is considerably more hazardous than most drivers realize. It is a main cause of deadly accidents. If you notice that you are becoming tire, do not hesitate to take a quick nap or even stop driving altogether and rest for the night.

Are You At Risk?

Before you begin to drive, determine if you:

- Are sleep-deprived or tired (your risk is tripled if you've had 6 hours of sleep or less)
- Have been experiencing sleeplessness (insomnia), sleep deprivation, or restless sleep
- Have been driving for a long time without resting
- Are driving during your typical sleep time (e.g. overnight or early morning). It is very common for CMV crashes to happen between the hours of midnight and 6 a.m.
- Are taking sedatives (antidepressants, cold tablets, antihistamines)
- Have been working over 60 hours per week, which increases your chances of falling asleep by 40 percent
- Are employed by more than one occupation, and your main job is comprised of shift work
- Will be driving by yourself or the route involves roads that are lengthy, isolated, dark, or monotonous
- Will be flying or dealing with time zone changes

Tips to Prevent Drowsiness Before a Trip

- Get at least 8 to 9 hours of sleep
- Map out the entire trip in advance, determining the total distance and identifying rest stops and other operational issues
- Plan to drive during the hours you are typically awake, not overnight
- Bring a passenger with you
- Do not take medications that cause drowsiness
- See a doctor if you are sleepy during the day, have trouble sleeping at night, or need to nap often
- Make exercise part to your routine to up your energy level

To Stay Alert While Driving

- Use sunglasses to protect yourself from glare and eyestrain
- Open the window or use the air conditioner to circulate air
- Don't eat rich foods just before a trip
- Take time to relax during the day
- Drive and take turns with a partner
- Have a rest break about every 100 miles or every 2 hours when driving long distances
- Take a break from driving to rest or take a nap
- Don't rely on caffeine, as it will make you alert at first—drowsiness will set in when it wears off.
- Drugs may cause you to stay awake, but not focused. Avoid taking them.

If you feel drowsy, you need to stop and sleep so you do not take chances with your life and the lives of others.

Roadway Factors

Poor Lighting

It is much more difficult to see clearly at night, particularly when driving on roads that are not well lit. Most of the time you will be solely relying on the light from your headlights. As a result, potential dangers will be much less obvious, especially those on or alongside the road who are not using lights or reflective gear. Be on the lookout for pedestrians, joggers, bicyclists, and animals.

Even when there is sufficient light to see, illuminated signs, buildings, and traffic signals can impede your view of the road. Slow down when the light is reduced or obscuring your vision. If you need to brake suddenly, you should be able to stop in the distance visible in front of you.

Drunk Drivers

Drivers who are inebriated from alcohol or drugs can pose a threat to themselves or other drivers. Beware of the times when bars and taverns are closing and look out for drivers who are drifting or driving erratically, stopping suddenly, or otherwise showing signs of drug or alcohol impairment.

Vehicle Factors

Headlights

When driving at night, your **headlights** are the main source of light for you to see by and for others to see you while on the road, so make sure they are clean, properly adjusted, and in good working order. It

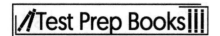

is important to keep in mind that you will not be able to see nearly as far with your headlights as you can during the day. Low setting lights allow you to see roughly 250 feet ahead of you, and high setting lights allow for visibility at about 350 to 500 feet. Your speed should be at such a range that you can still stop within the distance you can see with your headlights.

Other Lights
The following lights on your vehicle must be clean and in good working order so that others on the road can clearly spot you:

- Reflectors
- Marker lights
- Clearance lights
- Taillights
- Identification lights

Turn Signals and Brake Lights
It is even more important at night to have clear, properly working turn signals and brake lights at night so drivers are aware of your intentions.

Windshield and Mirrors
Make sure both the interior and exterior of your windshield and mirrors are clear. Light from the setting sun or bright lights during evening hours can enhance glare, impairing your view.

Night Driving Procedures

Pre-Trip Procedures
Before starting out on your trip, make sure you are well rested and fully alert. If you feel tired, go to sleep or take a nap before you drive. Make sure any necessary eyewear is clean and free of scratches— do not attempt to wear sunglasses at night. Thoroughly inspect your vehicle according to pre-trip procedures. Give special care to lights and reflectors, ensuring they are clean and working properly. Wipe any that appear dirty.

Avoid Blinding Others
Your headlights can blind drivers coming toward you and/or shine in the rearview mirrors of those traveling in the same direction. Set your lights so they are illuminated within 500 feet of an approaching vehicle and within 500 feet of a vehicle in front of you.

Avoid Glare from Oncoming Vehicles
Avoid staring directly at the lights of approaching vehicles. Instead, avert your gaze slightly to the right of the right lane or shoulder. If another driver is using their high beam lights and fails to switch to their low lights, it is best to avoid flashing them with your high beams. This could blind them and increase the possibilities of an accident.

Use High Beams Whenever Possible
While high beams enhance your night vision, they should only be utilized lawfully and at the proper distance from an oncoming vehicle (no less than 500 feet. Lights inside your vehicle can also be

distracting to other drivers. Keep your interior lights turned off and your instrument lights on as low a setting as possible to clearly see the controls.

If You Get Sleepy, Stop at the Nearest Safe Place

If you feel drowsy, check yourself in a mirror if you can safely do so. Even though you may think you are good to drive, it is best not to chance it. It is imperative to stop driving if you look or feel sleepy in order to prevent an accident. Sleep is the only remedy.

Driving in Fog

Fog is unpredictable and incredibly hazardous, particularly on highways, as it makes it very difficult to see the road ahead. If you encounter fog, be prepared to slow down. Don't presume that the fog will disperse quickly. The safest thing to do in foggy conditions is stop altogether until visibility improves. If driving conditions allow, you should pull over in a safe area until the fog lifts. If driving is unavoidable, make sure you do the following:

- Observe all fog-related warning signs.

- Reduce your speed before driving into fog.

- For the optimum visibility in foggy conditions, use fog lights and make sure your headlights are on the low-beam setting (even during the day), and be on the lookout for other drivers who did not switch on their lights.

- Use your four-way flashers to make your vehicle more visible to drivers behind you.

- Be on the lookout for vehicles parked on the side of the road. Foggy conditions distort your view. The taillights/headlights of other vehicles up ahead may not be driving on the road at all.

- Utilize highway reflector lights located along the side of the road to guide you through turns in the road.

- Listen for traffic out of your viewing range.

- Do not pass other vehicles.

- Don't pull over to the shoulder and stop, unless you feel it is absolutely essential.

Winter Driving

Vehicle Checks

You will need to take precautions to ensure that your vehicle can handle winter driving conditions. When making your pre-trip inspection, give special consideration to the following:

Coolant Level and Antifreeze Amount

A **coolant tester** can be used to confirm that the cooling system is at the proper capacity and that there is enough antifreeze to prevent freezing within the system.

Defrosting and Heating Equipment

Check to see that the defrosters are in good working order. They are essential to safe operation of your vehicle. Test the heater to make sure it works and you know how to use it properly. All other heaters located in the vehicle should be checked for its functionality. These might include mirror heaters, battery box heaters, and fuel tank heaters.

Wipers and Washers

Check the condition of the windshield wiper blades, making sure they glide against the window with enough force to clean the windshield; if not, they might not clear off any snow correctly. Test the windshield washer controls and make sure there is enough washer fluid in the chamber. Utilize windshield washer antifreeze to stop the washer fluid from freezing. If the wipers don't work properly once you start driving, safely stop and park your vehicle to fix them.

Tires

Check the tread level on your vehicle's tires. It should be a depth of *at least* 4/32 inches in each major groove of the front tires and a depth of *at* least 2/32 inches in the grooves of the remaining tires. These **grooves** provide the traction your vehicle needs to help you steer and navigate safely over wet roads and through snow, especially key during the winter. Use a gauge to verify if your vehicle's tread is deep enough to drive safely.

Tire Chains

Winter weather conditions may require using chains on your tires. Make sure you have enough chains and extra cross-links, and that they are the proper size for your drive tires. You will want to check the chains for any broken hooks, worn cross-links, or broken side chains. Confirm that you know to properly fit the chains on your vehicle's tires before you need to in snowy/icy conditions.

Lights and Reflectors

Ensure that the lights and reflectors are clear of any dirt or debris. It is particularly imperative that your lights and reflectors are clean during inclement weather conditions so your view is not compromised and others can see you. Re-check them when conditions are poor to ensure they are clean and in good working order.

Windows and Mirrors

Prior to starting out, clear any obstructions from the windshield, windows, and mirrors such as ice, snow, etc. using a snow scraper, brush, and your defroster as needed.

Hand Holds, Steps, and Deck Plates

Clear any ice and snow from the vehicle's handholds, steps, and deck plates to decrease your chances of slipping.

Radiator Shutters and Winterfront

You will want to clear any ice from the radiator shutters and make sure the winterfront is not too tightly closed. If these precautions are not in place, you take on the risk of the engine overheating and not working.

Exhaust System

When there isn't much air circulating inside the vehicle's cab, any leaks in the exhaust system are particularly dangerous. If connections are loose, carbon monoxide can leak inside, which causes drowsiness or even death. Inspect the exhaust system for loose fittings and other indications of leaks, such as odd noises.

Driving

Slippery Surfaces

Drive slowly and cautiously when roads are slippery. When conditions are extremely slick, pull over and stop at the first safe location.

Start Gently and Slowly

Use extreme care when starting out in wintry conditions. Ease onto the road and do not rush.

Check for Ice

Always be on the lookout for ice on the road surface, particularly bridges and overpasses, which often freeze first. If you do not see any water spraying up from other vehicles around you, this means the road is icy. Your mirrors and wiper blades are other indicators. If they are icy, then the road is probably slick as well.

Adjust Turning and Braking to Conditions

Turn as slowly as you can and don't brake suddenly or use the engine brake or speed retarder. Using these brakes can cause the wheels to slip or skid on slippery roads.

Adjust Speed to Conditions

Maintain a slow, steady speed so you don't have to repeatedly ease up and accelerate. Slow down and avoid braking when navigating a bend in the road and avoid passing slower vehicles unless absolutely necessary. Be aware that the road will become even more slippery if conditions warm and the ice begins melting.

Adjust Space to Conditions

Don't drive right next to or behind other vehicles. If you see traffic congestion in the distance, slow down or stop until it disperses. Concentrate on predicting when you will need to stop and slow down accordingly. Be on the lookout for snowplows and salt/sand trucks, and allow them a wide berth.

Wet Brakes

Your brakes will get wet if you are driving through heavy rain or road-flooding conditions, which can make the brakes weak, apply unevenly, or grab. If any of these happen, they can decrease your braking power, lockup your wheels, pull the vehicle from one side to another, and even jackknife the vehicle if it is pulling another heavy vehicle. If possible, stay clear of deep puddles or flowing water.

If you cannot avoid standing water, heed to the following:

- Decrease your speed and shift into a low gear.

- Apply your brakes gently so that the brake linings push against the drums or discs. This helps prevent debris and water from getting into the brakes.

57

- Rev the engine and drive through the water while gently applying the brakes.

- Once you have driven through the water, it is important to continue lightly pressing on your brakes for a short stretch at a time; this helps to keep the brakes warm and helps to dry them out.

When you reach a stretch of road where there are no vehicles following behind you, you should perform a safety check of your brakes. Then, press on the brakes to make sure they are working properly. If not, follow the step above to dry them out more. IMPORTANT: Do not press the brakes and accelerator too much simultaneously or the brake drums and linings can overheat.

Driving in Very Hot Weather

Vehicle Checks

When outside temperatures are extremely hot, perform an inspection before you begin your trip, and additional attention should be given to the following:

Tires

Inspect the tire mounting and air pressure, which will rise along with the temperature. As a result, you will need to check your vehicle's tires every 2 hours or 100 miles during exceptionally hot weather conditions. If you release air from the tires in extreme heat, the pressure will end up being too low once the tires end up cooling down. If a tire is too hot to touch, wait to start driving again until it cools down, or it may catch on fire or have a blowout.

Engine Oil

Oil helps cool and lubricate the engine. Make sure the vehicle has an ample supply. While you are driving, check the oil temperature gauge (if your vehicle is so equipped) to make sure the temperature stays within the proper range.

Engine Coolant

Before you start driving, make sure the vehicle has the required levels of water and antifreeze as per the manufacturer's directions. **Antifreeze** helps regulate engine temperature in hot weather as well as cold. While you are driving, make sure the water/coolant temperature gauge is staying within the normal range. If it rises above the upper safe temperature range, pull off the road as soon as it is safe to do so and try to troubleshoot the problem. High temperatures are dangerous and could cause engine failure or even a fire.

Some vehicles are equipped with a sight glass, a see-through coolant overflow container, or a coolant recovery container that allow you to check the coolant level even while the engine is still hot. If the coolant reservoir is not pressurized, you can safely remove the cap and add coolant even when the engine is warm. If it is part of a pressurized system, do not remove the cap until the system has cooled. Pressure can cause the steam and boiling water to spew out, causing serious burns. You should only open the radiator cap if it is cooled off. It if it cool to the touch, then it is probably safe enough to touch.

You should follow these steps if you need to replace a system's coolant without a recovery tank:

- Turn off the engine.

- Wait until the engine has cooled down.
- Protect your hands with gloves or a thick cloth.
- Slowly turn the radiator cap to release the pressure seal (the first stop).
- Step away from the vehicle while the cooling system releases pressure.
- Push down on the cap and turn to remove it once pressure has been released.
- Check the coolant level and add more if needed.
- Replace the cap; turn and tighten to the closed position.

Engine Belts

Make sure belts are not cracked or worn. Learn how to check whether your vehicle's v-belts are tight enough by pressing on them. If they are too loose, the water pump and/or fan will not work properly, causing the vehicle to overheat.

Hoses

Check that coolant hoses are in good working order—if a hose breaks while you are driving, the engine can fail or catch on fire.

Driving

Look Out for Bleeding Tar

During extremely hot weather conditions, tar often rises to the road surface, causing it to be slippery in spots.

Go Slowly Enough to Prevent Overheating

Driving at a high speed in hot weather can generate more heat for the tires and engine. In desert regions, this heat buildup can be hazardous, intensifying the chances of tire/engine failure or possibly even a fire.

Railroad-Highway Crossings

Always dangerous, railroad-highway crossings are intersections where the roadway goes over train tracks. You should approach these types of crossings with the assumption that a train is coming. The distance and speed of an approaching train can be very difficult to determine.

Types of Crossings

Passive Crossings

Since there are no traffic control mechanisms at **passive crossings**, you decide entirely on your own whether to stop or go ahead. You must acknowledge the crossing, look both ways for an approaching train, and determine if you can safely proceed.

Active Crossings

Crossings that are considered active are usually marked with a flashing red light (with or without bells) or some other form of a traffic control mechanisms. Sometimes, these **active crossing** have gates as well to help regulate traffic.

Warning Signs and Devices

Advance Warning Signs

Prior to approaching a public railroad-highway crossing, you will see a round, **black-on-yellow sign**. This is to warn and encourage you to slow down, look for signs of a train coming, and prepare your vehicle to come to a stop at the tracks if a train is coming down the tracks. It is a mandatory requirement for all passenger and hazmat carrying vehicles to stop.

See picture below for reference:

Pavement Markings

Sometimes an advanced warning sign is painted on the road. These are known as **pavement markings** and are in the shape of an "X" with the letters "RR" and a no passing marking on two-lane roads. See diagram below for reference.

Two-lane roads also have a no-passing zone sign. In some cases, a white stop line might be painted on the pavement before getting to the railroad tracks. If this line is present, school buses are required to stop behind this line while at the railroad crossing.

Crossbuck Signs
Signifying the grade crossing, **crossbuck signs** instruct you to give the train the right-of-way. If a white stop line is not painted on the road before the crossing, then you should take this to mean that you are required to stop and yield to the railroad tracks at a distance of at least 15 feet, but no more than 50 feet. If there is more than one track at the crossing, this will be designated with a sign below the crossbuck, distinguishing the number of tracks ahead. See the diagram below for reference.

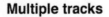

Flashing Red Light Signals
Flashing red lights and bells are often used at highway railroad crossings to indicate that a train is coming. You must yield to the train and stop as soon as you see the lights begin to flash.

Gates
In addition to flashing lights and bells, most highway crossings will use safety gates as well. It is critical to stop as soon as you notice the lights beginning to flash and before the arms lower. You must remain

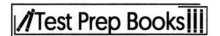

stopped until the gates have fully lifted and the lights have quit flashing. You can continue through the crossing once all warning signs have ceased and the train has passed.

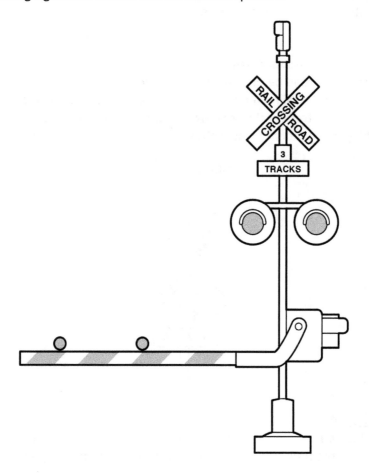

Driving Procedures

Never Race a Train to a Crossing

Do not try to beat a train to a crossing. It is incredibly dangerous and tough to gauge how fast a train is coming.

Reduce Speed

Slow your speed based on your capacity to see trains coming in both directions. You must be able to stop at tracks if needed.

Don't Expect to Hear a Train

Keep in mind that some crossings may not require or allow trains to use horns when approaching. These public crossings should have signs to indicate they are silent. You also may not hear the sound of a train coming due to noise inside your vehicle.

Don't Rely on Signals

Don't depend on signals, gates, or flagmen as your only source of caution regarding approaching trains. Make sure you are particularly aware at crossings without gates or flashing red lights.

<u>Double Tracks Require a Double Check</u>

When approaching a crossing with double tracks, always look both ways before proceeding—a train on one track may conceal a train on the other track. Once one train has passed, double check the tracks and make sure there are no other trains coming through the tracks.

<u>Yard Areas and Grade Crossings in Cities and Towns</u>

Use an equal amount of caution at yard areas and grade crossings located in cities and towns. They are just as hazardous as crossing in rural areas.

Stopping Safely at Railroad-Highway Crossings

It is essential that you completely stop your vehicle at grade crossings under the following circumstances:

- You are hauling cargo that necessitates coming to a full stop under state or federal regulations.
- It is a legal requirement.

When stopping, make sure you:

- Look for traffic in back of you while slowing to a stop.
- Utilize a pullout lane, if one is available.
- Switch on your four-way emergency flashers.

Crossing Railroad Tracks

Keep in mind that your vehicle can get hung up on railroad crossings with steep grades. Never get in a situation where you need to stop on the tracks. Make sure you'll be able to safely drive across before you attempt a crossing. You should give yourself at least 14 seconds to make it over a single track and at least 15 seconds to make it over double tracks, and do not shift gears while crossing.

Special Situations

Use special caution when driving one of the following vehicles that can get stuck on raised crossings:

- Those with low clearance underneath (lowboy, car carrier, moving van, possum-belly livestock trailer)

- A vehicle with a single-axle tractor pulling a long trailer with the landing gear on the tandem-axle tractor setting

If your vehicle gets stuck on the tracks, you need to immediately exit, abandon the vehicle, and get as far away as possible from the tracks. Check signs posted at the crossing for emergency information. Call 911 or another emergency number and notify personnel of the crossing location using landmarks, signage and the DOT number, if posted.

Mountain Driving

Gravity is a big factor when driving through mountainous areas. It will slow your vehicle when you are driving uphill and increase your speed when driving down. If you are driving up a hill that is especially

long or steep and/or you are hauling heavy cargo, you will have to shift into a lower gear in order to make it up the hill. When driving down a long, steep hill, make sure you slow down to a safe speed, stay in a low gear, and use correct braking methods. Plan your route ahead so you are aware of long, steep grades that might be difficult to navigate. If possible, consult other drivers who have traversed the hills to get an idea of a safe speed.

It is important to drive at a moderate enough speed so that the brakes work to slow your vehicle without getting too hot. Brakes that get too hot can begin to "fade," forcing you to press them harder and harder to make the vehicle stop. Continuously applying the brakes hard can cause them to keep fading until they do not work at all.

Select a "Safe" Speed

Selecting an appropriate speed should be based on:

- Combined weight of the vehicle and cargo
- Length of the hill
- Steepness of the hill
- Road conditions
- Weather

Pay attention to speed and grade length/steepness warning signs. Never exceed the speed limit or **"Maximum Safe Speed"** posted. Use the engine's braking effect as the main method to control your speed. This is most pronounced when the engine is near the governed rpms and the vehicle is in a low gear. Keep your brakes in good condition so that your vehicle is able to slow or stop when in traffic without creating a hazard for you and other drivers.

Select the Right Gear Before Starting Down the Grade

Before starting downhill, shift into a lower gear. Forcing the automatic transmission into a lower gear while the vehicle is in a state of acceleration has the potential to damage the transmission, and the vehicle could lose its braking effect as a result.

If you are driving an older vehicle, it is safest to put the vehicle in the same gear while traveling downhill as you would if driving uphill. However, newer trucks are more streamlined and often feature low friction mechanisms and stronger, more efficient engines. As a result, new models are able to climb hills in a higher gear and create less friction that would otherwise inhibit them driving down hills. If you are driving a newer vehicle, you may have to use a lower gear driving down a hill than climbing it. Know ahead of time how your vehicle operates best.

Brake Fading or Failure

The pressing down of a brake pad against brake drums is what causes a vehicle to slow down. This causes the brakes to get very hot, but brakes are built to withstand high levels of heat. However, using the brakes excessively or not taking advantage of the engine braking effect can cause brakes to overheat and fade or fail as a result.

Improper brake adjustment can also cause brakes to fade. If the workload is not equal throughout the vehicle, the brakes out of adjustment will not perform to their capacity. As a result, the vehicle will not

have enough braking power to stop properly. It doesn't take much for brakes to get out of adjustment, especially when they are used often. In addition, when brake linings are hot they can wear out much faster. It is important for your vehicle to have regular brake adjustment checks.

Proper Braking Technique

When you are driving on a steep downgrade, you should not use the brakes except to help strengthen the engine's braking effect. In other words, do not lay on the brakes for the full length of the downgrade. As soon as you shift the vehicle into the correct low gear, follow these braking techniques:

1. Depress the brake pedal with just enough pressure to feel the vehicle start to slow down.
2. Once your speed has decreased to about five mph lower than your "safe" speed, let up on the brakes. This process should take about three minutes.
3. After your speed has risen to your "safe" speed, repeat steps 1 and 2.

For example, if your "safe" driving speed on a downgrade is 45 mph, you should avoid using your brakes until you are traveling at 45 mph. Once you reach your "safe" speed, depress the brakes with enough pressure to gently lower your driving speed to 40 mph. Keep repeating this procedure as many times as you need until you are at the bottom of the hill.

Many roads on steep mountains have escape ramps. These are exit areas for drivers who have lost control driving down a hill. Escape ramps are often made of loose, soft material that help to slow an out of control vehicle. Sometimes these ramps guide the vehicle into going on an upgrade to contrast the momentum the vehicle had from initially going downhill. Accompanied by signs marking their location, it is important to be aware where escape ramps are situated along your route. Escape ramps help prevent accidents on roads with steep grades.

Driving Emergencies

There are two different types of driving emergencies:

- **Traffic emergencies**: when two vehicles are about to crash
- **Vehicle emergencies**: when critical components of a vehicle fail while in operation

You can help avoid emergencies by observing the safety procedures discussed throughout this guide. However, it is important to know how to react in case an emergency does occur.

Steering to Avoid a Crash

In an emergency situation, stopping is not always the safest choice. If there is not enough room on the road to stop, you might need to turn your vehicle to avoid the hazard. It is almost always quicker to steer a vehicle away than it is to stop. In these kinds of situations, be mindful that top-heavy vehicles or vehicles with multiple trailers are prone to flipping over. You will need to use caution when steering your vehicle away from a road hazard.

Keep Both Hands on the Steering Wheel
Do not remove either of your hands from the steering wheel for any reason. If you do need to turn quickly in response to an emergency, you'll need to grasp the steering wheel firmly in both hands.

How to Turn Quickly and Safely

It is possible to safely execute a rapid turn if it's done the right way. Some safety tips to follow include:

- Do not brake at the same time you are turning. This can cause your wheels to lock and make you skid out of control.

- Only turn as much as you need to avoid danger. Sharp turns increase the chances of a skid or rollover.

- Be ready to quickly "**countersteer**" (turn the wheel back in the other direction) as soon as you are clear of the obstacle. Emergency steering and countersteering go hand in hand.

Where to Steer

If a driver coming towards you drifts into your lane, it is best to steer to the right. This could prompt the other driver to return to the correct lane if he or she recognizes what happened.

If there is an obstacle in your way, the circumstance will dictate the best direction to turn. Using your mirrors will help you determine which lane is clear and safe to use. If the shoulder is free, steering to the right might be the best decision. It is less likely for a vehicle to be on the shoulder, but there could be a vehicle passing on your left. If there are vehicles surrounding you on both sides, turning to the right might be best. This will prevent you from forcing another vehicle into oncoming traffic and the possibility of a head-on collision.

Leaving the Road

Some emergencies may require you to drive off the road to avoid colliding with another vehicle. The shoulder is often a viable escape route, as they are usually strong enough to support the weight of a CMV. Some tips to follow if you do need to leave the road:

- Avoid braking; If feasible, do not brake until your speed has decreased to about 20 mph. Then slowly use your brakes to prevent your vehicle from skidding on the loose gravel.

- Try to keep at least one set on wheels in contact with the road. It is easier to keep control if at least one set of wheels is left on the road.

- Stay on the shoulder; If there are no obstacles on the shoulder, stay until your vehicle completely stops. Before returning to the main road, turn on your hazard lights and check your surroundings. Use your signal lights and carefully check your mirrors before turning back onto the road.

- Returning to the road; Sometimes a situation may require to get back on the road before being able to make a full stop. In these instances, use the following procedure:

- Hold onto the wheel firmly and make a sharp enough turn to return safely to the road.

- Don't try to slowly ease back onto the road. Your tires might spin on the loose gravel and cause you to lose control.

- Countersteer as soon as your vehicle's front tires are on the road. These two turns should be executed as a one "steer-countersteer" action.

66

How to Stop Quickly and Safely

You will most likely brake instinctively if another vehicle cuts in front of you. This is a good reflex to follow as long as you brake properly and have enough distance to safely stop. When you need to press on the brake, keep your vehicle as straight as possible, but still make sure you are able to turn if suddenly needed. There are two techniques—"controlled" or "stab" braking.

Controlled Braking
For **controlled braking**, depress the brakes as hard as you can; do not lock the wheels; and keep your steering wheel as tight as possible. If the wheels lock or you need to turn, let up on the brakes briefly, and then press down on them again as soon as you are able.

Stab Braking
Stab braking involves the following steps:

- Fully apply the brakes.

- Let up on the brakes when the wheels lock up.

- As soon as the wheels start going, apply the brakes again. Keep in mind that the wheels might take a moment to resume once the brakes have been released. If you apply the brakes again before the wheels have resumed, your vehicle will usually not straighten out in that moment.

Don't Slam on the Brakes
Contrary to popular belief, emergency braking does not refer to pushing on the brake pedal with all of your force. That method will only lock the wheels and cause you to skid, which affects your control of the vehicle.

Brake Failure

It is rare for brakes kept in good condition to fail. Most hydraulic brakes fail for one of two reasons: (1) Hydraulic pressure loss or (2) fading on long hills. Air brakes are discussed in another section.

Loss of Hydraulic Pressure
The brake pedal will have a spongy feel or it will drop to the floor if the system doesn't get enough pressure. Some steps to follow:

- Downshift: Moving into a lower gear will allow the vehicle to slow down.

- Pump the brakes: Sometimes the brake pedal needs to be pumped so as to create a sufficient amount of hydraulic pressure to cause the vehicle to stop.

- Turn on the parking brake: Since the parking or emergency brake is unconnected to the hydraulic brake system, it can be utilized to slow the vehicle. When using the parking brake, you have to activate the release button or lever while using the regular break. This will regulate the brake pressure and keep the wheels from locking up and losing function.

- Find an escape route: While trying to slow your vehicle, constantly scan your surroundings for a safe place to stop that will not cause you or others injury, such as an open field, side street, or

escape ramp. Steering the vehicle uphill is also a viable method to help slow down and stop. When you do stop, keep the vehicle from rolling back by putting it into a lower gear, using the parking brake, or, easing the back of the car into an obstacle that can help stop the vehicle.

Brake Failure on Downgrades

Navigating hills slowly and using correct braking techniques will stop brakes from failing most of the time. If the brakes do happen to fail, you will have to use something external to your vehicle to help it stop.

Look first for signs indicating an escape ramp, as this will be your best choice. Escape ramps are typically situated a few miles from the top of the hill. **Escape ramps** help prevent injuries and vehicle damage for hundreds of drivers every year. Some types of escape ramps are lined with soft gravel that counterbalances the vehicle's movement to bring it to a stop. Others feature an upturn that uses the grade to help stop the vehicle and soft gravel to keep it from moving.

If your brakes fail while traveling downhill and there is an escape ramp available, use it. It will help decrease the possibilities of a serious accident. If you cannot find an escape ramp close by, you can pull into an open field or an empty side road. Make your decision as soon as you realized your brakes have failed. The more time that goes by, the more speed your vehicle will pick up, making it increasingly difficult to stop.

Tire Failure

Recognizing Tire Failure

If you are able to promptly determine that a tire is having an issue, you will have more time to respond to the situation. Taking just a few extra seconds to run through the following checklist will help:

Sound
A **tire blowout** is accompanied by a loud, distinguishable "bang." You might not feel the impact right away, causing you to think it was another vehicle. However, to be on the safe side, always presume the sound of a tire blowout is from your vehicle.

Vibration
If your vehicle is making a thumping sound or severely vibrating, it may have a flat tire. If it is one of the rear tires, this vibration may be our only indication of a flat.

Feel
Often, a failed front tire will cause the steering to feel weighted and may make it difficult to steer the vehicle in general. If a rear tire fails, the vehicle will sometimes sway or "**fishtail**," although dual rear tires typically stop this from occurring.

Respond to Tire Failure

A tire failure places your vehicle in immediate danger. Respond by doing the following:

Hold the Steering Wheel Firmly
A front tire failure can cause you to lose your grip on the steering wheel. To avoid this from happening, always grasp the wheel firmly in both hands.

Stay Off the Brake

In an emergency situation, it's human nature to use the brakes. However, you could potentially lose control of the vehicle if you try to brake when a tire has failed. Unless you are in danger of hitting another object, do not brake until your vehicle has slowed down. Then slowly apply the brakes, pull over to the side of the road, and come to a complete stop.

Check the Tires

Once you have stopped and parked, get out and check all the tires, even if the vehicle appears to be driving ok. If the failure is in one of your dual tires, you may not be able to tell unless you do a visible inspection.

Antilock Braking Systems

Antilock braking systems (ABS) is a computerized system designed to prevent your wheels from locking when you apply them very hard. As an add-on to your vehicle's regular braking system, it does not reduce or intensify the brakes' capability. Though ABS is triggered when the wheels are about to lock up, it does not guarantee a decrease in the distance you will need in order to stop. ABS will, however, help you to maintain control of your vehicle during hard braking.

How Antilock Braking Systems Work

ABS is equipped with special instruments that sense situations that could cause the wheels to lock up. An **electronic control unit (ECU)** will then reduce and adjust pressure on the brakes to prevent the wheels from locking and provide the best possible braking capacity. In circumstances where your vehicle's wheels could lock up, ABS will react way quicker than you can. During all other situations, your brakes will function normally.

Vehicles Required to Have Antilock Braking Systems

As per the Department of Transportation, the following types of vehicles must be ABS-equipped:

- Truck tractors equipped with air brakes as of March 1, 1997

- Vehicles with air brakes, in addition to truck tractors, as of March 1, 1998

- Vehicles with hydraulic brakes, a gross vehicle weight rating exceeding 10,000 pounds, and built as of March 1, 1999;

A lot of CMVs manufactured before these mentioned dates have later been equipped with ABS.

How to Know if Your Vehicle is Equipped with ABS

Tractors, trucks, and buses equipped with ABS feature yellow ABS malfunction lights on the instrument panel. For trailers, yellow ABS malfunction lights should be located on the front or rear left side. Dollies built as of March 1, 1998, are required to have an ABS light positioned on the left side.

On newer vehicles, the ABS malfunction light flashes briefly to check the bulb when the vehicle is turned on and then quickly turns off. The light on some older systems might stay on until you reach a speed of 5 mph. If the light stays lit even after the bulb check or turns on after you start driving, the ABS may not

69

be working properly. It may be hard to determine if towed vehicles built prior to Department of Transportation requirements have ABS. To confirm these requirements, you will need to look under the vehicle for the ECU and wheel speed sensor wires come out of the back of the brakes.

How ABS Helps You

Vehicles without ABS are at risk for wheel lock up, skidding, jackknifing, and spinning if you have to brake hard on a slippery road. ABS is designed to help prevent your wheels from locking up and enable you to remain in control. Even though ABS does not necessarily allow for stopping abruptly, it should still help you avoid an obstacle in the road and even prevent your vehicle from skidding due to excessive braking.

ABS on the Tractor Only or Only on the Trailer

You will have better and more control when braking your vehicle even if ABS is only on the tractor, trailer, or only one axle. If the ABS is only on the tractor, you should have the ability to control your steering, and the possibility of jackknifing is decreased. However, if it starts to sway, keep an eye on the trailer and release pressure on the brakes. If ABS is only on the trailer, this decreases the chances of it swinging out, but in the event of losing control, you will want to release pressure on the brakes until control is maintained.

Braking with ABS

If your vehicle is equipped with ABS, use your brakes as you normally would:

- Use only enough brake pressure as is required to safely stop and retain control.
- Brakes should be used the same way, regardless of where ABS is equipped.
- As you slow your speed, watch your tractor and trailer and decrease brake pressure to maintain control.

This method has just one exception. If your vehicle is a truck or combination equipped with ABS on each of its axles, you can fully apply the brakes as needed for an emergency stop.

Braking if ABS is Not Working

Your brakes will still work fine even without ABS; drive and brake just as you normally would. A yellow malfunction light on the dash will turn on if something isn't functioning properly. On newer vehicles, the ABS malfunction light will briefly flash when the vehicle is started up. On some older systems, the light might stay on until you reach a speed of 5 mph. If the ABS malfunction light remans lit after the bulb check, or comes on after you start driving, there is a possibility that you have lost ABS functionality on one or more wheels. It is important to keep in mind that you still have your standard brakes even if the ABS isn't working properly. You can continue to drive, but make sure to get the system checked soon.

Safety Reminders

Keep the following in mind when driving an ABS equipped vehicle:

- You won't be able to drive faster, follow behind another vehicle more closely, or drive more recklessly.

- ABS is specifically for preventing skids caused by abrupt braking; it does not protect against skids caused by taking turns too fast.

- Don't assume the distance you need to stop will be shorter—ABS will help you retain control of your vehicle, but it doesn't necessarily decrease stopping distance.

- Your maximum stopping power won't be boosted or reduced—ABS is a supplement for your normal brakes, not a substitute.

- Your standard braking will not be affected. ABS will only be a factor if one of your wheels would have become locked due to braking too much.

- ABS can't take the place of bad brakes or improper brake maintenance.

- Remember: A safe driver is still the best safety feature on your vehicle.

- Remember: Drive in a manner that you will never need to use your ABS.

- Remember: ABS is a great technology that can help to prevent critical accidents.

Skid Control and Recovery

Your vehicle will skid if its tires stop gripping the road, the result of one of the following conditions:

- Over-braking. If you brake too hard, the wheels can lock up. In slippery conditions, use of the speed retarder can also cause your vehicle to skid.

- Over-steering. Executing a sharper turn than the vehicle can handle.

- Over-acceleration. Making the drive wheels spin by giving them too much power.

- Driving Too Fast. Driving faster than the road conditions allow is the most common cause of serious skids. By modifying your driving to your surroundings, you won't be traveling too fast and therefore won't over-brake or make a sharper turn than your vehicle can handle.

Drive-Wheel Skids

Most **skids** occur because the rear wheels cannot keep traction on the road due to braking or acceleration. Those caused by accelerating typically occur in ice or snow conditions. If you find yourself skidding when conditions are slippery, take your foot off the accelerator. If the road is very slick, push in the clutch. Otherwise, the engine might prevent the wheels from moving freely and regaining traction.

Sometimes when the brakes are pressed too hard, the rear wheels will lock up, and this will cause skidding to happen. Locked wheels typically have less traction on the road, and this can cause the rear wheels to slide to the side in an attempt to match the front-end wheels. Buses and straight trucks will usually "spin out" in these situations; vehicles with trailers or a **drive-wheel skid** will usually spin sideways and cause a jackknife.

See the diagram below for reference:

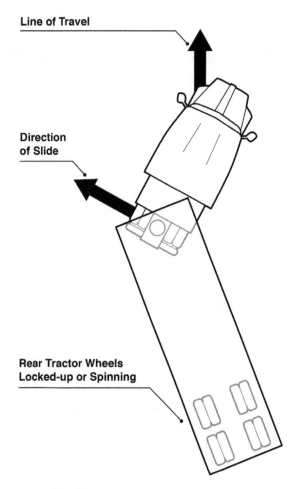

Correcting a Drive-Wheel Braking Skid

The following steps will help correct a drive-wheel braking skid:

1. Stop Braking. Taking pressure off the brakes will allow the rear wheels to move and help prevent them from sliding.
2. Countersteer. As a vehicle re-rights itself, it may continue to turn. By quickly turning the steering wheel in the other direction, you can prevent skidding the opposite way.

While in a skid, it requires quite a bit of practice to lay off the brake, quickly turn the wheel, press in the clutch and countersteer. Make sure to practice these skills on a large driving range or "skid pad."

Front-Wheel Skids

Most **front-wheel skids** are caused when vehicles travel faster than the road conditions allow. Front-wheel skids can also be caused by a not having a lack tread on the front tires and cargo that is unevenly distributed. Under these circumstances, the front end of the vehicle will typically continue in a straight line, regardless of how you are turning the steering wheel. This can be problematic if the road is wet and you are not able to control the vehicle through a turn or curve. If you experience a front-wheel skid, the only way to stop is by slowing your vehicle as fast as you can without turning or braking hard.

Accident Procedures

If you have an accident and aren't critically injured, you must take steps to stop any additional harm. The procedure to follow at the scene of an accident includes:

- Protecting the area.
- Notifying authorities.
- Caring for the injured.

Protect the Area

You will first need to make sure another accident does not occur in the same location.

Protect the area by doing the following:

- If your vehicle was involved in the accident, do your best to move it over to the shoulder. This will let other vehicles get around the scene and help avoid another accident.

- If you pull over to help, park your vehicle away from the accident. Emergency vehicles will need to have a clear amount of space surrounding the accident.

- Turn your flashers on.

- Place reflective triangles on the road as a warning to other vehicles. Make sure they are visible so that drivers can see them in plenty of time to get around the accident.

Notify Authorities

If you have a mobile phone or CB radio, call for help before leaving your vehicle. If a phone or radio is not available, stay where you are until the scene of the accident is protected; once it is safe, locate a device to call, or send someone to call for authorities. Try to pinpoint your location via landmarks or road signs so you can tell the dispatcher where to find you.

Care for the Injured

If someone at the scene has emergency experience and is assisting with injuries, stay clear unless asked to help. Otherwise, do your best to help anyone who is hurt, making sure to follow these steps:

- Don't move someone who is seriously injured unless it is essential to move them away from heavy traffic or a fire hazard.

- Applying direct pressure to a wound can help stop excessive bleeding.
- Make sure the injured person is kept warm.

Fires

Truck fires are very dangerous. Make sure you know what causes fires, how to prevent them, and the procedure for putting them out.

Causes of Fire

Some causes of vehicle fires include:

- The scene of an accident. Leaking fuel, incorrect use of flares.
- Tires. Tires that are under-inflated and dual tires that make contact.
- Electrical system. Short circuits caused by damaged insulation and loose connections.
- Fuel. Ignited by a driver who is smoking, incorrect fuel procedures, or loose fuel connections.
- Cargo. Freight that is flammable or inadequately closed or loaded, bad ventilation.

Fire Prevention

In order to prevent fires from happening, go through the following checklist:

- Pre-trip inspection. Thoroughly check the electrical, fuel, exhaust systems, tires, and freight. Make sure the fire extinguisher is fully charged.

- En route inspection. Whenever you stop during a trip, inspect the tires, wheels, and truck body to make sure they are not too hot.

- Follow safe procedures. Take appropriate measures for fueling, braking, using flares, and other activities involving flammable materials or processes.

- Monitoring; Glance periodically at the vehicle's instruments and gauges to make sure none of the systems are overheating, and utilize your mirrors to check for signs of smoke from the vehicle or tires.

- Caution. Handle anything flammable with special care.

Fighting Fires

It is imperative that you are aware of how to fight fires. Drivers without this knowledge have made a fire situation worse. Make sure you read and understand the instructions printed on the fire extinguisher located in your vehicle so that you know how to operate it before you need to in an emergency. If a fire does occur, follow these procedures:

Pull Off the Road
First and foremost, get your vehicle off the road and come to a complete stop. Park in a spacious area, away from anything that could catch on fire or put others in danger. Do not pull into a gas station! Call the authorities to alert them of your situation and location.

Keep the Fire from Spreading

You will need to make sure the fire doesn't spread before you attempt to extinguish it. If the fire is in the engine, turn off the ignition as soon as possible and avoid opening the hood if you can. Spray the extinguisher through the vehicle's louvers, radiator, or underneath. If the fire starts in your freight, and you are driving a van or trailer, keep the doors closed, especially if the cargo contains flammable hazardous materials. Opening the doors will "feed" the fire with oxygen, possibly increasing its intensity.

Extinguish the Fire

When using a fire extinguisher, make sure you stand as far away from the fire as you can. Aim the nozzle at the source or bottom of the fire, not higher up near the flames.

Use the Right Fire Extinguisher

The diagrams below explain which fire extinguisher works best for each type of fire. B:C extinguishers are intended for electrical fires and burning liquids. A:B:C types can be used for wood, paper, and cloth fires as well.

Class/Type of Fires	
Class	Type
A	Wood, paper, ordinary combustibles; can be extinguished with water or dry chemicals to quench the fire
B	Gasoline, oil, grease, greasy liquids; can be extinguished with carbon dioxide or dry chemicals to smother, cool, or heat shield the fire
C	Electrical equipment fires; can be extinguished with carbon dioxide or dry chemicals; Do not use water.
D	Fires in combustible metals. Extinguish by using specialized extinguishing powders.

Class of Fire	Type of Extinguisher
B or C	Regular dry chemical
A, B, C, or D	Multipurpose dry chemical
D	Purple K dry chemical
B or C	KCL dry chemical
D	Dry powder special compound
B or C	Carbon dioxide (dry)
B or C	Halogenated agent (gas)
A	Water
A	Water with anti-freeze
A or B	Water, loaded steam style
B, on some A	Foam

Other Tips:

- Water is safe to use for fires on wood, paper, or cloth. Never try to use water to extinguish an electrical fire (it can cause shock) or a gasoline fire (it will make the flames spread).

- A burning tire should be cooled. May require a good deal of water.

- Wait for the firefighters to arrive if you are unsure of how to safely extinguish the fire.

75

- Allow the wind to carry the extinguisher to the fire by standing upwind.

- Continue to put out the fire until the burning material is cooled. The fire can restart even if you don't see smoke or flames.

Alcohol, Other Drugs, and Driving

Alcohol and Driving

It is very hazardous to drive after drinking alcohol. Drinking and driving is the cause of over 20,000 deaths every year. Alcohol affects muscle coordination, reaction time, depth perception, night vision, judgment and inhibition—all necessary for safe driving. Some drivers can be affected by just one drink.

How Alcohol Works
When you have an alcoholic beverage, the alcohol enters your blood stream, where it first travels to your brain. Your body will emit a small amount through your urine, perspiration, and via breathing, but the rest goes to your liver. The liver is only able to process $\frac{1}{3}$ of an ounce of alcohol per hour, much less than the alcohol contained in a standard drink. As a result, only time will help remove the effects of alcohol. If you drink more quickly than your body can process the alcohol, more alcohol will remain in your bloodstream, impairing your driving even more. **Blood Alcohol Concentration (BAC)** is used to measure the level of alcohol in the body.

The following drinks all contain the same amount of alcohol:

- A 12-ounce glass of 5% beer.
- A 5-ounce glass of 12% wine.
- A $1\frac{1}{2}$ ounce shot of 80 proof liquor

What Determines Blood Alcohol Concentration?
A number of factors determine BAC:

- The quantity of alcohol (more alcohol equals a higher BAC)
- How quickly the alcohol is consumed (drinking more rapidly equals a higher BAC)
- Weight (Smaller people don't have to drink as much to reach the same BAC)

Alcohol and the Brain
As BAC builds up in the body, the alcohol increasingly affects your brain and the various body functions it controls. Judgment and self-control are the first to be influenced, which can prevent you from realizing you are getting drunk. This is particularly dangerous for someone who plans to drive, as good judgment and self-control are absolutely essential to drive safely.

As BAC increases, other body functions that are affected include muscle control, vision, and coordination. Effects on driving may include:

- Drifting into another lane.
- Rapid, jerky starts.
- Not using signals or lights.

76

- Going through stop signs and red lights.
- Passing incorrectly.

All of these effects increase the possibilities of an accident and loss of your driver's license.

According to statistics, it is much more likely for drivers who have been drinking to get into an accident than those who have not.

How Alcohol Affects Driving

Drinking alcohol affects the judgment, vision, coordination, and reaction time of all drivers. This results in dangerous driving mistakes, such as:

- Slower reaction time
- Driving too fast or too slow
- Driving in the wrong lane
- Hitting the curb
- Weaving

Other Drugs

In addition to alcohol, other drugs (both legal and illegal) may also impair driving performance. As a commercial driver, many of these are illegal to use or have in your possession while on a work assignment. These include any type of "controlled substance" that could influence your ability to drive safely, such as amphetamines ("pep pills," "uppers," and "bennies"), narcotics, and prescription and over-the-counter drugs (cold medicines), which may cause drowsiness or other impairments. Medicines given to a driver by a doctor are allowed if the doctor has stated that the drug will not affect driving capability.

It is important to check the warning labels on medicines and to heed a doctor's recommendations about potential side effects. Avoid using any illegal drugs and any drug that masks tiredness. Rest is the only remedy for exhaustion. Alcohol or drugs (even those that are over-the-counter) used in tandem with other drugs can exacerbate their effects. The best rule of thumb is to avoid mixing drugs and driving. Driving under the influence of drugs can cause a crash resulting in death, injury, and property damage. It can also cause you to be arrested, fined, or jailed, not to mention the end of your driving career.

Illness

Occasionally you might be too sick to drive safely. If this is the case, you should not operate your CMV under any circumstances. If you fall ill while driving, navigate to the closest location where you can safely stop.

Hazardous Materials Rules for All Commercial Drivers

As a commercial driver, you need to be able to identify hazardous cargo and be aware if you need a hazardous materials endorsement on your CDL license to haul it.

What Are Hazardous Materials?

Hazardous materials are goods that are risky to transport. See the diagram below for reference:

Hazard Class Definitions		
Class	**Class Name**	**Example**
1	Explosives	Ammunition, dynamite, fireworks
2	Gases	Propane, oxygen, helium
3	Flammable	Gasoline, fuel, acetone
4	Flammable solids	Matches, fuses
5	Oxidizers	Ammonium nitrate, hydrogen peroxide
6	Poisons	Pesticides, arsenic
7	Radioactive	Uranium, plutonium
8	Corrosives	Hydrochloric acid, battery acid
9	Miscellaneous Hazardous Materials	Formaldehyde, asbestos
None	ORM-D (other regulated material-domestic)	Hairspray or charcoal
None	Combustible liquids	Fuel oils, lighter fluid

Why Are There Rules?

The safety rules regarding hauling hazardous materials are intended to:

- Contain the product.
- Communicate risk.
- Ensure that drivers and equipment remain safe.

To Contain the Product

Many hazardous goods are so dangerous that they can cause bodily harm or death on contact. To protect drivers and other people, the companies shipping these products follow regulations regarding how to package them safely for transport. Similar containment rules are in place to guide drivers about how to load, transport, and unload bulk tanks.

To Communicate the Risk

To alert dockworkers and drivers of risky cargo, shippers are required to utilize special documentation and diamond shaped hazard labels.

If you have an accident or experience a leak or spill while hauling hazardous cargo, you might not be able to alert emergency personnel about the dangerous goods you are transporting. To help alleviate

78

this problem, keep your hazardous material documentation in an easily accessible spot on top of your other shipping papers:

- In a pouch on the driver's door, or
- In clear view within reach while you are driving, or
- On the driver's seat when you need to leave the vehicle.

Lists of Regulated Products

Placards are designed to alert others that you are hauling hazardous cargo. They are signs placed on the exterior of a vehicle identifying the cargo's hazard classification. Vehicles with placard identification must have at least 4 placards that are exactly the same, located on the front, rear, and both sides and clearly displayed from all 4 directions. They must be at least $10\frac{3}{4}$ inches square, in a diamond shape that is turned upright on a point. Cargo tanks and other bulk packaging vehicles show the identification number of their materials on placards or orange panels.

Identification Numbers are a four-digit code used by emergency personnel to classify hazardous materials for transport purposes. An identification number may signify more than one chemical shipping documentation. Each identification number begins with the letters "NA" or "UN." A list of chemicals and their corresponding identification numbers can be found in the **US DOT Emergency Response Guidebook (ERG)**.

Most (but not all) vehicles hauling hazardous materials are required to have placards. Specific regulations regarding the use of placards are listed in a later section of this guide. You are permitted to operate a vehicle carrying hazardous cargo if placards are not required. If the materials do require placards, you are not allowed to carry them unless you have the hazardous materials endorsement on your driver's license.

79

See diagram below for more information:

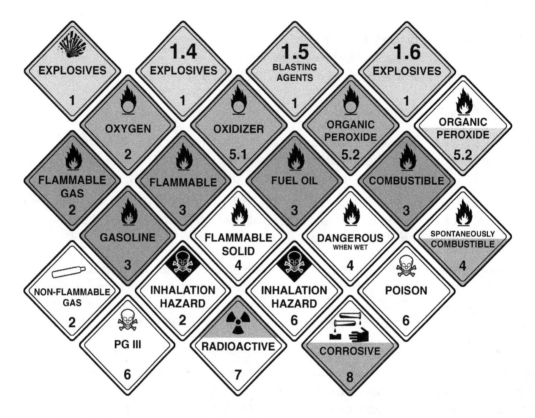

If you drive a placarded vehicle, you must have the hazardous materials endorsement on your driver's license and know how to load and transport hazardous materials safely. This requires passing a written test on hazardous cargo.

Some vehicles carrying liquid or gases require a tank endorsement. These include:

- Vehicles that are Class A or B CDL with permanently mounted cargo tanks of any capacity; or

- Vehicles hauling portable tanks with capacities of 1,000 gallons or greater

You must have a working knowledge of placard regulations if you plan on having a hazardous materials endorsement. Ask your employer if you are not sure whether your vehicle requires placards. If you do not have the hazardous materials endorsement, you should never drive a vehicle that requires placards. This is a criminal offense. If you are pulled over, you will receive a citation and no longer be able to drive your vehicle, costing you time and money. If you fail to display a placard when carrying hazardous materials, you are risking your own life and the life of others in the event of an accident. First responders will have no idea you are hauling dangerous materials.

Drivers of hazardous cargo must also be aware which materials can be combined together in a load and which cannot. The list of regulations is available in a later section of this guide. If you are unsure, refer to this list and consult your employer.

Transporting Cargo Safely

In order to get a CDL, you must know fundamental cargo safety rules. If the material you are carrying is loaded incorrectly or improperly secured, it can be dangerous to yourself and others. Cargo that falls off of your vehicle while you are driving can impact traffic or injure or kill others on the road. It could also injure or kill if you need to stop quickly or get into an accident. Overloading could also damage your vehicle or make it more difficult to steer.

Regardless of whether you pack and safeguard the cargo yourself, you are responsible for:

- Inspecting your cargo.
- Identifying overloaded materials and improperly balanced weight.
- Being aware that the cargo you are carrying is correctly secured and does not block your view in any way.
- Being aware that your cargo does not limit your access to emergency equipment.

If you are hauling hazardous cargo requiring placards, you must also have a hazardous materials endorsement on your license. The information needed to pass the hazardous materials test can be found in a later section of this guide.

Inspecting Cargo

Ensuring that your vehicle is not overloaded and the cargo is correctly distributed and secured is part of your pre-trip inspection procedure.

After Starting
Within the first 50 miles of starting out on a trip, stop to check that the cargo is secured, making any necessary adjustments.

Re-Check
Inspect the cargo and the devices used to secure it as often as needed during a trip to make sure the materials are properly in place. Do a re-check:

- After driving for 3 hours or 150 miles.
- After every break during your trip.

Federal, state, and local laws vary by location regarding CMV weight, securing and covering cargo, and where it is legal to drive large vehicles. Before heading out on a trip, be aware of the regulations on your route.

Weight and Balance

It is your responsibility to make sure the cargo you are carrying is not overloaded. Here is a list of important weight considerations:

- **Gross Vehicle Weight Rating (GVWR):** The loaded weight of a single vehicle as stipulated by the manufacturer.

- **Gross Combination Weight Rating (GCWR):** The loaded weight of a combination (articulated) vehicle as stipulated by the manufacturer. If the manufacturer does not specify a GCWR, the figure is determined by adding the GVWR of the powered vehicle together with the total weight of the unit being towed and any cargo.

- **Axle Weight:** The weight transferred to the ground by one axle or one set of axles.

- **Tire Load:** The maximum weight a tire can safely bear as defined by the pressure rating listed on the side of each tire.

- **Suspension Systems:** The capacity rating as specified by the manufacturer.

- **Coupling Device Capacity:** The maximum weight rating specified for that device.

Legal Weight Limits

The weight of the cargo you are hauling must not be higher than the maximum GVWR, GCWR, and axle weight for the state(s) on your route. The maximum axle weight is often determined via a bridge formula, which allows a lower maximum axle weight for axles that are situated closer together. This is designed to avoid carrying too much weight over bridges and roadways.

If your vehicle is overloaded, it can also affect your steering, braking, and speed control. Trucks that are overloaded travel uphill very slowly and too fast when going down hills. It takes longer for overloaded vehicles to stop, and brakes are more likely to fail if forced to work too hard.

It might not be safe for you to drive in inclement weather or a mountainous region even if your cargo is within the legal maximum weight limit. Make sure to take this into consideration before starting out.

Don't Be Top-Heavy

It is imperative that your cargo is not piled too high or too heavy. If the vehicle's center of gravity is too high, you are more likely to tip over, particularly when driving around a bend or if you need to veer quickly to avoid an obstacle. Make sure the materials you are hauling are loaded as low as possible and the lighter cargo is stacked on top of heavier items.

Balance the Weight

It is also important that the cargo you are hauling is properly balanced. If the steering axle is bearing too much weight, it can be difficult to steer and damage the steering axle and tires. The vehicle may also not steer correctly if the front axles aren't bearing enough weight (the result of cargo shifting to the back). If the driving axles are under-loaded, the vehicle may not get enough traction. This can cause the drive

wheels to spin, making it difficult for the vehicle to operate when weather conditions are poor. There is an increased possibility of rollover if there is too much weight in the center of the hauled unit. If your towed unit is a flatbed, the cargo is also more likely to shift or fall off if it is loaded too heavy.

See diagram below for reference:

Loading Cargo

Wrong	Right

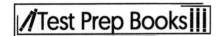
Securing Cargo

Blocking and Bracing

Blocking is secured to the cargo deck and placed tightly against the material being hauled to prevent it from sliding. Cargo is also held in place with bracing, which extends from the upper section of the cargo to the floor and/or walls of the cargo compartment.

Cargo Tiedown

Cargo on flatbed trailers or trailers without sides must be securely tied down to prevent it from shifting around or falling off. **Tiedowns** can also be used in closed vans to stop materials from moving around. You must be sure to use tiedowns that are the correct kind and strength for the cargo being hauled. According to federal regulations, the collective limit of any securement system used to prevent cargo from shifting must be at least $\frac{1}{2}$ times the weight of the cargo. Appropriate tiedown equipment is required, including ropes, straps, chains, and tensioning devices such as winches, ratchets, and clinching components. These tiedowns must be properly attached to the vehicle with fasteners such as hooks, bolts, rails, and rings. See diagram below for reference:

Tie - Down Devices

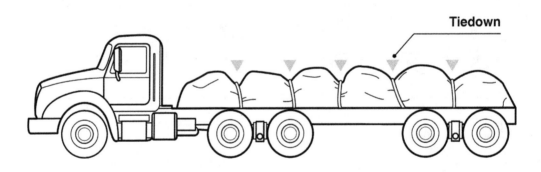

Tiedown

The material you are hauling should have at least a minimum of 2 tiedowns, with at least one tiedown for each 10 feet of cargo. There should be at least 2 tiedowns holding the cargo, no matter how small it is. Make sure your cargo has enough tiedowns to meet these requirements. If you need to secure various heavy pieces of metal, there are special regulations to follow. You will need to determine what these requirements are if you are hauling this type of load.

Header Boards

Front-end header boards (also called "**headache racks**") are designed to prevent the cargo from hitting the driver in case of an accident or sudden stop. Check that the front-end structure is in good working condition so that it will be able to block any cargo being hauled from pitching forward.

Covering Cargo

Why cargo needs to be covered:

- To protect people from spilled cargo.
- To protect cargo from weather conditions.

Many states require spill protection for safety reasons. You need to be aware of the regulations for the states on your route.

As you are driving, check your mirrors to ensure your cargo covers are secure. If a cover appears to be flapping, it could indicate it is about to tear away, which could expose the cargo, potentially blocking your view or another driver's.

Sealed and Containerized Loads

Cargo is loaded into containers for situations where freight is transported by rail or ship for part of its journey. The container is moved to a truck either at the beginning and/or end of the trip. Some container units have their own devices to tie them down or latches that connect the unit directly to a special frame. Other containers are placed on flat bed trailers. All containers need to be correctly secured the same as other cargo.

Containers are typically already sealed, so you won't be able to check the contents, but you should make sure gross weight and axle weight limits are within the proper range.

Cargo Needing Special Attention

Dry Bulk

If you are carrying a dry bulk tank, pay special attention when navigating bends and sharp turns, as these loads have a high center of gravity, which can cause materials to shift.

Hanging Meat

If you are hauling a refrigerated vehicle containing hanging meat, drive slowly and pay special attention when navigating bends and off/on ramps, as these loads are often unstable with a high center of gravity.

Livestock

Livestock is basically moving cargo and requires special care. If you are carrying less than a full load, use false bulkheads to prevent livestock from moving around. But keep in mind that even when livestock are grouped together, they can lean on turns, shifting the center of gravity and increasing the possibility of a rollover.

Oversized Loads

Oversized loads are typically only allowed on the road at particular times and usually require special transit permits. Specific equipment may be required such as "wide load" signs, flashing lights, flags, etc.

A police escort or accompanying vehicles carrying warning signs and/or flashing lights may be necessary. Use extra caution when hauling these types of oversized loads.

Transporting Passengers Safely

If you wish to drive a bus, you will most likely need a CDL and must have a passenger endorsement. The number of multiple passengers requiring a CDL varies from state to state, so check with your local state DMV to make sure. To get the endorsement you must pass a knowledge test on the "Driving Safely" and "Transporting Passengers Safely" sections of this guide. If the bus has air brakes, you will also need to pass a knowledge test on Air Brakes. In addition, you will be required to pass the skills tests for your vehicle class.

Vehicle Inspection

Prior to driving your bus, ensure it is safe by reviewing the inspection report written up by the previous driver. Sign this report only if issues reported earlier have been repaired or deemed not necessary for repair. This certifies that previous issues have been repaired.

Vehicle Systems

Before you begin driving your bus, make sure the following items are working properly:

- Service brakes, including air hose couplings (if your bus is equipped with a trailer or semitrailer)
- Parking brake
- Steering unit
- Lights and reflectors
- Tires (those on the front should not be recapped or regrooved)
- Horn
- Windshield wiper(s)
- Rear-view mirror(s)
- Coupling devices (if so equipped)
- Wheels and rims
- Emergency gear

Access Doors and Panels

Walk around and inspect the exterior of the bus, closing any open emergency exits and access panels (for luggage, restrooms, engine, etc.) prior to driving.

Bus Interior

Since buses left unattended are sometimes vandalized, inspect the inside prior to driving to ensure the safety of your passengers. The aisle and steps leading up to the bus should be clear of any debris and the following sections should be in safe and proper working order:

Do not drive with an open emergency exit door or window. The "Emergency Exit" sign must be clear and/or lit if the bus has lights. Make sure it is on in the evening and any other time outside lights are used.

Roof Hatches

If needed, some of the emergency roof hatches can be left partially open to allow fresh air to circulate. However, make sure they are not left open all the time, and pay special attention to the fact that your bus will have a higher clearance while they are open. Your bus must have legally required fire extinguisher and emergency reflectors, and spare electrical fuses (unless it has built-in circuit breakers). Make sure all these items are present and in good working order.

Use Your Seatbelt!

Check that the driver's seatbelt is in good working order and make sure you always use it for safety reasons.

Loading and Trip Start

The aisle should be completely free of luggage and other items so that passengers have a clear pathway. Make sure your passengers stow their baggage and other belongings in a secure place in order to:

- Prevent damage
- Allow you (the driver) to move freely without restrictions
- Allow passengers to exit through a window or door in the event of an emergency
- Protect passengers from injury if any belongings fall out of the overhead compartment or jostle about

Hazardous Materials

Be on the lookout for any passenger luggage or belongings that may contain hazardous materials. Most hazardous materials are not allowed on buses. The **Federal Hazardous Materials Table** lists the types of items that are considered hazardous and risky to public health, safety, and property during transport. These items must be clearly marked with one of the 9, 4-inch, diamond-shaped hazard labels, listing the name, identification number, and hazard classification of the substance. Check passenger baggage and belongings for these diamond shaped labels. Do not allow any hazardous material on your bus unless you are absolutely certain it is within the proper legal regulations.

See table below for reference:

Hazard Class Definitions		
Class	Class Name	Example
1	Explosives	Ammunition, dynamite, fireworks
2	Gases	Propane, oxygen, helium
3	Flammable	Gasoline, fuel, acetone
4	Flammable solids	Matches, fuses
5	Oxidizers	Ammonium nitrate, hydrogen peroxide
6	Poisons	Pesticides, arsenic
7	Radioactive	Uranium, plutonium
8	Corrosives	Hydrochloric acid, battery acid
9	Miscellaneous Hazardous Materials	Formaldehyde, asbestos
None	ORM-D (other regulated material-domestic)	Hairspray or charcoal
None	Combustible liquids	Fuel oils, lighter fluid

Forbidden Hazardous Materials

Small-arms ammunition labeled ORM-D, emergency hospital supplies, and drugs are permitted on buses. Small amounts of other hazardous materials are also allowed if the shipper cannot transport them any other way.

Buses must never carry:

- Division 2.3 poison gas, liquid Class 6 poison, tear gas, irritating material.
- More than 100 pounds of solid Class 6 poisons.
- Explosives in the same area people are situated, except small arms ammunition.
- Substances considered radioactive in same area people are situated.
- Over 500 pounds of legally permitted hazardous materials, and no more than 100 pounds of any one class of hazardous materials.

Passengers may try to get on your bus with a hazardous substance that is not labeled. Do not permit everyday hazards such as car batteries or gasoline on your bus.

Standee Line

Passengers must stand behind the driver's seat. Buses that have an area for standing room must be clearly marked with a 2-inch line on the floor (called the **standee line**) or some other indicator communicating the standing area to passengers. All standing passengers must stay behind this line.

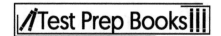

At Your Destination

Once you arrive at the designated or intermediate stop(s), you should announce:

- The location
- Reason for stopping
- Next departure time
- Bus number

Remind disembarking passengers to take all belongings with them. If the aisle is located on a lower level than some of the seats, remind these passengers to watch their step prior to coming to a complete stop. If you are driving a charter bus, do not permit passengers to get on the bus until the slated departure time in order to help prevent theft and/or vandalism of the bus or passenger belongings.

On the Road

Passenger Supervision

Most charter and intercity bus companies have specific regulations pertaining to the comfort and safety of passengers. Before you begin driving, make sure you clarify any rules regarding smoking, drinking, or the use of electronic devices that might disturb others. Spelling out the rules at the beginning will help prevent issues from happening down the road. While driving, use your mirrors to check the inside of the bus as well as the road ahead, the sides, and the rear. You may have to repeat the rules to passengers and/or ask them to refrain from placing their arms or heads outside the window.

At Stops

Make sure to warn passengers to watch their step when exiting the bus, as they may trip when stepping on or off, or when the bus starts or stops. Wait for them to take their seat or hold onto something before starting. Make sure to start up and come to a stop as smoothly as you can to prevent passengers from getting hurt.

On occasion, you may have a passenger who is drunk or unruly. Take care to keep this passenger as safe as the others. Don't let them get off in an unsafe location. It might be best to wait until the next stop that is better lit with more people. Many bus companies have guidelines for handling unruly passengers.

Common Accidents

Most bus accidents occur at intersections. It's best to approach them carefully, even if the traffic flow is directed via signal or stop sign. Sometimes school and commuter buses bump their mirrors or run into passing vehicles when disembarking from a bus stop. Be aware of the clearance area required by the bus you are driving and look out for poles and tree limbs at stops. Have a thorough understanding of the space your bus needs to accelerate and merge into traffic. Wait until a large enough space opens up before pulling away from a stop. Do not presume that other drivers will slow down to allow you to merge in front of them.

Speed on Curves

Accidents are often the result of navigating a bend too fast, often when the road is slippery due to poor weather conditions such as rain or snow. Banked curves feature a safe "design speed." The speed posted is typically safe for cars during decent weather conditions, but it may be too high for many buses. The bus could roll over or skid off the road, depending on the traction level. Make sure you slow your speed on curves—if you are navigating a banked curve and the bus is leaning toward the outside, you are driving too fast.

Railroad-Highway Crossing/Stops

Stop at RR Crossings

- Stop your bus between 15 and 50 feet before approaching a railroad crossing.
- Look and listen in both directions for trains. Open your front door to check if it improves your ability to see or hear an approaching train.
- After a train has gone by, make sure another train is not coming in the other direction before crossing.
- If your bus has manual transmission, never switch gears while driving across the tracks.
- For these circumstances, you are not required to stop, but you must slow down and carefully check for other vehicles:
- At streetcar crossings
- Sites where a policeman or flagman is directing traffic
- At a green traffic signal
- At "exempt" or "abandoned" crossings

Drawbridges

Come to a complete stop at drawbridges lacking a signal light or someone to monitor traffic control. Stop the bus at least 50 feet ahead of where the bridge rises up and make sure the bridge is completely closed before proceeding to cross.

It is not necessary to stop, but you need to slow down and check that the bridge is safe to cross, when:

- The traffic light is green.
- The bridge has someone monitoring traffic when the bridge is open.

After-Trip Vehicle Inspection

Check your bus following each shift. If you drive for an interstate bus company, you will be required to fill out a written inspection report for each bus you operate. Indicate any issues that could lead to crash safety or repair. If there are no problems, mark this on the report.

Sometimes safety-related items such as handholds, seats, emergency exits, and windows need repair. If this damage is reported at the end of a shift, the parts can be fixed before the next trip. If you drive a commuter bus, make sure passenger signaling devices and brake door interlocks are in good working order.

Prohibited Practices

Do not stop to get gas while passengers are on board unless absolutely essential. Never add fuel in a closed building while carrying passengers.

While you are driving, refrain from having conversations or participating in any activity that could divert your attention.

Do not tow or push a bus that is disabled while passengers are inside, unless it would be dangerous for them to exit the bus. Make sure the bus is only towed or pushed to a nearest safe spot to allow passengers to get off. Follow the guidelines of your bus company regarding towing or pushing disabled buses.

Use of Brake-Door Interlocks

City commuter buses may be equipped with a brake and accelerator **interlock system**. The interlock engages the brakes and puts the throttle in idle position when the back door is open. When the back door is closed, the interlock releases. Make sure you do not use this safety feature instead of the parking brake.

Air Brakes

This section is essential if you want to drive a truck or bus with air brakes, or pull a trailer with air brakes. If you want to pull a trailer with air brakes, you also need to read the next section covering Combination Vehicles.

Air brakes utilize compressed air to operate the brakes. Although they are a useful and safe method of stopping big, heavy vehicles, it is essential that they are used correctly and have regular maintenance. Air brakes are comprised of 3 different types of braking systems:

- **Service brake**: employs and releases the brakes when the brake pedal is utilized during normal driving.

- **Parking brake**: employs and releases the parking brakes when the parking brake control is engaged.

- **Emergency brake**: uses components of both the service and parking brake systems to stop the vehicle in case the brake system fails.

These systems are discussed in greater detail below.

Parts of an Air Brake System

An air brake system has many different components. Make sure you have knowledge of the parts reviewed below.

Air Compressor

Attached to the engine through gears or a v-belt, the **air compressor** pumps air into the air storage reservoirs. Either air or the engine cooling system may cool the compressor. It might have its own oil supply or get its lubrication from engine oil. If it has its own oil supply, check the oil level prior to driving.

Air Compressor Governor

The air compressor's governor regulates the air pumped into the air storage tanks. When the air tank pressure reaches its maximum level (around 125 pounds per-square-inch or "psi"), the governor will prevent the compressor from pumping air. When the air tank pressure goes back to a normal level (around 100 psi), the compressor will start pumping air again.

Air Storage Tanks

Compressed air is stored in **air storage tanks**. Although the amount and size of air tanks vary among commercial vehicles, the stored air is enough to supply the brakes for several uses, even if the compressor stops working.

Air Tank Drains

Compressed air often contains small quantities of water and compressor oil, which can be detrimental to the air brake system. In cold weather conditions, the water can freeze, causing the brakes to fail. The water and oil have the tendency to drip to the bottom of the air tank. It is very important to make sure the air tanks in your vehicle are completely drained via the drain valve in the bottom. There are two types of drain valves:

- Manual: operated by turning the valve a quarter turn or pulling a cable. These tanks must be drained manually at the end of each day of driving or trip.

- Automatic: water and oil are automatically ejected. These tanks may also have manual drains. Some automatic air tanks are equipped with electric heating devices, which help prevent the automatic drain from freezing in cold weather.

Alcohol Evaporator

Some air brake systems are equipped with an **alcohol evaporator**. This deposits alcohol into the air system, helping to prevent ice from building up in the air brake valves and other parts during cold weather. If ice gets inside the air brake system, the brakes can freeze up and stop working. Check the alcohol reservoir level and refill every day during cold weather or as needed. It is still necessary to drain the air tanks every day to expel water and oil. (Unless the vehicle is equipped with automatic drain valves.)

Safety Valve

The first tank in the air compressor system has a **safety relief valve**, which is designed to protect the tank and the rest of the system from becoming too pressurized. The open setting for this valve is typically 150 psi. If the safety valve is releasing air, it needs to be checked by a mechanic.

Brake Pedal

The brakes are engaged by pressing on the **brake pedal** (also known as the foot valve or treadle valve). The harder the pedal is pressed, the more air pressure is released. Taking your foot off of the brake pedal disengages the brakes, decreasing air pressure. This causes some compressed air to escape, reducing air pressure in the tanks and requiring the air compressor to kick in. Needlessly pushing in and letting up on the pedal can release air faster than the compressor can replenish it. If the air pressure level is too low, the brakes will not function properly.

Foundation Brakes

Each wheel has **foundation brakes**, with the s-cam drum brake being the most common. The various brake components are listed below.

Brake Drums, Shoes, and Linings

Located on each end of the vehicle's axles, the **brake drums** are bolted to the wheels and house the braking mechanism. The vehicle stops by pressing the **brake shoes** and linings up against the inside of the drum. This pressure causes friction, slowing the vehicle (and generating heat). The degree of heat a

drum can handle before getting damaged depends on how hard and how long the brakes are used. The brakes can stop working if they get too hot.

S-cam Brakes

Pressing the brake pedal releases air into each brake chamber. The air pressure pushes the rod out, engaging the slack adjuster and twisting the brake camshaft. This causes the s-cam to turn (named as such because of its "S" shape).

The **s-cam** pushes the brake shoes away from each other, pressing them against the inside of the brake drum. When the brake pedal is released, the s-cam falls back and a spring forces the brake shoes away from the drum, allowing the wheels to move. See diagram below:

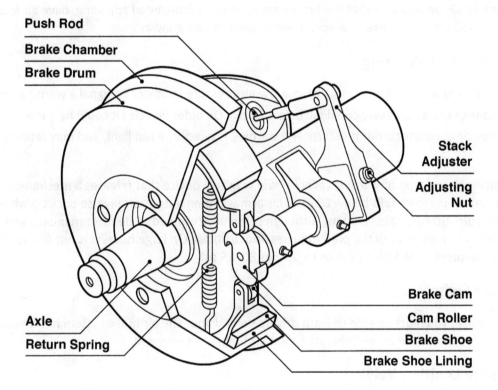

Wedge Brakes

Wedge brakes feature a brake chamber push rod that ejects a wedge directly between two brake shoes, forcing them apart and pushing them against the inside of the brake drum. These types of brakes can contain just one brake chamber, or they might have two chambers that force the wedges in at both ends of the brake shoes. Wedge brakes may need manual adjustment or they could be self-adjusting.

Disc Brakes

Air-operated disc brakes use air pressure to operate a brake chamber and slack adjuster, like s-cam brakes. However, a "power screw" is used rather than a s-cam. The **power screw** is turned as a result of the pressure placed on the slack adjuster by the brake chamber. Similar to a large c-clamp, the power

screw clamps onto the disc or rotor located between the brake lining pads of a caliper. S-cam brakes are more common than wedge or disc brakes.

Supply Pressure Gauges

All vehicles with air brakes have a **pressure gauge** to indicate the amount of pressure in the air tanks. If the system has dual air brakes, each will have its own gauge, or one gauge with two pressure needles. (Dual systems are covered later in this guide).

Application Pressure Gauge

The **application pressure gauge** indicates the level of air pressure being applied to the brakes. Not all vehicles are equipped with this feature. If you need to increase the application pressure to maintain your speed, this is an indicator that the brakes are starting to fade, need adjusting, have air leaks, or mechanical problems. Decrease your speed and downshift into a lower gear.

Low Air Pressure Warning

Vehicles equipped with air brakes must have a low air pressure indicator to signal a warning when there's a chance the air pressure could fall below 60 psi. On older vehicles it could be $\frac{1}{2}$ the amount of the compressor governor cutout pressure. The warning is typically a red light, and may feature a buzzer as well.

Some vehicles have a type of warning called a "**wig wag**"—a device that releases a mechanical arm when the system pressure falls below 60 psi. This arm will then automatically rise back up when the system pressure increases above 60 psi, although some devices need to be reset manually and will not remain in the up position until the pressure rises above 60 psi. On large buses it is not unusual for signals on low-pressure warning devices to buzz at 80–85 psi.

Stop Light Switch

When you brake, you must be able to warn drivers behind you. The air brake system has an electric switch that illuminates the brake lights when the air brakes are engaged.

Front Brake Limiting Valve

A **front brake limiting valve** and a **control knob** can be found in the cab area of some older vehicles (manufactured prior to 1975). The knob is typically labeled "normal" and "slippery." When the knob is placed in the "slippery" position, the limiting valve reduces "normal" air pressure to the front brakes by half. Although limiting valves were designed to prevent the front wheels from skidding on slick roads, they decrease a vehicle's braking power. Front wheel braking is sufficient to use in all circumstances. According to braking tests, it is unlikely to experience a front wheel skid as a result of using the brakes, even during icy conditions. If this knob is present, make sure it stays in the "normal" position.

Automatic front wheel limiting valves decrease the air applied to the front brakes, except in hard braking situations (60 psi or more application pressure). Since they are engaged automatically, they are not driver-operated.

Spring Brakes

Every commercial vehicle is required to have both emergency and parking brakes held in place mechanically (since air pressure can leak). Most CMVs use spring brakes for this purpose, held in place by air pressure when driving. If there is no air pressure, the brakes are engaged via the springs. The driver releases the air from the spring brakes through a parking brake mechanism located in the cab that signals the springs to engage the brakes. The springs will also apply the brakes if all the air is leaked from the air brake system.

The **spring brakes** on tractor and straight trucks will completely engage when air pressure drops to a level of 20 to 45 psi (typically 20 to 30 psi). It is important to safely stop the vehicle as soon as you see the low air pressure warning light and hear the buzzer go off. Do not wait for the brakes to automatically engage; apply the brakes yourself while you still have control. Spring brakes must be adjusted properly in order to retain the required level of braking power and to ensure both the regular brakes and emergency/parking brakes function correctly.

Parking Brake Controls

Newer vehicles with air brakes are equipped with a yellow, diamond-shaped control knob to operate the **parking brakes**. To apply the parking brakes (spring brakes), the knob is pulled out; when the brakes need to be released, it is pushed in. Older vehicles often have a lever to operate the parking brakes, which must be utilized whenever the vehicle is parked.

Caution
The brake pedal should never be pressed when the spring brakes are on, as the combined forces of the springs and the air pressure could damage the brakes. Although most brake systems have a built-in failsafe to prevent this from occurring, not all feature this type of design, and those that do may not always work. As a general rule, it is best to make sure you never press down on the brake pedal when the spring brakes are on.

Modulating Control Valves
Some vehicles feature a control mechanism called a **modulating valve** to steadily engage the spring brakes. It is spring-loaded to give drivers a feel for the braking action. The more pressure that is placed on the mechanism, the more difficult it is to apply the spring brakes. This is designed so the driver can control the spring brakes in the event of a failure to the service brakes. If you need to place a vehicle in park that has a modulating control valve, make sure you pull the lever as far as it will go and make sure the locking device snaps it in place.

Dual Parking Control Valves
The spring brakes are applied when the main air pressure is diminished. Certain vehicles, such as buses, are equipped with air tanks specifically designed to release the spring brakes so the vehicle can be operated in case of an emergency. A push-pull valve is utilized to engage the spring brakes for parking purposes. The other valve is spring loaded in the "out" position; when it is pressed in, air from this separate tank releases the spring brakes so the vehicle can move. Letting go of the control engages the spring brakes again. Since this separate tank only has enough air to do this procedure a few times, it is important to plan carefully before operating the vehicle, or else you might end up in an unsafe place when the separate air supply is out.

Antilock Braking Systems (ABS)

A computerized system designed to prevent your wheels from locking up during hard braking situations, **antilock brakes** are required on the following types of vehicles:

- Truck tractors equipped with air brakes manufactured on or after March 1, 1997

- Other vehicles equipped with air brakes (trucks, buses, trailers, and converter dollies) manufactured on or after March 1, 1998

Many CMVs manufactured prior to these dates have also been updated with ABS. In order to determine whether your vehicle has ABS, check the manufacture date on the vehicle's certification label.

If there is an issue with a vehicle's ABS, a yellow malfunction light will illuminate. These are located:

- On the instrument panel if it is a tractor, truck, or bus
- On the left side (either on the front or rear corner) if it is a trailer
- On the left side if it is a dolly manufactured on or after March 1, 1998

If the vehicle is newer, the malfunction light will illuminate briefly when the vehicle is first turned on for a bulb check, and then turn off. If the vehicle is older, the light may stay lit until you are traveling at a speed higher than five mph. If the light remains on after the bulb check, or lights up as you are driving, the ABS might not be working on one or more wheels.

It might be difficult to discern whether a towed unit built prior to DOT requirements is equipped with ABS. To check, inspect the **electronic control unit (ECU)** located under the unit and the wheel speed sensor wires in the back of the brakes.

Supplementary to the normal brakes, it is important to note that ABS not diminish or increase the brake's normal proficiency. ABS is only activated when wheels are about to lock up. It does not necessarily lessen the vehicle's stopping distance, but it does help control the vehicle during hard braking.

Dual Air Brake

Most CMVs utilize a **dual air brake system**—two separate air brake systems, each with its own air tanks, hoses, lines, etc., that share a single set of brake controls. The "**primary system**" is designed to control the regular brakes on the rear axle(s), and the "**secondary system**" controls the regular brakes on the front axle (and sometimes one rear axle). Both systems deliver air to the trailer.

Prior to operating a vehicle with a dual air system, you will need to let the air compressor rise to a pressure of at least 100 psi in both systems. Check the gauges for both the primary and secondary air pressure (or needles, if the system has two needles in one gauge), keeping an eye on the low air pressure warning light and buzzer. When air pressure in both systems rises to the pre-set level determined by the manufacturer (must be greater than 60 psi), they should turn off.

A drop in air pressure (just prior to dipping below 60 psi in either system) will trigger the warning light and buzzer. If you are driving when this occurs, stop as soon as possible and safely park the vehicle. If

just one air system is experiencing very low pressure, either the front or rear brakes will not be working properly, taking you longer to stop. Safely stop the vehicle and have the air brakes repaired.

Inspecting Air Brake Systems

When inspecting a vehicle with air brakes, follow the same basic seven-step inspection procedure described earlier in this guide, with the addition of the following items listed below in the order they fit into the seven-step method:

During Step 2 Engine Compartment Checks

If the air compressor is belt-driven, check to make sure the air compressor drive belt is snugly in place and in good condition.

During Step 5 Walkaround Inspection

Check the slack adjusters on the S-cam brakes. Make sure the vehicle is parked on level ground and the wheels are chocked to prevent it from moving. Release the parking brakes so you can manually manipulate the slack adjusters. Wearing gloves, pull hard on each slack adjuster within reach. If one of them shifts more than an inch from where it is connected to the push rod, adjust it or have it realigned. You may have difficulty stopping your vehicle if there is too much brake slack. Brakes that are out-of-adjustment are the most common issue spotted during roadside inspections. Check the slack adjusters to ensure safety.

Automatic slack adjustors are available on all vehicles manufactured after 1994. Even though they are self-adjusting when the brakes are fully applied, they still need to be inspected. They do not require manual adjusting except when the brakes are undergoing maintenance and the slack adjusters are being installed. When the pushrod stroke exceeds the legal brake adjustment limit in a vehicle with automatic adjusters, it indicates one of the following:

- There is a mechanical problem in the adjuster
- There is an issue with the related foundation brake parts
- The adjuster was incorrectly installed

If manual adjustment of an automatic adjuster is needed in order to place the brake pushrod stroke within legal limits, it is likely concealing a mechanical problem. In addition, adjusting most automatic adjusters too often can prematurely wear them out. When brakes with automatic adjusters are out of adjustment, it is best to take the vehicle to a repair shop to safely fix the problem. Manually adjusting automatic slack adjusters can be a risky undertaking, since it can mask the effectiveness of the braking system.

It is best to view the manual adjustment of an automatic adjuster as a temporary fix used only in emergency situations. The brake will typically revert back to being out of adjustment anyway since this method does not correct the underlying adjustment problem.

Note: Because different companies manufacture automatic slack adjusters, operation methods vary between systems. You will need to consult the manufacturer's Service Manual before attempting to determine a brake adjustment problem.

Check Brake Drums (or Discs), Linings, and Hoses

The **brake drums** (or discs) should not contain cracks greater than half the width of the friction area. Linings (friction material) need to be tight and clean (not drenched with oil or grease) and not extremely thin. All mechanical parts should be snugly in place, with no broken or missing components. The air hoses attached to the brake chambers should not be cut or worn from excessive rubbing.

Step 7 Final Air Brake Check

Perform the following inspections instead of the hydraulic brake check shown in the earlier section: Check Brake System.

Test Low Pressure Warning Signal

Turn the engine off once the air pressure level is sufficient and the low pressure warning light is not on. Turn on the electrical power and press up and down on the brake pedal to reduce pressure in the air tanks. The low air pressure warning light should illuminate prior to the pressure dropping below 60 psi in the air tank (or in dual air systems, the tank with the lowest air pressure). See diagram below for reference. If the warning light does not go on, you could unknowingly lose air pressure, causing abrupt emergency braking in a single tank system, or increased stopping distance in a dual system. Until the spring brakes engage, braking would be limited.

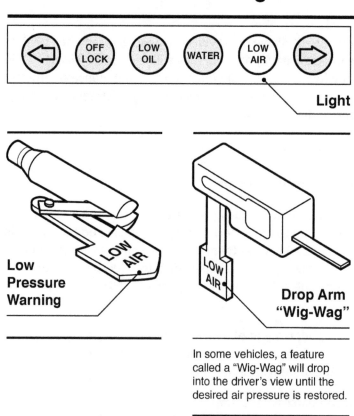

Low Air Pressure Warning Devices

In some vehicles, a feature called a "Wig-Wag" will drop into the driver's view until the desired air pressure is restored.

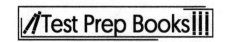

Check That Spring Brakes Come On Automatically

Continue to step up and down on the brake pedal to reduce tank pressure. When the air pressure falls to the manufacturer's specification level (20 to 45 psi), the tractor protection valve and parking brake valve should close (pop out) if the vehicle is a tractor-trailer combination. On other types of vehicles, the parking brake valve should close (pop out). This action should prompt the spring brakes to engage.

Check Rate of Air Pressure Buildup

In vehicles with dual air systems, the pressure should rise from 85 to 100 psi within 45 seconds when the engine is operating at a normal rpm. If the vehicle's air tanks are larger than the minimum required, it could take longer, but still within the safe range. Check the manufacturer's specifications. In single air systems (built before 1975), the pressure typically rises from 50 to 90 psi within 3 minutes with the engine idling at a speed of 600 to 900 rpms. If your vehicle takes too long to build up air pressure, the level might fall too much while you are driving, forcing you to make an emergency stop. Get the issue repaired prior to driving the vehicle.

Test Air Leakage Rate

Check the air leakage rate by following these steps:

- Make sure the air system is completely charged (around 125 psi)
- Turn the engine off
- Chock the wheels
- Release the tractor protection valve (if necessary)
- Push in the parking brake
- Fully apply the foot brake and hold it for one minute

Look at the air gauge. If the air pressure falls more than 3 pounds in one minute (for a single vehicle) or 4 pounds in one minute (for a combination vehicle), the vehicle is losing air too quickly. Before driving the vehicle, check for air leaks. If any leaks are discovered, get them repaired right away or the brakes could fail while you are driving.

Check Air Compressor Governor Cut-in and Cut-out Pressures

The air compressor should begin pumping air around 100 psi and stop around 125 psi. Check the manufacturer's specifications to be sure. Operate the engine at a fast idle. The air governor should cut-out the air compressor while in the manufacturer's specified pressure range and the air pressure on your vehicle's gauge(s) should stop increasing. While the engine is still idling, press up and down on the brake in order to reduce pressure in the air tank(s). The compressor should cut-in around the manufacturer's specified pressure range and the pressure should start rising. If the air governor is not working as described above, it might not retain enough air pressure to ensure safe driving and require repair.

Test Parking Brake

Stop the vehicle, engage the parking brake, and gently pull against it while in a low gear to check that it will hold.

Test Service Brakes

Once at a normal air pressure, release the parking brake, drive the vehicle slowly forward (going about 5 mph), and firmly step on the brake pedal. If the vehicle "pulls" to one side, has an unusual feel, or a delayed stopping action, this could indicate an issue requiring repair.

Using Air Brakes

Normal Stops

For normal stops, press down on the brake pedal, regulating the pressure so that the vehicle comes to a smooth, safe stop. If the vehicle has a manual transmission, don't press in the clutch until the engine rpm is near idling. When you are stopped, select a gear to start up again.

Emergency Stops

It is typical to react by slamming on the brakes if another vehicle pulls or swerves in front of you. This is fine, as long as there's enough distance to stop and properly use the brakes. When you brake, make sure your vehicle stays in a straight line and you can safely turn if needed. There are two braking methods you can use, "**controlled braking**" or "**stab braking**."

Controlled Braking

This technique involves using the brakes with as much force as you can without causing the wheels to lock up, while keeping your steering wheel movements very small. Let up on the brakes if you need to widen your steering or if the wheels lock up, then go back to applying the brakes as soon as you can.

Stab Braking

This style involves fully using your brakes and then quickly letting up once the wheels lock. As soon as the wheels move again, once more completely use the brakes. At least a second might go by before the wheels begin rolling after the brakes are released. If you engage the brakes before the wheels move, the vehicle won't stay straight.

Stopping Distance

Stopping distance was previously described in the section on "Speed and Stopping Distance." However, if you drive a vehicle with air brakes, you will have to factor in "brake lag," which will cause an additional delay when stopping. Brake lag is the amount of time it takes the brakes to engage after the brake pedal is pushed. Hydraulic brakes (the type used on cars and light/medium trucks), work right away, but air brakes need time (at least $\frac{1}{2}$ second) for the air to pass through the lines and reach the brakes.

As a result, there are 4 different factors that need to be added together to determine the total stopping distance for vehicles with air brake systems:

$$Perception\ Distance\ +\ Reaction\ Distance\ +\ Brake\ Lag\ Distance\ +\ Braking\ Distance\\ =\ Total\ Stopping\ Distance$$

A vehicle traveling at a speed of 55 mph on decent road conditions will have an air brake lag distance of about 32 feet, or a total stopping distance of over 450 feet.

102

Brake Fading or Failure

Brakes slow down a vehicle by using brake shoes or pads to create friction against the brake drum or disks. This causes the brakes to get very hot, but brakes are built to withstand high levels of heat. However, using the brakes excessively and/or not taking advantage of the engine braking effect can cause brakes to overheat and fade or fail as a result.

Extreme use of the service brakes can cause them to fade and overheat. The intense heat causes chemical changes in the brake lining, reducing friction and causing the brake drums to expand. As the overheated drums swell, the distance the brake shoes and linings have to move to touch the drums increases, reducing the intensity of this interaction. If the brakes continue to be stressed, brake fade could increase enough that you may not be able to slow or stop the vehicle.

Improper brake adjustment can also cause brakes to fade. If the workload is not equal throughout the vehicle, the brakes out of adjustment will not be performing to their capacity. As a result, the vehicle will not have enough braking power to stop properly. It doesn't take much for brakes to get out of adjustment, especially when they are used often. In addition, when brake linings are hot, they can wear out much faster. It is important for your vehicle to have regular brake adjustment checks.

Low Air Pressure

If your vehicle's low air pressure warning light illuminates, this could indicate an air leak in the system. You need to find a safe place to stop and park immediately—if there is not enough air in the air tanks, controlled braking will be impossible. If the air pressure falls between 20 to 45 psi, the spring brakes will engage. If the vehicle is carrying a large load, it will take longer to stop since the spring brakes are not available on all axles. A vehicle traveling on a slick road or carrying a light load can potentially skid out of control when the spring brakes engage. Play it safe and stop the vehicle while it still contains enough air in the tanks to use the foot brakes.

Parking Brakes

The parking brakes should be used every time you need to park, (except as indicated below.) If the vehicle is a newer model, the **parking brake control knob** is typically a yellow, diamond-shaped knob marked "parking brakes." On older vehicles, the knob might be blue and round or some other shape, such as a lever that swings from side to side or up and down. To engage the parking brake, pull the knob out. When you start up again, push it in to release.

Exceptions:

Do not use the brakes if they are:

- Excessively hot. The heat can damage them.

- Extremely wet in freezing conditions. The brakes can freeze up and make the vehicle impossible to move.

In these situations, park on level ground and use wheel chocks to hold the vehicle in place. If the brakes are too hot, allow them to cool down before using the parking brakes. If the brakes are wet, heat and dry them gently while driving in a low gear.

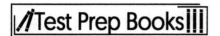

If automatic air tank drains are not present on your vehicle, drain the air tanks at the end of each shift to remove moisture and oil to prevent the brakes from failing.

You should never leave your vehicle unattended without first applying the parking brakes or chocking the wheels. The vehicle could roll, causing injury and damage.

Combination Vehicles

This section details the basic information required to pass the knowledge tests for combination vehicles (tractor-trailer, doubles, triples, straight truck with trailer). If you need to take the knowledge exam for doubles and triples, you should also study the next section.

Driving Combination Vehicles Safely

Driving a combination commercial vehicle is more complicated and demanding than a single CMV, as these vehicles are typically heavier, longer, and require more complex skill set. This section highlights essential safety issues that pertain expressly to combination vehicles.

Rollover Risks

Truck rollovers cause over half of all CMV driver crash fatalities. Towed units that are heavily loaded are 10 times more likely to tip over in an accident than those that are empty. These units have a higher center of gravity, making them easier to tip over.

To help prevent your vehicle from turning over, make sure the cargo is loaded as low to the ground as possible, and navigate around turns very slowly. When driving a combination vehicle, it is even more imperative to load the cargo low and properly centered than when driving a straight truck. If the cargo is located on one side of the truck bed, it can make the trailer lean to that side, increasing the chances of a rollover. It should be positioned in the center and distributed as much as possible.

Since a rollover is most likely to occur when a CMV takes a turn too quickly, make sure to navigate corners and exit/on ramps at a slow pace, and do not attempt quick lane changes, especially when your vehicle is fully loaded.

Steer Gently

Because CMV trailers have the tendency to sway back and forth, quick lane changes can cause them to tip easily. It is not uncommon for accidents to occur where only the trailer has turned over.

This swaying motion is caused by "**rearward amplification**." Vehicles with a rearward amplification of 2.0 are twice as likely to have their trailer tip over than the tractor. Triples have a rearward amplification of 3.5, which means the chances of tipping the last vehicle on a triple unit are 3.5 times more likely than a 5-axle tractor.

When operating a vehicle that is hauling a trailer, you should drive gently and smoothly. Any quick movement with the steering wheel could cause the trailer to turn over. Maintain a safe following distance behind other vehicles, at least one second for each 10 feet of the vehicle's length, plus another second if traveling over 40 mph. Make sure to scan far enough ahead so you won't need to change lanes quickly. At night, drive at a slow enough pace to ensure you can spot any road obstructions before it is too late to make a lane change or stop. Shift down in to a low gear in order to take turns safely.

Brake Early

Whether the load you are hauling is empty or full of cargo, make sure to maintain and control your speed. When a large combination vehicle is empty, it takes longer to stop than when it is fully loaded. In addition, the stiff suspension springs and robust braking system provide poor traction, causing the wheels to lock up easily and increasing the chances of the trailer swaying out and hitting other vehicles. It doesn't take much for the tractor to jackknife.

"**Bobtail**" tractors (tractors without semitrailers) require special caution, as they have been shown to be very difficult to stop smoothly and quickly. They often require a longer stopping time than a fully loaded tractor-semitrailer. When driving any combination vehicle, leave ample distance ahead so you can brake safely without being caught off-guard and needing to stop suddenly.

Railroad-Highway Crossings

Railroad-highway crossings can be problematic for combination vehicles, as they can get easily hung up on raised crossings. The following types are most likely:

- Low clearance units (e.g. lowboy, car carrier, moving van, possum-belly livestock trailer).

- Single-axle tractors hauling a long trailer with its landing gear formulated to handle a tandem-axle tractor.

If you get stuck on the tracks, exit the vehicle immediately and get away from the tracks. Check nearby signage for an emergency number to contact. Call 911 or some other emergency number, giving the operator the crossing location and all identifiable landmarks, particularly the DOT number, if indicated.

Prevent Trailer Skids

When a trailer's wheels lock up, it has the tendency to sway and swing, particularly when carrying very little or no cargo. This is referred to as a "**trailer jackknife**."

The procedure for stopping a trailer skid is:

Recognize the Skid

Checking your mirrors is the best first course of action if you think your trailer has started to skid. Any time you need to brake hard, scan the mirrors to ensure the trailer is staying in place. It is very tough to avoid a jackknife situation once the trailer sways into another lane.

Stop Using the Brake

Let up on the brakes to regain traction and refrain from using the trailer hand brake to "straighten out the rig." This will only make the situation worse, as the trailer wheel brakes were the initial cause of the skid. When the trailer wheels are able to regain firm contact with the road, the trailer will realign behind the tractor.

Turn Wide

When navigating a bend in a CMV, keep in mind that the rear wheels will not be in line with the front wheels. This is called **offtracking** or **"cheating."**

The diagram below demonstrates how offtracking creates a wider route than the rig itself, with longer vehicles offtracking even more. The rear wheels of the CMV offtrack a little, but the trailer's rear wheels offtrack even more. If the vehicle has more than one trailer, the rear wheels of the last one will offtrack the most.

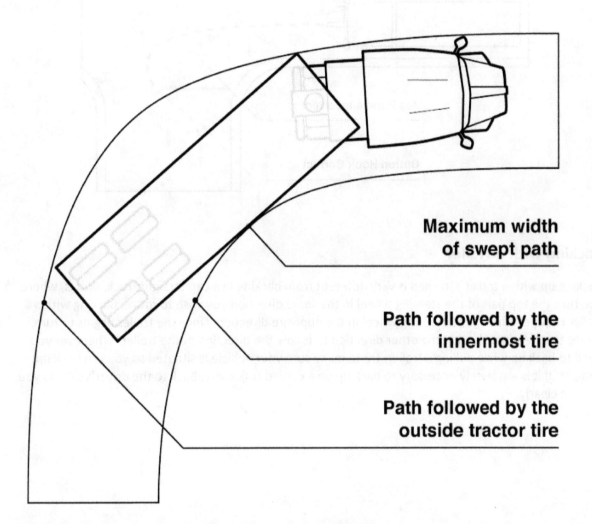

Maximum width of swept path

Path followed by the innermost tire

Path followed by the outside tractor tire

You will need to steer the front end of the vehicle in a wide enough turn when rounding a corner so that rear end does not hit the curb, pedestrians, or anything else on the side of the road or sidewalk. At the same time, you will need to keep the rear of the vehicle close to the curb in order to prevent other drivers from passing you on the right side. If you find you cannot make the turn without entering into

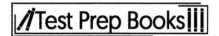
another traffic lane, turn wide as you complete the turn. This is a more effective strategy than curving wide to the left before starting the turn because it stops other drivers from passing on your right side.

See the diagram below for reference.

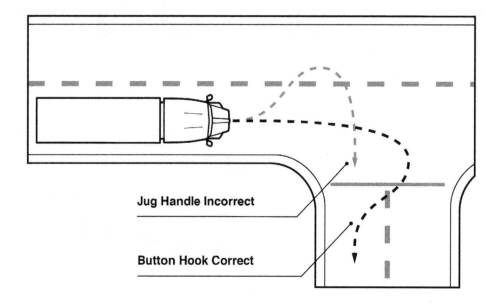

Jug Handle Incorrect

Button Hook Correct

Backing with a Trailer

Backing up with a trailer attached is very different from backing in a car, straight truck, or bus, where you turn the top part of the steering wheel in the same direction you wish to move. Backing with a trailer requires turning the steering wheel in the opposite direction. Once the trailer begins to turn, rotate the steering wheel in the other direction to follow the direction of the trailer. Whenever you need to back up while pulling a trailer, try to make sure your vehicle is situated so you can back up straight. If it is absolutely necessary to back up on a curved trajectory, back to the driver's side so you can see clearly.

See the diagram below for reference.

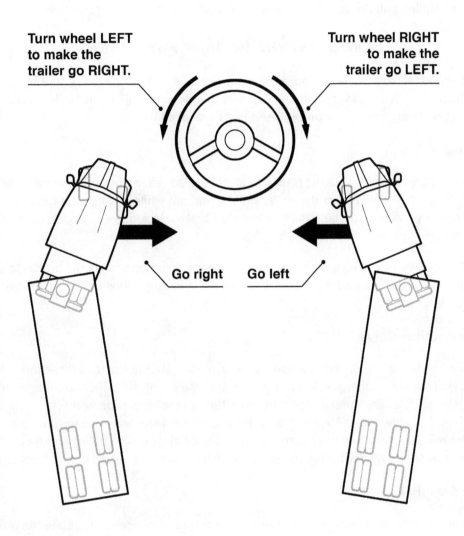

Turn wheel LEFT to make the trailer go RIGHT.

Turn wheel RIGHT to make the trailer go LEFT.

Go right   Go left

Look at Your Path
Before you attempt to back up, get out of your vehicle and walk all around, scanning the path you will travel. Make sure the path behind the vehicle is clear and there is enough room around the sides and top of the vehicle.

Use Mirrors on Both Sides
Repeatedly scan the outside mirrors on both sides of the vehicle. If you are not sure whether there is enough clearance, get out and re-check your route.

Back Slowly
This will allow you to make any necessary modifications before getting too far off track.

Correct Drift Immediately
As soon as you notice the trailer deviating too much from the correct course, adjust its path by turning the top of the steering wheel in the direction the trailer is moving.

Pull Forward

When backing a trailer, pull the vehicle forward as necessary to make re-alignments.

Combination Vehicle Air Brakes

Prior to reading the information below on combination vehicle air brakes, re-read the prior section on air brakes. The braking system in combination vehicles involves controlling the trailer brakes, in addition to the air brake parts explained previously. These parts are listed below.

Trailer Hand Valve

The **trailer brakes** are controlled via the trailer hand valve, also called the **trolley valve** or **Johnson bar**. You should only use this valve to test the trailer brakes, and not while driving, as it can cause the trailer to skid. The foot brake distributes air to all of a vehicle's brakes, including the trailer(s), and is much less likely to cause the vehicle to skid or jackknife.

Do not use the hand valve when you park, as the air might leak out and cause the brakes to unlock. When parking, always use the parking brakes. If the trailer is lacking spring brakes, use wheel chocks to prevent the trailer from rolling.

Tractor Protection Valve

Regulated by a "trailer air supply" control valve located in the cab, the **tractor protection valve** is designed to retain air within the vehicle's brake system in the event the trailer disengages or the air brakes start leaking. You can manually open and shut the tractor protection valve via this control valve. If air pressure gets too low (20 to 45 psi), the tractor protection valve will close automatically, preventing the release of air from the tractor. It also releases air from the trailer emergency line, prompting the trailer emergency brakes to engage, which could cause you to lose control of the vehicle.

Trailer Air Supply Control

On most newly manufactured vehicles, the **trailer air supply control** used to regulate the tractor protection valve is a red, eight-sided knob. Push it in to provide air to the trailer, and pull it out to stop the airflow and engage the trailer emergency brakes. When the air pressure falls to 20 to 45 psi, the valve will automatically pop out, which causes the tractor protection valve to close.

Older vehicles may have a different design for the "emergency" or **tractor protection valve control**. It might not work spontaneously and could feature a lever instead of a knob. If you are pulling a trailer, the lever will be set in the "normal" position. Move the lever into the "emergency" position if you need to turn off the air and use the trailer emergency brakes.

Trailer Air Lines

Every combination vehicle contains two lines to carry air: (1) the service line and (2) the emergency line. These lines run between the vehicle components (from tractor to trailer, trailer to dolly, dolly to second trailer, etc.)

Service Air Line

The **service line**, also called the **control line** or **signal line**, transports the air that is regulated by the foot brake or the trailer hand brake. The level of pressure applied to the foot brake or hand valve determines the force of air in the service line, which is attached to a series of relay valves. These valves help the trailer brakes work more quickly.

Emergency Air Line

The **emergency line**, also called the supply line, has two objectives:

- To transport air to the trailer air tanks.
- To regulate the emergency brakes on combination vehicles

If the emergency line loses air pressure, the trailer emergency brakes will turn on and the tractor protection valve will close (causing the air supply knob to pop out). This loss of pressure could be due to the trailer coming loose from the tractor, causing the emergency air hose to tear, or the breakdown of a hose, metal tubing, or some other part.

Emergency line components (hose, couplers, etc.) are often red in color to avoid confusion with the blue service line.

Hose Couplers (Glad Hands)

The **coupling devices** used to join the service and emergency air lines between the vehicle components are called glad hands. Featuring a rubber seal, the couplers prevent air from escaping. Make sure the couplers and rubber seals are clean before attaching them to the glad hands. To make the connection, press the two rubber seals together with the couplers facing each other at a 90-degree angle. Turn the glad hand connected to the hose to attach and lock the couplers. It is important to make sure that you couple the correct glad hands together. The components are sometimes color-coded to distinguish the various parts that fit together; typically blue for the service lines and red for the emergency (supply) lines. Some vehicles may have metal tags that are attached to the lines labeled with the words "service" and "emergency."

See the diagram below for reference.

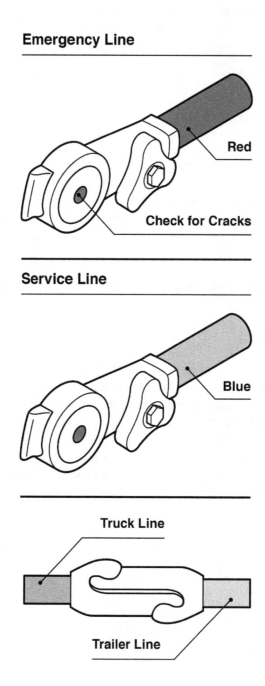

Emergency Line

Red

Check for Cracks

Service Line

Blue

Truck Line

Trailer Line

If the air lines are crossed, supply air will be carried through the service line instead of the trailer air tanks. As a result, the trailer spring brakes (parking brakes) won't have the ability to release. Make sure to check the air line connections if the spring brakes aren't releasing when you press the trailer air supply control, as they could be improperly connected.

Since older trailers lack spring brakes, the trailer wheels will spin and the emergency brakes will not function if the air supply in the trailer air tank leaks out. Before you drive, make sure you always test the

112

trailer brakes by using the hand valve or pulling the air supply (tractor protection valve) control. While in a low gear, pull against them lightly to ensure the brakes are working.

The air supply needs to be kept clean and clear. Some vehicles have "dead end" or dummy couplers in order to keep water and dirt from clogging the components. Attach the hoses to these dummy couplers when the air lines are not connected to a trailer. On some vehicles, the glad hands can be locked together in lieu of dummy couplers.

Trailer Air Tanks

One or more air tanks supply the air pressure for the trailer brakes on every trailer and converter dolly. The air becomes the tractor's emergency (supply) line. The air tanks carry pressure to the brakes via relay valves.

The brake pedal regulates the service line pressure. The pressure in the service line indicates the amount of pressure that should be transported to the trailer brakes by the relay valves.

The air tanks need to be checked frequently for water and oil accumulation; if they get clogged, the brakes might not work properly. Open the drain valve on each tank daily to extract any debris, even if the tanks on your vehicle feature automatic drains.

Shut-Off Valves

The service and supply air lines located in the rear of trailers designed to tow other trailers feature **shut-off valves** (also called **cut-out cocks**). These valves close the air lines when the trailer is not towing another unit. To make sure they will function as intended, check that all the shut-off valves are open except the ones in the rear of the last trailer, which must remain closed.

Trailer Service, Parking and Emergency Brakes

Newer model trailers feature spring brakes just like trucks and truck tractors. However, on converter dollies and trailers that were manufactured prior to 1975, spring brakes were not a requirement. Those lacking spring brakes have emergency brakes, which are supplied by the air stored in the trailer air tank. The emergency brakes will come on whenever the emergency line loses air pressure, which could be the result of the following:

- The air supply knob being pulled out of the trailer is disconnected.
- A major leak in the emergency line, causing the tractor protection valve to close.

As long as there is air pressure in the trailer air tank, the brakes will work. However, when all the air leaks out, the brakes will fail. Since these trailers have no parking brake, it is very important to use wheel chocks when parking a trailer without spring brakes.

A major leak in the service line may not be detected until you attempt to use the brakes. The leak will cause the air tank pressure to drop rapidly and the trailer emergency brakes to come on if the pressure plunges low enough.

Antilock Brake Systems

Trailers Required to Have ABS

ABS is a requirement on trailers and converter dollies manufactured on or after March 1, 1998. However, for those manufactured before this date, ABS was a voluntary requirement. Trailers equipped with ABS feature yellow malfunction lights on the front or rear corner on the left side. Dollies built on or after March 1, 1998, are required to have an ABS light on the left side.

It may be hard to discern whether a vehicle built prior to the required date is equipped with ABS. To make sure, check under the vehicle for the ECU and wheel speed sensor wires projecting out of the back of the brakes.

ABS is a computerized system that is supplemental to your vehicle's regular brakes. It is designed to prevent your wheels from locking when you apply them very hard. An add-on to your vehicle's regular braking system, it does not reduce or intensify the brakes' capability. Triggered when the wheels are about to lock up, ABS may not decrease the distance you will need to stop, but it will help you control your vehicle during hard braking.

Braking with ABS

The system's computer can detect when the wheels are about to lockup, reducing the braking pressure to a safe level and enabling you to remain in control. Even if the ABS is only present on the trailer, or just one axle, you will still have more control when braking. The chances of the trailer swinging out are lower when only the trailer features ABS. However, if you lose control of the steering or start to jackknife, decrease pressure on the brakes (if you can do so safely) until you regain control.

Brake as you normally would when operating a tractor-trailer combination featuring ABS, i.e. use the minimum level of braking power that is absolutely necessary to stop safely and maintain control. This holds true whether you have ABS just on the tractor, just on the trailer, or on both units. As you decrease your speed, pay close attention to the various vehicle components. Step off the brakes (if you can safely do so) to maintain control.

It is important to keep in mind that you still have your standard brakes even if the ABS fails. You can continue to drive, but make sure to get the system checked soon. ABS is strictly supplementary; it won't enable you drive faster, follow behind other vehicles more closely, or drive less cautiously.

Coupling and Uncoupling

In order to safely operate a combination vehicle, it is imperative that you know how to couple and uncouple properly. It is very dangerous if the vehicle is not coupled and uncoupled correctly. Common steps regarding coupling and uncoupling are listed below. However, you will need to be aware of the coupling and uncoupling instructions specific to your CMV, as there are variances between different vehicles.

Coupling Tractor-Semitrailers

Step 1. Inspect Fifth Wheel

Inspect for parts that may be damaged/missing and make sure the fifth wheel is firmly mounted to the tractor, with no cracks in the frame, etc. Check that the plate for this wheel is well greased. If the fifth wheel plate is not lubricated enough, friction between the tractor and trailer could cause steering problems. Make sure the fifth wheel is correctly positioned for coupling:

- The wheel should be tilted down toward the back of the tractor.
- The jaws should be open.
- The safety-unlocking handle is in the automatic lock position.
- Make sure the sliding fifth wheel is locked (if the vehicle is so equipped)
- Check that the trailer kingpin is not bent or broken.

Step 2. Inspect Area and Chock Wheels

Check that the area surrounding the vehicle is clear and the trailer wheels are chocked or the spring brakes are on. Make sure any cargo is snugly in place to guard against movement from the tractor/trailer combination.

Step 3. Position Tractor

Move the tractor so that it is positioned directly in front of the trailer without backing under the trailer at an angle. This can thrust the trailer sideways, breaking the landing gear. Check the position by scanning all along both sides of the trailer using both mirrors.

Step 4. Back Up Slowly

Back up slowly just until the fifth wheel is touching the trailer—do not hit it with any force.

Step 5. Secure Tractor

Engage the parking brake and move the transmission into neutral.

Step 6. Check Trailer Height

The trailer height should be low enough so that it rises up a bit when the tractor is backed underneath. If it is too low, the tractor could collide with the trailer nose, causing damage; if the trailer is positioned too high, it might not couple correctly. Raise or lower the trailer as necessary and make sure the kingpin and fifth wheel are aligned.

115

Step 7. Connect Air Lines to Trailer

Inspect the seals on the glad hands. Connect the tractor emergency air line to trailer emergency glad hand and the tractor service air line to the trailer service glad hand. Make sure air lines are positioned so they aren't crushed or wedged in when you back the tractor under the trailer.

Step 8. Supply Air to Trailer

Check the air supply to the trailer brake system by pressing the "air supply" knob located inside the cab or shift the tractor protection valve control from the "emergency" to the "normal" position. Wait until the air pressure reaches a normal level.

Check the brake system for any crossed air lines:

- Shut off the engine so you can hear the brakes working.

- Step on and off the trailer brakes, listening for the sound of the trailer brakes being applied and released. You should hear the sound of the brakes being pressed and the escape of air when the brakes are released.

- Check the air brake system pressure gauge for indications of major air loss.

- Once you are positive the trailer brakes are in good working order, start engine. Check that the air pressure level is in the normal range.

Step 9. Lock Trailer Brakes

Pull the "air supply" knob out or shift the tractor protection valve control from "normal" to "emergency."

Step 10. Back Under Trailer

To prevent striking the kingpin too hard, back the tractor slowly under the trailer using the lowest reverse gear. Come to a complete stop once the kingpin is locked into the fifth wheel.

Step 11. Check Connection for Security

Slightly lift the trailer landing gear off the ground. Slowly move the tractor ahead while the trailer brakes are still in a locked position to make sure the two units are still connected.

Step 12. Secure Vehicle

Shift the transmission into neutral and turn on the parking brakes. Turn off the engine and make sure you have the key to prevent someone from moving the truck while you are underneath.

Step 13. Inspect Coupling

You may need to get a flashlight in order to do a thorough inspection of the coupling. Check that the area between the upper and lower fifth wheel is snug. Space between them indicates some kind of issue. If the kingpin is wedged on top of the closed fifth wheel jaws, the trailer could easily detach from the tractor. Crawl underneath the trailer and scan the rear of the fifth wheel to ensure that the fifth wheel jaws are firmly closed around the shank of the kingpin and the locking lever is in the "lock" position. Make sure the safety latch is positioned over the locking lever. The catch on some fifth wheels needs to be positioned manually. Do not operate the coupled vehicle if the coupling is incorrect; take it in for repair.

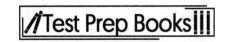

Step 14. Connect the Electrical Cord and Check Air Lines

Plug the electrical cord into the trailer and secure the safety catch. Make sure the air and electrical lines are in good working order and are out of the way of any of the vehicle's moving components.

Step 15. Raise Front Trailer Supports (Landing Gear)

Raise the landing gear using a low gear range (if the vehicle is so equipped). Switch to a higher gear and raise the landing up all the way once the vehicle is no longer bearing any weight. Do not operate the vehicle with landing gear partially in the up position—it could snag on railroad tracks or other obstructions. Once the landing gear is up, make sure the crank handle is safely secured.

When the full weight of the trailer is resting on the tractor:

- Make sure there is enough space between the back of the tractor frame and the landing gear. The tractor should not strike the landing gear when making sharp turns.

- Make sure there is sufficient space between the upper part of the tractor tires and the trailer's nose.

Step 16. Remove Trailer Wheel Chocks

Remove and safely stow wheel chocks.

Uncoupling Tractor-Semitrailers

The following steps will help you safely uncouple your vehicle units.

Step 1. Position the Rig

Check that the parking area pavement is strong enough to support the weight of the trailer.

Move the tractor in line with the trailer. The landing gear can be damaged if you attempt to pull out at an angle.

Step 2. Ease Pressure on the Locking Jaws

Lock the trailer brakes by turning off the trailer air supply and then back up slowly to reduce pressure on the fifth wheel locking jaws. While the tractor is pressing against the kingpin, engage the parking brakes. This holds the vehicle in place while keeping pressure off the locking jaws.

Step 3. Chock the Trailer Wheels

If the trailer lacks spring brakes, or if it is unclear whether it does, make sure to chock the trailer wheels. If air leaks out of the trailer air tank, the emergency brakes will release, causing the trailer to roll if chocks are not in place.

Step 4. Lower the Landing Gear

If the trailer does not contain any cargo, lower the landing gear until it solidly touches the ground. If trailer is full of cargo, turn the crank a few extra turns in a low gear once the landing gear makes solid contact with the ground to relieve the tractor of some of the load. However, make sure you do not lift the trailer off the fifth wheel. Following these steps will:

- Make it easier to unhook the fifth wheel.

- Make it easier to couple the units when you resume driving.

Step 5. Disconnect the Air Lines and Electrical Cable
Detach the air lines from the trailer and join the air line glad hands to the dummy couplers in the rear of the cab or couple them together. Make sure the electrical cable is hung up with the plug facing downward to keep moisture out. Check that the lines are out of the way of any obstructions so the tractor does not damage them.

Step 6. Unlock the Fifth Wheel
Elevate the release handle lock and move the release handle to the "open" position while making sure your legs and feet are out of the way of the rear tractor wheels in the event the vehicle rolls backward.

Step 7. Pull the Tractor Partially Clear of Trailer
Move the tractor forward until fifth wheel comes free from under the trailer. Stop the vehicle once the tractor frame is positioned under the trailer. This will prevent the trailer from crashing to ground if the landing gear drops or gives way.

Step 8. Secure Tractor
Put the transmission in neutral and put on the parking brake.

Step 9. Inspect Trailer Supports
Check that the pavement is able to support the trailer weight and the landing gear is undamaged.

Step 10. Pull Tractor Clear of Trailer
Release the parking brakes, make sure the area ahead is clear, and drive the tractor forward until it is free of the trailer.

Inspecting a Combination Vehicle

Follow the seven-step inspection directions outlined in Section 2 to check your combination vehicle. However, keep in mind a combination vehicle has more of the same items to inspect (e.g. tires, wheels, lights, reflectors, etc.), as well as some new components, which are listed below:

Additional Things to Check During a Walkaround Inspection

Do these checks in addition to those already listed in Section 2.

Coupling System Areas
Check the fifth wheel (lower section).

- Make sure the coupling system is firmly mounted to the frame.
- Check for any missing or damaged parts.
- Make sure components are well greased.
- Make sure there is no space between the upper and lower fifth wheel.

- Check that the locking jaws are positioned around the shank, not the kingpin head. (See diagram below)
- Make sure the release arm is positioned correctly and the safety latch/lock is on.

Kingpin

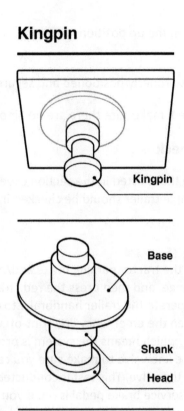

Check the fifth wheel (upper section).

- Make sure the glide plate is firmly mounted to the trailer frame.
- Check for any damage to the kingpin.

Air and electric lines to trailer.

- Check that the electrical cord is securely in place and plugged in.
- Make sure the air lines are free of leaks, attached correctly to the glad hands, and suitably positioned, allowing enough slack for turns.
- Make sure all lines are undamaged.

Sliding fifth wheel.

- Check to see that there is no damage or missing parts to the slide.
- Make sure it is well greased.
- Check for all the locking pins and make sure they are securely locked.
- Make sure no air is leaking if the vehicle is air powered.

- Make sure the fifth wheel is properly positioned. It needs to be back far enough so that the tractor frame won't strike the landing gear, or the cab won't come in contact with the trailer, when you are navigating turns.

Landing Gear
- Make sure the landing gear is in the up position, and none of the components are missing, bent or broken.

- Check that the crank handle is properly positioned and secured.

- If the system is power operated, make sure there are no air or hydraulic leaks.

Combination Vehicle Brake Check

Do the following checks in addition to those listed in the section covering the inspection of air brake systems. The brakes on a double or triple trailer should be checked in the same manner as those on any combination vehicle.

Check That Air Flows to All Trailers
Keep the vehicle in place by engaging the tractor parking brake and/or chocking the wheels. Wait for air pressure to drop within the normal range, and then press the red "trailer air supply" control to transport air to the emergency (supply) lines. Operate the trailer handbrake to carry air to the service line. Go around to the back of the unit and open the emergency line shut-off valve in the back of the last trailer. Listen for the sound of air coming out, which means the system is properly charged. Close the emergency line valve. Open the service line valve to make sure you can hear service pressure air carried through all the trailers, and then shut the valve. This test is conducted under the assumption that neither the trailer handbrake nor the service brake pedal is on. If you do NOT hear air coming out of both lines, check to see that the shut-off valves on the trailer(s) and dolly(ies) are in the OPEN position. Air must be transported all the way to the back in order for all brakes to work.

Test Tractor Protection Valve
Charge the trailer air brake system by bringing the air pressure to a normal level and pressing the "air supply" knob. Turn off the engine and press the brake pedal up and down several times to decrease air pressure in the tanks. Make sure the trailer air supply control (also called the tractor protection valve control) pops out (or changes from a "normal" to "emergency" position) when the air pressure drops to the pressure range stipulated by the manufacturer. (Typically 20 to 45 psi.)

If the tractor protection valve is not working properly, a leaking air hose or trailer brake could drain all the air out of the tractor, causing the emergency brakes to come on and making the vehicle difficult to control.

Test Trailer Emergency Brakes
Charge the trailer air brake system as directed in the previous step (testing the tractor protection valve) and make sure the trailer wheels are rolling freely. Then stop and pull out the trailer air supply knob, or put it in the "emergency" position. Move the trailer slowly forward using the tractor to make sure the trailer emergency brakes are on.

Test Trailer Service Brakes

To test the service brakes, you will need to ensure there is adequate air pressure flow, release the parking brakes, bring the vehicle forward, and then apply the trailer brakes. It should be obvious that the brakes are on, alerting you that they are attached and working properly. While the trailer brakes are tested with the hand valve, the foot pedal is used for their operation. This will carry air to the service brakes located on all the wheels.

Doubles and Triples

This section encompasses the necessary information of the CMV knowledge test for safe operation of double and triple trailers. It contains important information surrounding cautious driving while operating a CMV with more than one trailer, properly coupling and uncoupling vehicle units, and thoroughly inspecting doubles and triples.

Pulling Double/Triple Trailers

Enhanced awareness is required when pulling double or triple trailers, as they are typically less steady than other CMVs, increasing the chances of issues arising. This section will cover some areas of concern.

Prevent Trailer from Rolling Over

Steering steadily and navigating turns and on/off ramps slowly is necessary when pulling multiple trailers in order to avoid them from turning over. You will need to be mindful that when pulling a double or triple trailer, you will have to slow down. You cannot take the curve at the "normal" speed as you might in a straight or single trailer combination truck.

Beware of the Crack-the-Whip Effect

The **"crack-the-whip" effect** is even more pronounced in double/triple trailers, making them even more likely to flip over than other combination vehicles, particularly the last trailer in a combination.

Inspect Completely

Vehicles with two or three trailers contain a greater number of components that need inspecting. Make sure to check all of them by following the procedures listed later in this section.

Look Far Ahead

Double and triple combination vehicles require steady and smooth operation to prevent them from flipping over or jackknifing. Make sure to always scan the road far enough in the distance so you can slow the vehicle or make a gradual lane change if needed.

Manage Space

Keep in mind the extra distance that is required around double and triple combinations. Not only is their length more extensive, but they also need more room for turning and stopping. As a result, more space will need to be kept between you and the vehicle in front of you. Also, make sure your vehicle has enough clearance when entering or crossing traffic and making lane changes.

Adverse Conditions

Harsh driving conditions, including inclement weather, slick roads, and driving in mountainous areas, require even more caution when pulling doubles and triples. Keep in mind that the longer vehicle length and greater number of axles increase the possibility of skids and the loss of traction.

Parking the Vehicle

Park in a location where you'll be able pull straight ahead. Make sure you know parking lot configurations so that you can get out quickly and easily when you need to resume driving.

Antilock Braking Systems on Converter Dollies

Antilock brakes must be equipped on converter dollies on or after March 1, 1998. These brakes should be detectable with a single yellow light placed on the dolly's left side.

Coupling and Uncoupling

Incorrectly coupling and uncoupling of double and triple trailers is very dangerous. Proper steps are listed below.

Coupling Twin Trailers

Secure Second (Rear) Trailer

If the second trailer is without spring brakes, you will need to make sure the tractor is near the trailer, secure the emergency line, charge the trailer air tank, and then detach the emergency line. This will make sure that the trailer emergency brakes are firmly in place, as long as the slack adjusters are properly adjusted. If you think the brakes are not holding, make sure to chock the wheels.

For safety reasons, the trailer with the heaviest cargo should be right behind the tractor, and the trailer carrying lighter weight should be in the last position. There are some dollies equipped with a device called a converter gear. These are designed to couple semitrailers to the rears of tractor-trailer combinations, resulting in a doubled bottom vehicle.

See the diagram below for reference.

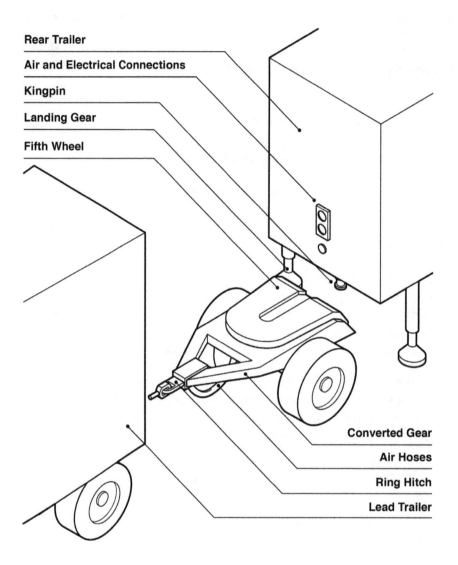

Position Converter Dolly in Front of Second (Rear) Trailer

To release the dolly brakes, open the air tank petcock. If the dolly is equipped with spring brakes, then engage the parking brake control. If the two units are not situated too far apart, manually move the dolly so it is aligned with the kingpin. Or, pick up the converter dolly using the tractor and first semitrailer:

- Place the two units as close as you can to the converter dolly.
- Couple the dolly to the back of the first semitrailer.
- Secure the pintle hook.
- Raise and secure the dolly support.
- Position the dolly as close as possible to the second semitrailer.
- Lower the level of the dolly support.

124

- Unfasten the dolly from the first trailer.
- Move the dolly so it is aligned with the kingpin in front of the second trailer.

Connect Converter Dolly to Front Trailer
- Back up the first semitrailer into place so it is in front of the dolly tongue.
- Fasten the dolly to the front trailer.
- Lock the pintle hook.
- Raise and secure the converter gear support.

Connect Converter Dolly to Rear Trailer
- Firmly secure the trailer brakes and chock the wheels if necessary.
- Position the trailer at the appropriate height. It should be slightly lower than the fifth wheel's center, making the trailer raise up when the dolly is positioned under it.
- Back the converter dolly underneath the rear trailer.
- Raise the landing gear a little bit to prevent damage in the event the trailer rolls.
- Pull against the pin of the second semitrailer to make sure the coupling is secure.
- Visually inspect the coupling to make certain that there is not any space between the upper and lower fifth wheel. The locking jaws should be tightly closed around the kingpin.
- Secure each of the safety chains, air hoses, and light cords to ensure proper function.
- Shut the converter dolly air tank petcock and shut-off valves at the back of the second trailer (service and emergency shut-offs).
- Open the shut-off valves located at the back of the first trailer (and on the dolly if it has them).
- Completely raise the landing gear.
- Charge trailer brakes by pressing in the "air supply" knob, and open the emergency line shut-off at the back of the second trailer to check for air. If you are unable to detect any air pressure, this indicates there is some kind of issue and the brakes are not in working order.

Uncoupling Twin Trailers

Uncouple Rear Trailer
- Park the vehicle in a straight line on a stable level surface.
- Engage the parking brakes so the vehicle won't roll.
- If the second trailer vehicle is lacking spring brakes, chock the wheels.
- To lessen the weight on the dolly, bring the landing gear of the second semitrailer to a lower position.
- Close the air shut-offs in the back of the first semitrailer (and on the dolly if it has them).
- Detach and lock in place each air and electric line of the dolly.
- Release the brakes of the dolly.
- Release the dolly's fifth wheel latch converter.
- Cautiously move the tractor, front semitrailer, and dolly forward. This will give the dolly room to come out from under the second semitrailer.

Uncouple Converter Dolly
- Lower the dolly landing gear.
- Unfasten the safety chains.
- Depress the converter gear spring brakes or chock the wheels if necessary.

125

- Unfasten the pintle hook on the first semi-trailer.
- Slowly move ahead clear of the dolly.

Never unfasten the pintle hook while the dolly is positioned under the rear trailer, as the dolly tow bar could spring up, potentially causing damage, and making it hard to re-couple.

Coupling and Uncoupling Triple Trailers

Couple Tractor/First Semitrailer to Second/Third Trailers
- The tractor should be coupled to the first trailer.
- Follow the aforementioned steps for coupling tractor and semitrailers.
- Positions the converter dolly into place; then, couple the first and second trailers following the steps outlined for coupling doubles.
- The triples vehicle is now properly coupled.

Uncouple Triple-Trailer Rig
- To uncouple the third trailer, remove the dolly and unfasten it using the uncoupling procedure for doubles.

- Once those steps are completed, you can uncouple the rest of the following the standard procedure for uncoupling any double-bottom rig.

Coupling and Uncoupling Triple Trailers

Couple Tractor/First Semitrailer to Second/Third Trailers
Couple the tractor to the first trailer using the previously explained procedure for coupling tractor-semitrailers. Move the converter dolly into its position and couple the first and second trailers using the previous steps for coupling doubles.

Uncouple Triple-Trailer Rig
Uncouple the rear trailer by pulling the dolly out and unlatching the dolly via the procedure used to uncouple doubles. Then uncouple the rest of the vehicle following the same method previously described for uncoupling double-bottom rigs.

Coupling and Uncoupling Other Combinations

The coupling and uncoupling procedures listed above pertain to the more typical tractor-trailer combinations. However, it is important to keep in mind that there are many other methods depending on the type of rig. As a result, you will need to know the coupling and uncoupling procedure specific to your vehicle(s).

Inspecting Doubles and Triples

Combination vehicles have more parts that need to be checked than on a single vehicle. When inspecting doubles and triples, you will use the seven-step inspection procedure described previously, but some components will require multiple checks since there are more of them (e.g. tires, wheels, lights, reflectors, etc.). There are also some new items that will need inspecting, which are listed below.

Additional Checks

Do the following checks in addition to the Walkaround inspection discussed earlier in this guide:

<u>Coupling System Areas</u>
Check fifth wheel (lower)

- Make sure it is securely mounted to the frame.
- Check for missing or damaged parts.
- Make sure it is well greased.
- Check that the upper and lower fifth wheel does not have any gaps.
- Ensure the locking jaws get placed around the shank rather than the kingpin head.
- Check that the release arm is correctly in place and the safety latch/lock is on.

Check fifth wheel (upper)

- The glide plate should be mounted firmly on the trailer frame.
- Check that the kingpin is undamaged.

Air and electric lines to trailer

- Make sure the electrical cord is securely plugged in and tightly in place.
- Check that the air lines and the glad hands are connected, that no air leaks are present, and that their positioning allows for slack during turns.
- Make sure none of the lines show signs of damage.

Sliding fifth wheel

- Make sure there are no missing components or signs of damage on the slide.
- Check that the fifth wheel is well greased.
- Do a check for all locking pins and make sure they are firmly latched.
- For an air powered vehicle, check that it is absent of air leaks.
- The fifth wheel should be positioned far enough back to avoid having the tractor frame strike the landing gear; otherwise, the cab may collide with the trailer when the vehicle is being turned.

<u>Landing Gear</u>
- Make sure the landing gear is in the up position and there are no missing components or visible damage.
- Check that the crank handle is firmly secured.
- For a power operated vehicle, there should not be any air or hydraulic leaks.

<u>Double and Triple Trailers</u>
The shut-off valves on the back-ends of each trailer, in the service, and in the emergency lines need to be in the correct positions:
   o Beck of front trailers: OPEN
   o Back of end trailer: CLOSED
   o Drain valve of converter dolly air tank: CLOSED

127

Make sure the air lines are secured and the glad hands are correctly attached.
If there is a spare tire on the dolly, it must be in the right placement.
Make sure the pintle-eye of the dolly is correctly positioned in the pintle hook of the trailer(s).
Check that the pintle hook is locked in place.
Make sure the safety chains are fastened to the trailer(s).
Check that the light cords are securely locked in the trailer(s) sockets.

Additional Things to Check During a Walkaround Inspection

Do the checks listed below in addition to the checks listed in the section on "Inspecting Air Brake Systems."

Doubles/Triples Air Brake Check

The brakes for a double or triple trailer should be checked just as any other vehicle, following the instructions discussed in the previous section of this guide. In addition, you will need to perform the following checks that pertain to double or triple trailers:

Additional Air Brake Checks

Check That Air Flows to All Trailers (Double and Triple Trailers)

Securely stop the vehicle via the tractor parking brake and/or chocking the wheels. Once the air pressure is at a normal level, press the red "trailer air supply" knob in order to supply air to the emergency (supply) lines. The trailer handbrake can be used to move air to the service line. Walk around to the back of the last trailer and open the emergency line shut-off valve. Listen for the sound of air escaping, which so that air pressure can travel through each trailer, and after, close the valve. The handbrake or service brake pedal must deployed while running this test. If the air escaping from both lines is not audible, double check that the trailer and dolly shut-off valves are actually OPEN. The brakes will not work unless air is carried all the way through the unit.

Test Tractor Protection Valve

The air brake can be charged by balancing the air pressure to a and engaging the "air supply" knob. The engine needs to be shut off and then you can pump the brake pedal multiple times to release air pressure in the tanks. When the air pressure drops into the pressure range specified by the manufacturer (typically 20 to 45 psi), the trailer air supply control (also known as the tractor protection valve control) should pop out (or move from "normal" or "emergency" mode). If there is an error with the functionality of the protection valve, there is a risk that air could leak from the tractor through a hose or brake leak and cause the emergency brakes to switch on, resulting in loss of control of the rig. y

Test Trailer Emergency Brakes

Charge the trailer air brake system and make sure the trailer wheels can move freely. After checking these components, bring the vehicle to a stop and switch the trailer air supply control to the "emergency" position. Using the tractor, pull the trailer slowly ahead to make sure the trailer emergency brakes are working.

Test Trailer Service Brakes

Once the air pressure is in the normal range, release the parking brakes, bring the vehicle forward, and use the hand control to trigger the trailer brakes, if the vehicle has one. You should feel the brakes engage, indicating that the trailer brakes are correctly attached and in good working order. The trailer brakes can be tested with the hand valve and operated with the foot pedal to ensure air makes it to each wheel's service brake.

Tank Vehicles

You will need a tank endorsement for some vehicles carrying liquids or gases. These include:

- Class A or B CDL, and the transported goods have an individual rated capacity surpassing 119 gallons as well as an aggregate rated capacity of no less than 1000 gallons; this includes materials that are attached permanently or temporarily to the vehicle.

- Class C vehicles when the vehicle is used to haul hazardous liquid or gas cargo in the type of tanks described above.

You must inspect the tanker prior to loading, unloading, or driving a tanker in order to ensure that the vehicle is in good working order and can safely transport the liquid or gas.

Inspecting Tank Vehicles

When inspecting your tank vehicle, keep in mind that there are numerous types and sizes, each with components specific to that unit. Refer to the vehicle's operator manual so you know the particulars of inspecting the tank vehicle you will be driving.

Leaks

Since you are transporting a gas or liquid, **leaks** are the most important detail to look for when checking all tank vehicles. It is against the law to transport liquids or gases in a leaking tank. If caught, you will receive a citation, be banned from driving, and might be held responsible for the cleanup of any spilled materials. You will need to look underneath and all around the vehicle for any indications of leaks, checking the following in particular:

- Make sure the body or shell of the tank is free of dents or leaks.
- The intake, discharge, and cut-off valves need to be inspected.
- Make sure all valves are properly positioned prior to loading, unloading, or operating the vehicle.
- The pipes, connections, and hoses need to be checked.
- Check the manhole covers and vents to ensure that the covers contain gaskets, close properly, and the vents are clear.

Check Special Purpose Equipment

If your vehicle is equipped with any of the following items, make sure they are in good working order:

- Vapor recovery kits.
- Grounding and bonding cables.
- Emergency shut-off systems.
- Built-in fire extinguisher.

Do not try to operate a tank vehicle whose valves are exposed or whose manhole covers are open.

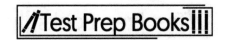

Special Equipment

Inspect the emergency equipment specific to your vehicle. Determine which items are required and make sure you they are present and in good working order.

Driving Tank Vehicles

Because of the elevated center of gravity and specific movements of the materials, special training is required for someone who transports liquids in tank containers.

High Center of Gravity

Tank vehicles carry the majority of the cargo at a higher elevation, and this causes the vehicles weight to unevenly distribute to its top; this makes it more likely to tip over, particularly liquid tankers. Because tests have indicated that tank vehicles can roll over while traveling the normal speed limits posted for curves, you will need to navigate bends and on ramps/off ramps well below the posted speeds.

Danger of Surge

If the tank you are hauling is partially full, the liquid can slosh around inside, disrupting your driving. For example, when you stop, the wave of liquid from the surge can strike the end of the tank, causing the vehicle to move in the same direction as the wave. If you are driving on a slick road when this happens, the wave can push the tanker out into the middle of an intersection. It is important to know how the vehicle you are operating handles.

Bulkheads

Some liquid tanks use **bulkheads** to break the tank into several smaller units. Carefully distribute these smaller tanks during the loading and unloading process, making sure not to place too much weight in the front or back of the vehicle.

Baffled Tanks

Baffled tanks have holes to encourage the flow of the liquid in a way that controls the liquid surging. However, side-to-side surge is still a possibility and can cause the vehicle to tip over.

Un-Baffled Tanks

Forward-and-back surge is very prevalent in **un-baffled liquid tankers** (sometimes called "**smooth bore**" tanks), since they have nothing inside to slow down the liquid movement. These types of tankers typically carry food products such as milk. Sanitation requirements prohibit the use of baffles since they make cleaning out the inside of the tank much more difficult. Use extra caution when operating smooth bore tanks, particularly when starting and stopping.

Outage

Because heat causes liquids to expand, make sure you always leave a little extra room when loading a tanker. This is called "**outage.**" Since the degree of expansion varies according to each liquid, know the outage requirement of the liquid you are hauling.

How Much to Load?

Liquids which are dense in weight and may surpass the legal limits. If you are transporting a liquid of this type, you may need to only partially fill the tank. The amount of liquid you will need to load depends on:

- How much the liquid will expand in transit.
- The weight of the liquid.
- Legal weight limits.

Safe Driving Rules

Safe driving rules regarding tank vehicles include:

Driving Smoothly

The high center of gravity and liquid surge of a tank vehicle require smooth driving, particularly starting, slowing, navigating curves, and lane changes and stopping.

Controlling Surge

In order to control liquid surge, make sure you steadily work the brakes and do not release too quickly when stopping. Use your brakes well ahead of the time you need to stop and increase the distance you are following behind the vehicle ahead of you. Use controlled or stab braking if you need to stop quickly to avoid an accident. These methods are covered in a previous section—review if necessary. Keep in mind that the tanker could tip over if you veer suddenly while braking.

Curves

Slow down when approaching a curve, and then increase your speed slightly as you navigate the curve, keeping in mind that the posted speed may be too fast for your vehicle.

Stopping Distance

Be aware of the distance required to stop your vehicle. Keep in mind that wet roads double the typical distance needed to stop and an empty tanker may take longer to stop than one that is fully loaded.

Skids

To avoid skids, refrain from over steering, driving too fast and braking too hard. If the drive or trailer wheels on a tanker begin to skid, the vehicle could jackknife. When driving any vehicle that begins to skid, work quickly to regain wheel traction.

Hazardous Materials

Cargo that is risky to health, safety, and property during transport is called **hazardous materials**. Things like explosives, gases, solids, flammable and combustible liquid, and others count as hazardous materials. They are often referred to on road signs as **HAZMAT**, or **HM** in government regulations. Since these materials are dangerous, they are heavily regulated at every level of government.

Parts **100–185 of title 49 of the Code of Federal Regulations** contains information about Hazardous Materials Regulations (HMR). **49 CFR 100–185** outlines the regulations for these materials.

These regulations include a Hazardous Materials Table. However, because regulation definitions can vary, the list does not include all items. The type of cargo and the shipper's decision regarding whether or not the material falls under the hazardous material definition determine which items will be labeled as hazardous materials. Some vehicles used for transporting hazardous materials must display specific placards, or warning signs.

This section will help you understand your role and responsibilities when transporting hazardous materials. However, bear in mind that because government regulations are continually changing, it is essential to always refer to the most current copy of the complete regulations, which includes a comprehensive glossary of terms.

According to **49 CFR 383.5**, your CDL must feature an endorsement for hazardous materials before you operate a vehicle transporting these kinds of materials. A written test regarding the regulations surrounding the transport of hazardous materials must be passed in order to gain this endorsement for your license.

This section outlines the information required to pass this exam. It is critical that you keep up-to-date on federal and state regulations and requirements regarding the transportation of hazardous materials. These classes are typically provided by your employer, colleges/universities, and related associations. Copies the required regulations can be accessed through a local Government Printing Office bookstore as well as an industry publisher. In addition, union and/or company offices often have copies on hand.

The regulations stipulate that all drivers carrying hazardous materials must undergo training and testing provided by your employer or a designated representative. Employers are required to maintain training records for every driver who transports hazardous materials for a period of ninety days. Drivers who transport hazardous materials must renew their education and testing results every three years. .

This includes training regarding the security risks of carrying hazardous materials, particularly how to identify and react to potential security threats.

Specialized training is required for drivers who:

- Transport some types of flammable gas or radioactive materials.
- Transport cargo tanks and portable tanks.

The driver's employer or representative is responsible for providing the necessary training.

In some regions, permits are required to carry particular explosives or bulk hazardous wastes, and drivers may need to follow specific hazardous materials routes. In addition, especially dangerous

material (such as rocket fuel) may need a federal permit or exemption. You will need to be aware of permits, exemptions, and special routes for the locations in which you will be operating.

The Intent of the Regulations

Containing the Material

Because hauling hazardous materials is a potentially dangerous matter, regulations are designed to protect the driver, anyone nearby, and the environment. These "containment rules" specify how to safely prepare the materials for transport and outline the proper methods for loading, carrying and unloading this type of cargo.

Communicating the Risk

The shipped must communicate the risks of hazardous cargo by labeling them with the appropriate warning labels as well as inserting the correct papers regarding shipping information, emergency protocol, and warning signs. By following these steps, the shipper, carrier, and the driver are all aware of the potential risks.

Assuring Safe Drivers and Equipment

You must pass a written exam covering the protocol for hazardous materials transportation before you will be eligible for the CDL endorsement. In order to pass the exam, you will need to know how to:

- Identify various hazardous materials.
- Safely load cargo.
- Properly placard your vehicle as per regulations.
- Safely transport cargo.

Study and follow the hazardous materials regulations in order to reduce the possibility of damage and injury. Failure to abide by the rules is not only dangerous, but it can result in fines and time in prison. It is important to inspect your vehicle before and during each trip, as you could be pulled over by a police officer for a spot check. A spot check may include inspection of shipping papers, warning signs, and verification of your endorsement and knowledge of the cargo you are transporting.

Hazardous Materials Transportation—Who Does What

The Shipper

Prior to sending the cargo to its proper destination via truck, rail, vessel, or airplane, the shipper refers to the hazardous materials regulations in order to determine the cargo's:

- Identification number
- Proper shipping name.
- Hazard class.
- Packing group.
- Proper packaging.

- Proper label and markings.
- Proper placards.

The shipper is responsible for:

- Packaging, marking, and labeling the hazardous items.
- Preparing the shipping papers.
- Supplying emergency response information.
- Providing placards.
- Preparing the shipment according to regulations.

The Carrier

The **carrier** transports the material from the shipper to its destination. Before taking the cargo, the carrier makes sure the shipper has properly described, marked, labeled, and organized the items, rejecting any that are incorrectly prepared. The carrier is also responsible for informing the appropriate government agency of any hazardous materials accidents and/or incidents.

The Driver

The driver is responsible for:

- Reviewing the hazardous materials classifications, marks, and labels done by the shipper.
- Refusing any packages and cargo that is leaking.
- Placarding the vehicle while loading the cargo, if so required.
- Safely transporting the material in a timely manner.
- Following the regulations specific to transporting hazardous materials.
- Keep up with the shipping papers and information regarding emergency response procedures.

Communication Rules

Definitions

Many terms used to classify hazardous materials vary from the typical term definitions you may have seen in the past. There are nine different hazard classes used to describe the potential dangers correlated with each item.

The types of materials included in these nine classes are listed in the table below; definitions of other significant hazardous materials terms can be found in the glossary at the end of this section.

Class	Division	Name of Class or Division	Examples
1	1.1	Mass explosives	Dynamite
	1.2	Projection hazards	Flares
	1.3	Mass fire hazards	Display fireworks
	1.4	Very insensitive	Ammunition
	1.5	Extreme insensitive	Blasting Agents
			Explosive devices
2	2.1	Flammable gases	Propane
	2.2	Non-flammable gases	Helium
	2.3	Poisonous/toxic gases	Fluorine, compressed
3	-	Flammable liquids	Gasoline
4	4.1	Flammable gases	Ammonium Picrate,
	4.2	Spontaneously combustible	Wetted white
	4.3	Spontaneously combustible when wet	phosphorus sodium
5	5.1	Oxidizers	Ammonium nitrate
	5.2	Organic peroxides	Methyl ethyl ketone
			Peroxide
6	6.1	Poison (toxic material)	Potassium cyanide
	6.2	Infectious substances	Anthrax virus
7	-	Radioactive	Uranium
8	-	Corrosives	Battery fluid
9	-	Miscellaneous	Polychlorinated
		Hazardous materials	Biphenyls (PCB)
e	-	ORM-D (other regulated material-domestic)	Food flavorings,
			medicine
	-	Combustible liquids	Fuel oil

Hazardous Materials Table

Shipping papers (including shipping orders, bills of lading, and manifests) list and specify the hazardous cargo being transported.

Each hazardous material must be correctly listed and be assigned an **emergency response number**. Carriers and drivers are required to make sure they have quick access to these papers and the necessary emergency response information is clearly indicated. To make sure the papers are handy, drivers should keep them in one of the following places:

- In a pouch on the driver's door
- Within immediate reach while driving—in clear view while the seat belt is on
- On the driver's seat when exiting the vehicle

These shipping papers help alert emergency personnel of the hazardous material you are transporting. Depending on the kind of accident you get into, you may not be able to personally notify anyone, so the papers will be essential in this time.

Package Labels

Most cargo containing hazardous materials will be marked with a diamond-shaped hazard-warning label to make others aware of the potential danger. If a label cannot fit on a package, the shipper can secure the package with a tag containing the label. For example, compressed gas cylinders can be difficult to attach labels to, so they often feature tags or decals with the needed information.

Lists of Regulated Products

Placards

These are warning signs that indicate a vehicle or package contains hazardous materials. These **placards** must be positioned on the outsides of their containers so as to notify any cargo handlers. There must be at least four identical placards on a placarded vehicle, placed on the front, rear, and both sides so that they are visible from all four directions. At least 250 mm (9.84 inches) on each side, placards are square-on-point, in a diamond shape. Cargo tanks and bulk packaging should display their identification numbers on placards or other designated signs.

Emergency personnel use these identification numbers to identify hazardous materials. Some numbers may be used to classify more than one chemical. The letters "NA" or "UN" precede each 4-digit number. The United States Department of Transportation's **Emergency Response Guidebook (ERG)** has a listing of hazardous chemicals and their designated identification numbers. There are three major lists that shippers, carriers, and drivers refer to when classifying hazardous materials. A driver should always check a material's name against all three lists before transporting it, since some items are found on all lists, but others just one. Always check the following lists:

- Section 172.101, the Hazardous Materials Table.
- Appendix A to Section 172.101, the List of Hazardous Substances and Reportable Quantities. Appendix B to Section 172.101, the List of Marine Pollutants.

The Hazardous Materials Table

The diagram below displays a section of the Hazardous Materials Table. Column 1 lists the shipping mode(s) affected by each hazardous item and other data regarding the shipping description. The next bullet points indicate the shipping name, hazard class, identification number, packaging group, and their specified labels. The first column may contain up to 6 different symbols:

- (+) Signifies the correct shipping name, hazard class, and packing group, even if the material isn't technically defined as hazardous.

- (A) Indicates that the hazardous material listed in the second column falls under the Hazardous Materials Regulation (HMR) only when slated for air transport unless it is considered a hazardous substance or waste material.

- (W) Means the hazardous material displayed in the second column falls under HMR only when slated for water transport unless it is considered a marine pollutant, or hazardous substance or waste material.

- (D) Signifies that the shipping name can be used to describe cargo hauled domestically, but may not be suitable for international transport.

137

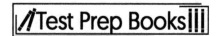

- (I) Indicates a shipping name appropriate for materials transported internationally; a different shipping name may be assigned when the transport is domestic.

- (G) Means the hazardous material described in the second column has been given a basic shipping name and a technical name, as well as a hazardous marker for the shipping paper.

The second column shows the correct shipping names and descriptions of hazardous substances that are regulated. They are listed alphabetically to make finding the correct entry easier. The shipping paper must list the proper shipping names for each item, which should be displayed in regular typeface. Those listed in italics are not the proper shipping names.

49 CFR 172.101 Hazardous Materials Table									
Symbols	Hazardous materials description and proper shipping names	Hazard class or division	Identification numbers	PG	Label Codes	Special provisions (172.102)	Packaging (173. ***)		
							Exceptions	Non bulk	Bulk
(1)	(2)	(3)	(4)	(5)	(6)	(7)	(8A)	(8B)	(8C)
A	Acetaldehyde ammonia	9	UN1841	III	9	IB8, IP6	155	204	240

The third column lists the class or division of the hazardous material. Sometimes a "forbidden" status is listed—these items are strictly prohibited from transport. Hazardous cargo shipments should be placarded based on the quantity and hazard class of the item(s). You should be able to determine the proper placard based on the following:

- The hazard class of the material
- The amount of the item(s) being shipped.
- The total amount of the hazardous material(s) en route

The fourth column displays the identification number for each proper shipping name. Each identification number begins with the letters "UN" or "NA"—"NA" numbers are used to designate shipments within the United States and to and from Canada. The identification number visible on the hazardous material's packaging, tanks, and shipment papers. In the event of an accident or other incident, emergency personnel can use this number to quickly identify the hazardous materials.

The fifth column lists the hazardous material's packing group (displayed in Roman numeral format).

The sixth column lists the hazard warning label(s) required by shippers of hazardous materials. Some cargo may need more than just one label if there is more than one type of hazard present.

The seventh column displays any additional stipulations. Refer to the federal regulations for special information if there is an entry in this column. If it is a number between one and six, the hazardous material is a poison inhalation hazard (PIH). PIH materials require specific instructions regarding shipping papers, marking, and placards.

The eighth column features three parts that reflect the section numbers and requirements for packages of each material present.

The ninth and tenth columns are disregarded for highway transportation.

Appendix A to 49 CFR 172.101: The List of Hazardous Substances and Reportable Quantities

Any spills of a reportable quantity of the hazardous items listed in the chart below must be reported to the DOT and the EPA by either you or your employer.

The column on the right lists the reportable quantity (RQ) for each item. When the items on this list are carried in one package in an RQ or more, the shipper much mark "RQ" on the corresponding packaging and papers.

If "INHALATION HAZARD" is marked anywhere on the packaging or papers, "POISON INHALATION HAZARD" or "POISON GAS" placards must be placed as regulated by the product's hazard category. Make sure the hazard class placard and the POISON INHALATION HAZARD placard are always in clear view, even if you are transporting small quantities.

Hazardous Substances and Reportable Quantities	
Hazardous Substance	Reportable Quantity (RQ) Pounds (Kilograms)
Phenyl mercaptan @	100 (45.4)
Phenylmercury acetate	100 (45.4)
N-Phenylthiourea	100 (45.4)
Phorate	10 (4.54)
Phosgene	10 (4.54)
Phosphine	100 (45.4)*
Phosphoric acid	5,000 (2270)
Phosphoric acid, diethyl 4-nitrophenyl ester	100 (45.4)
Phosphoric acid, lead salt	10 (.454)
*Spills at or in excess of 10 pounds require reporting.	

Appendix B to 49 CFR 172.101: List of Marine Pollutants

Appendix B lists chemicals that are toxic for marine life. The list of marine pollutants is specifically for chemicals whose container has a capacity of at least 119 pounds and does not have a label as suggested by the HMR when transported via highways. Any bulk packages of a Marine Pollutant must display the **Marine Pollutant** marking (white triangle with a fish and an "X" through the fish). This marking is required to be place on the outside of the vehicle. Additionally, "Marine Pollutant" must be labeled at the top of the shipping papers.

The Shipping Paper

The hazardous material shipping papers require:

- Page numbers (if more than one page is included). The total number of pages must be listed on the first page (i.e. "Page 1 of 4").
- The correct shipping description for each hazardous material.
- Proper certification signed by the shipper stating that the shipment was prepared as per regulations.

The Item Description

If a shipping paper contains hazardous and non-hazardous materials, the hazardous information must be:

- Listed first.

- Highlighted with a contrasting color, OR

- Identified by an "X" in the "HM" column located in front of the shipping description (ID#, Shipping Name, Hazard Class, Packing Group). "RQ" can be signed instead of "X" if it is necessary to identify a reportable quantity.

The correct order and listing of hazardous materials is as follows:

- Identification number
- Proper shipping name
- Hazard class or division
- Packing group, if any (displayed in Roman numerals and may be preceded by "PG")

The identification number, shipping name, and hazard classification should not be abbreviated unless permitted by hazardous materials regulations.

It must also include:

- The total amount and unit of measure of the cargo.
- The total number and item type (e.g.: "6 Drums").
- The letters RQ, if the cargo is a reportable quantity.
- The name of the hazardous substance if the letters RQ are present (if not included in the shipping name).
- The technical name of the hazardous material for all items classified with the letter "G" (Generic) in Column 1.

Shipping papers are also required to list an emergency response telephone number designated by the shipper (unless excepted). If an accident or emergency occurs, emergency professionals can reference the number to figure out what hazardous content are involved in the incident. The telephone number must belong to:

- The person advocating for transportation of the hazardous material (if this person is the emergency response information (ERI) provider); or

- An agency or organization able to accept responsibility for providing the detailed information listed in paragraph (a)(2) of this section. The person connected with the ERI provider must disclose their name, contract number, or a unique identifier permitted by the ERI provider.

Shippers must submit **emergency response information** for their material being shipped to the person transporting the shipment. This must be accessible outside of the CMV and it is required to have

information explaining how to securely manage circumstances involving the cargo. The following information is required:

- The basic description of the material and its technical name
- Immediate health hazards
- Fire or explosive dangers
- Precautions to be taken in case of an accident or incident
- Procedures for dealing with fires
- Instructions for handling spills or leaks without a fire
- Initial first aid procedures

This information can be listed on the shipping paper, as part of a separate document that includes the hazardous cargo's technical name and basic description, or in a guidebook such as the Emergency Response Guidebook (ERG). Some transport carriers include an ERG inside each vehicle hauling hazardous items. The driver is responsible for communicating their emergency response information to the authority figure(s) that arrive at or investigate an accident involving the hazardous materials.

The total amount, number, and type of material must be posted with the basic description information. The package type and measurement unit may be shown in an abbreviated format. For example: 10 ctns. UN1263, Paint, 3, PG II, 500 lbs.

If the material is hazardous waste, the shipper must include the word WASTE in front of the correct shipping name on the shipping paper (hazardous waste manifest). For example: UN1090, Waste Acetone, 3, PG II.

For a non-hazardous material, it does not need a hazard class or identification number.

Shippers must keep a record (electronic or physical) for two years (three years for hazardous waste) after the material has been collected. If the company is not the actual initiator of a shipment and only provides transportation for it, they must maintain records for at least only a year.

Keep in mind: The **Code of Federal Regulations**, **Title 49**, **Parts 100–185** contains the requirements for transporting hazardous materials.

Shipper's Certification

The certification (signature) of the shipper should be present on the original shipping paper, indicating the shipper's guarantee that the material has been prepared as per regulations. Exceptions include:

- A private carrier transporting their own material
- The package is provided by the carrier (for example, a cargo tank)

Unless there is a blatantly dangerous or nonconforming component of a package, it is safe to assume that certification concerning the proper packaging is appropriate. Some carriers may have additional requirements regarding the transport of hazardous materials. When accepting shipments, make sure you adhere to the rules imposed by your employer.

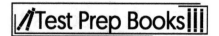

Package Markings and Labels

The shipper provides the required classification for the hazardous cargo, which varies according to the material size and type. It is typically placed on the package, a label, or a tag. The identification of the material must be identical to what is stated on the shipping paper. As necessary, the following information should be visible on the packaging:

- Information, including name and address of shipper or consignee.
- The name and identification number of the hazardous material.
- The necessary labels.

Make sure you compare the shipping paper with the labels/markings on the hazardous cargo. The correct description must be on the shipping paper, and it must be verified that the appropriate labels are on the packaging. If the material is unrecognizable, the shipped needs to contact the carrier's office.

If required by the regulations, the shipper will include the classifications RQ, MARINE POLLUTANT, BIOHAZARD, HOT, or INHALATION-HAZARD on the package. Liquid containers must be placed in the proper upright direction. Their labels should depict the hazard class of the material. If there are multiple labels needed, they needs to be placed adjacent to each other and their correct shipping names.

Recognizing Hazardous Materials

Learn how to identify shipments of hazardous materials. Checking the shipping paper will help you determine whether a shipment contains hazardous items. Look for:

- An item with the proper shipping name, hazard classification, and identification
- A highlighted entry, or if an X or RQ is in the corresponding column

Other indicators of hazardous materials:

- The business category of the shipper. The examples listed below often manufacture hazardous products:
- Paint dealer
- Chemical supply
- Scientific supply house
- Pest control or agricultural supplier
- Explosives, munitions, or fireworks dealer
- Tanks with diamond labels or placards at the shipping location
- The type of package being shipped
- Cylinders and drums are often used to carry hazardous materials
- A hazard classification label, correct shipping name, or proper identification number on the package
- Any safety precautions

Hazardous Waste Manifest

If the material you are hauling is considered hazardous wastes, you will be required to sign and carry a **Uniform Hazardous Waste Manifest** cataloging the identifier and **EPA registration number** of the

intended shippers, carriers, and destination. This manifest must be prepared, dated, and signed by the shipper and should be regarded like a shipping paper while the waste is being transported. Make sure you hand over the shipment only to another designated carrier or disposal facility. The manifest must be hand signed by each carrier transporting the hazardous waste. Retain your copy once the shipment is delivered. Make sure each record includes the necessary signatures and dates, as well as information from the final delivery destination.

Placarding

Before driving the vehicle, make sure all the necessary placards are in place. An incorrectly placarded vehicle can only be moved during an emergency as a precautionary measure to protect life and property.

Placards must be present on both sides/ends of the vehicle. Each placard must be:

- Clearly seen from its facing direction
- Situated so that the words or numbers are even and readable from left to right
- No less than three inches from another label placement
- Away from any equipment or components such as ladders, doors, and tarpaulins
- Clear from damage so that all necessary information is visible
- Attached to a background that has a contrasting color.

The front-end warning sign may be attached to the tractor or the trailer. "Drive Safely" and other slogans are forbidden.

To decide the which placards are necessary, you will need to know:

- The hazard class of the items
- The amount of hazardous materials being shipped
- The net weight of the total hazardous materials being transported

Placard Tables

There are two placard tables to help determine the correct placards to use. Table 1 indicates which items must be labeled with warning signs regardless of the amount being transported. See diagram below for reference.

Placard Table 1: Any Amount	
If your vehicle contains any amount of…	Placard as…
1.1 Mass Explosives	Explosives 1.1
1.2 Project Hazards	Explosives 1.2
1.3 Mass Fire Hazards	Explosives 1.3
2.3 Poisonous/Toxic Gases	Poison Gas
4.3 Spontaneously combustible when wet	Dangerous When Wet
5.2 (Organic peroxide, Type B, liquid or solid, Temperature controlled)	Organic Peroxide
6.1 (Inhalation hazard zone A & B only)	Poison
7 (Radioactive Yellow III label only)	Radioactive

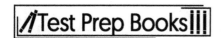

With the exception of bulk packaging, the materials in Table 2 must be labeled with warning signs if the amount being transported exceeds 1,001 pounds (including the package). Include the amount from all the shipping papers for the total number of items listed on Table 2 that you are carrying. See diagram below for reference.

Placard Table 2: 1,001 Pounds or More	
Category of Material (Hazard class or division number and additional description, as appropriate)	Placard Name
1.4 Very Insensitive	Explosives 1.4
1.5 Extreme Insensitive	Explosives 1.5
1.6	Explosives 1.6
2.1 Flammable Gases	Flammable Gas
2.2 Non-Flammable Gases	Non-Flammable Gas
3 Flammable Liquids	Flammable
Combustible Liquid	Combustible*
4.1 Flammable Gases	Flammable Solid
4.2 Spontaneously Combustible	Spontaneously Combustible
5.1 Oxidizers	Oxidizer
5.2 (other than organic peroxide, Type B, liquid or solid, Temperature Controlled	Organic Peroxide
6.1 (other than inhalation hazard zone A or B)	Poison
6.2 Infectious Substances	(None)
8 Corrosives	Corrosive
9 Miscellaneous Hazardous Materials	Class 9**
ORM-D	(None)
*Flammable may be interchangeable for combustible on cargo or portable tanks.	
**Class 9 is not necessary for transportation domestically.	

You are permitted to attach DANGEROUS placards rather than separate placards for each class expressed in Table 2 when:

- 1,001 pounds or more of two or more these are being carried, necessitating distinctive placards, and

- 2,205 pounds or more of any Table 2 materials have not been loaded in a single location. You must use the specific placard for this material.

If "**INHALATION HAZARD**" is present on the packaging or papers, warning labels with "POISON GAS" or "POISON INHALATION" will need to be included as well as any other warning labels as mandated by its hazard classification. The 1,000-pound exception is not applicable to these items.

Items that have an additional "dangerous when wet" classification are required to display a "**DANGEROUS WHEN WET**" warning label as well as any additional label mandated by its classification. The 1,000-pound exception is not applicable in these instances.

Placards which separate a primary or subsidiary classification of a material are required to clearly display its hazard class or division number on the lower corner of the warning label. Subsidiary hazard labels lacking the hazard class number but are permanently attached, are allowable as long as they meet the requirements for their corresponding color codes. Placards can be places on hazardous materials regardless of requirement as long as they accurately describe what is being transported

A single container with an equal amount or excess of 119 gallons is referred to bulk packaging. They must be labeled appropriately even if there is only hazardous residue present. Some bulk packages need placarding on each of the vehicle's side or may show its labels. All others need to warning labels on all four sides.

Loading and Unloading

Make sure you treat containers of hazardous materials with special care. Using unnecessary tools during the loading process risks damage to the containers being loaded.

General Loading Requirements

Make sure you set the parking brake prior to loading or unloading hazardous material to ensure the vehicle will not move. Hazardous cargo should not be loaded near a heat source, as many products become even more dangerous when exposed to heat.

Be on the lookout for packages that are leaking or damaged. Remember: LEAKS INDICATE TROUBLE! Do not transport any containers that are leaking. Not only could it put you, the vehicle, and others around you in danger, but it is also illegal to drive a vehicle containing hazardous materials that are leaking.

Make sure you securely fasten any hazardous materials cargo prior to a trip to help avoid shifting of packages during transport.

No Smoking
Keep away from fire when loading or unloading hazardous materials—do not allow anyone to smoke near your vehicle. Absolutely no smoking around the following items:

- Class 1 (Explosives)
- Class 2.1 (Flammable Gas)
- Class 3 (Flammable Liquids)
- Class 4 (Flammable Solids)
- Class 5 (Oxidizers)

Secure Against Movement
Firmly secure all hazardous cargo so that it doesn't fall, shift, or move around during transport. Use caution when loading containers with valves or other fixtures.

After the packages are loaded, do not open any of them during your trip, including transferring hazardous items from one package to another while you are hauling them. Only a cargo tank is allowed to be emptied while on your vehicle—all other containers are not permitted to be opened while in transit.

Cargo Heater Rules

There are specific regulations for cargo heaters during the loading process:

- Class 1 (Explosives)
- Class 2.1 (Flammable Gas)
- Class 3 (Flammable Liquids)

Cargo heaters and air conditioner units are usually not permitted. It is advised against storing any of the above mentioned items with a heater in a cargo space.

Use Closed Cargo Space

Overhang or tailgate loads of the following items are forbidden:

- Class 1 (Explosives)
- Class 4 (Flammable Solids)
- Class 5 (Oxidizers)

A closed off cargo space is needed to store the above mentioned item, with exceptions to:

- Fire and water-resistant materials
- Materials covered with a tarp that is fire and water-resistant

Precautions for Specific Hazards

Class 1 (Explosives) Materials

Prior to loading or unloading any explosives, turn off your engine and then inspect the cargo area. Make sure to:

- Disable cargo heaters.

- Disconnect the heater power source(s) and drain heater fuel tank(s).

- Check for any sharp points that might damage the items you are transporting. Can the area for exposed screws, broken panels, and broken floorboards.

- A floor lining should be utilized with Division 1.1, 1.2, or 1.3. The floors need to be tightly sealed and the liner material should be either non-metallic or non-ferrous metal (any metal not made out of iron or iron alloys).

- Use extra care to protect cargo that contains explosives:

    o Avoid using hooks or other metal tools.
    o Avoid mishandling packages.
    o Keep it clear of other cargo that might be damaging.

Division 1.1, 1.2, or 1.3 cargo should not be switched over to another vehicle while on a main highway. In the event that an emergency transfer must take place, you must place the appropriate warning signs along the highway and vehicle to warn other drivers on the road.

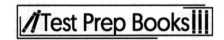

Never transport packages containing explosives that are damaged or show signs of dampness or an oily stain.

Division 1.1 or 1.2 should not be transported in vehicle combinations under the following circumstances:

- One of the vehicles contains a marked or placarded cargo tank.

Avoid transportation if a vehicle in the combination contains:

- Division 1.1 A (Initiating Explosives)
- Packages of Class 7 (Radioactive) materials labeled "Yellow III"
- Division 2.3 (Poisonous Gas) or Division 6.1 (Poisonous) materials
- Portable tanks containing hazardous materials, on a DOT Spec 106A or 110A tank

Class 4 (Flammable Solids) and Class 5 (Oxidizers) Materials

Solids that react spontaneously or to water, heat, and air (including fire or explosion) are considered Class 4 materials.

Materials that fall under Class 4 and 5 must be securely sealed off or covered during transport. Cargo that becomes unstable and dangerous when exposed to liquid needs to be kept dry during transit and loading and unloading. Items that are susceptible to spontaneous combustion or heat must be transported in properly ventilated vehicles.

Class 8 (Corrosive) Materials

When loading items by hand, carry breakable containers containing corrosive liquid one at a time, making sure they are right side up. Load them in an area with an even floor surface, being careful not to drop or roll the containers. Carboys should only be stacked if the bottom containers can comfortably withstand the weight of the top containers without posing a hazard or risk their contents.

Avoid stacking nitric acid on top of other materials during transport or storage. Charged storage batteries should be loaded right side up, so no liquid spills out and away from other cargo that could damage them.

Corrosive liquids should never be loaded next to or above:

- Division 1.4 (Explosives C).
- Division 4.1 (Flammable Solids).
- Division 4.3 (Dangerous When Wet).
- Class 5 (Oxidizers).
- Division 2.3, Zone B (Poisonous Gases).

Corrosive liquids should never be loaded with:

- Division 1.1 or 1.2.
- Division 1.2 or 1.3.
- Division 1.5 (Blasting Agents).
- Division 2.3, Zone A (Poisonous Gases).
- Division 4.2 (Spontaneously Combustible Materials).
- Division 6.1, PGI, Zone A (Poison Liquids).

147

Class 2 (Compressed Gases) Including Cryogenic Liquids

If the vehicle lacks the proper shelving for safely storing cylinders, they should then be stored on a flat floor of the vehicle. The cylinders must be:

- Held upright.
- Stored in racks secured to the vehicle or placed inside boxes to prevent them from rolling over

They can be stored on their sides only if the relief valve is placed in the vapor space.

Division 2.3 (Poisonous Gas) or Division 6.1 (Poisonous) Materials

Never carry poisonous gas or materials in containers with interconnections. Never load cargo that is labeled POISON or POISON INHALATION HAZARD in the driver's cab, sleeper compartment or near food products meant for humans or animals. You must have specific training in order to load and unload Class 2 materials in cargo tanks and follow the regulations for handling this type of cargo.

Class 7 (Radioactive) Materials

Some Class 7 (Radioactive) materials have a "transport index" number. They should be classified Radioactive II or Radioactive III by the shipper and have a transport index on the label. These packages will be surrounded by radiation, which will also permeate all packages within close vicinity. To deal with this issue, regulations limit the number of packages that can be loaded together and their proximity to people, animals, and unexposed film. The **transport index** indicates the required boundaries during transit. A vehicle's transport index of all cargo in transit cannot exceed 50. The table below lists the rules for each transport index, indicating the proximity for loading Class 7 (Radioactive) materials to people, animals, or film. Consider: a package's transport index of 1.1 cannot be loaded within two feet of people or cargo walls.

Radioactive Separation Table A						
Total Index/Transport	Minimum distance in feet to nearest undeveloped film					To People or Cargo Compartment Partitions
	0-2 hours	2-4 hours	4-8 hours	8-12 hours	Over 12 hours	
None	0	0	0	0	0	0
0.1 to 1.0	1	2	3	4	5	1
1.1 to 5.0	3	4	6	8	11	2
5.1 to 10.0	4	6	9	11	15	3
10.1 to 20.0	5	8	12	16	22	4
20.1 to 30.0	7	10	15	20	29	5
30.1 to 40.0	8	11	17	22	33	6
40.1 to 50.0	9	12	19	24	36	

Mixed Loads

Regulations forbid some products to be loaded in the same cargo area. They must be loaded separately. See table below for examples.

Do Not Load Table	
Do Not Load	**In the Same Vehicle With**
Division 6.1 or 2.3 (POISON or poison inhalation hazard labeled material)	Food of any kind; General toiletries do not fall into the "foodstuff" category.
Division 2.3 (Poisonous) gas Zone A or Division 6.1 (Poison) liquids, PGI, Zone A	Division 5.1 (Oxidizers). Class 3 (Flammable Liquids). Class 8 (Corrosive Liquids). Division 5.2 (Organic Peroxides). Division 1.1, 1.2, 1.3 (Class A or B) Explosives. Division 1.5 (Blasting Agents). Division 2.1 (Flammable Gases). Class 4 (Flammable Solids).
Charged storage batteries	Division 1.1 (Class A Explosives)
Class 1 (Detonating primers)	Other explosives unless less otherwise authorized dur to special packaging.
Division 6.1 (Cyanides or cyanide mixtures)	Corrosive materials, or acidic materials that may release hydrocyanic acid; Including: Cyanides, Inorganic, n.o.s. Silver cyanide Sodium cyanide
Nitric acid (Class B)	Can be loaded as long as the nitric acid is not positioned above other items in transit.

Other materials that must be separated are listed on the Segregation Table for Hazardous Materials.

Bulk Packaging Marking, Loading, and Unloading

Since cargo tanks are bulk packaging permanently affixed to a vehicle, they remain attached during the loading and unloading process. Portable tanks are considered bulk packaging except they are not secured to a vehicle. Cargo is loaded or unloaded while these tanks are out of the vehicle and then placed on the vehicle for transport. While there are several different types of cargo tanks in use, the most common are MC306 for liquids and MC331 for gases.

Markings

The **identification number** of any and all hazardous materials in transit must be obviously visible on the carrier. According to regulations, there must be orange panels, placards, or a white diamond-shaped sign with black 100 mm (3.9 inch) numbers displayed on the vehicle. Specification cargo tanks must be labeled with a re-test date.

Portable tanks must indicate the name of the lessee or owner and the shipping name of the material being transported on two opposite sides. Portable tanks with capacities of more than 1,000 gallons must have the shipping name clearly visible at two-inches tall, and the shipping name must be at least one-inch tall on tanks less than 1,000 gallons. The identification number should be visible on all sides and

ends of portable tanks transporting more than 1,000 gallons; This number should be visible on both opposite sides of a tank transporting less than 1,000 gallons. If all qualifying identification numbers are not visible when the tank is secured on the CMV, the numbers will need to be displayed additionally on both sides and ends of the transport vehicle.

Intermediate bulk containers (IBCs) are not required to display the shipping name or owner of the vehicle.

Tank Loading

It is the responsibility of the worker who loads and unloads the cargo tank to verify that the correct person is in attendance and monitoring this process. The overseer of the loading and unloading process must:

- Be alert.
- Have clear sight of the cargo tank.
- Stand within 25 feet of the tank.
- Be aware of the cargo hazards.
- Know emergency procedures.
- Be sanctioned and able to move the cargo tank if needed

Cargo tanks carrying propane and anhydrous ammonia have special requirements for those who must be present.

In order to prevent leaks or hazardous materials, all valves need to be closed before traveling, every time. As regulated by 49 CFR 173.29, operating such a vehicle with open valves is illegal with the exception being only if it is empty of all contents.

Flammable Liquids

Your vehicle must be shut off before engaging in loading or unloading flammable liquids. The engine should be running only if necessary to operate a pump. Ground a cargo tank properly before opening and filling it with the flammable liquid. Make sure the ground is maintained until the filling hole is closed.

Compressed Gas

Liquid discharge valves on compressed gas tanks should always be closed, unless of course they are being filled or empties. The engine needs to be turned off during the filling or emptying process unless it needs a pump to complete the transfer. If the engine is needed for transferring the contents, you should still turn it off once the contents have been transferred but before the transfer hose is taken off. All connections that were used for filling or emptying the tank should be removed before coupling, uncoupling, or transferring the actual cargo tank. Make sure trailers and semi-trailers are chocked to prevent movement when unfastened from the power unit.

Hazardous Materials—Driving and Parking Rules

Parking with Division 1.1, 1.2, or 1.3 Explosives

If Division 1.1, 1.2, or 1.3 explosives are being transported, it is imperative that you refrain from parking within five feet of the main road. With exception for unavoidable vehicle operations (like filling the vehicle with gas), you should not park the hazardous vehicle within 300 feet of:

- Bridges, tunnels, or buildings
- Common areas where people congregate
- Open fires

If you need to park because of job responsibilities, make it brief. Don't park on private property unless you make sure the owner knows the risks. Make sure an individual is always supervising the parked vehicle. You may allow another person to look out for your vehicle only if it is:

- On the shipper's property.
- On the carrier's property.
- On the consignee's property

A safe haven refers to an area where drivers may leave their vehicles with explosive cargo unattended. Local authorities typically authorize them.

Parking a Placarded Vehicle Not Transporting Division 1.1, 1.2, or 1.3 Explosives

Contrary to the rule regarding vehicles transferring explosives, a placarded vehicle (without explosives) can be parked within five feet of the main road for a brief moment. There must be an additional person to monitor the vehicle while it is stopped on a main road. A trailer carrying hazardous materials may not be left on a main road and then abandoned within 300 feet of an open fire.

Attending Parked Vehicles

A placarded vehicle must be monitored by someone who is:

- Inside the vehicle, awake, and not inside the sleeper berth, or within 100 feet of the vehicle and have it clearly within their sight
- Knows the danger level of the materials being transported
- Is aware of proper emergency procedures
- Is able to move the vehicle, if necessary

No Flares!

Reflective triangles or red lights should be used to warn surrounding drivers if your vehicle breaks down. Flares should be avoided, especially around:

- Vehicles that carry or have carried Class 3 (Flammable Liquids) or Division 2.1 (Flammable Gas)
- Vehicles with Division 1.1, 1.2, or 1.3 Explosives contents

Route Restrictions

Permits are required to transport hazardous materials or wastes in some states and counties, which may limit your routes in these locations. Since local route and permit regulations often vary, you must determine any deviations and ensure you have the required paperwork prior to starting out.

When working for a carrier, and not independently, route restrictions or required access permits will typically be communicated before beginning your route. If you are an independent trucker and the route is a new one for you, inquire the agencies of the states you will be traveling through before your trip.

Educating yourself on travel restrictions for hazardous materials along your route before beginning can help you to avoid any conflict or hang-ups once the route is in progress. For a placarded vehicle, you will need to refrain from driving in densely populated communities, tunnels, narrow streets, or alleys. Even if it is not convenient, choose another route unless that is the only way you can go. Always avoid open fires while driving a placarded vehicle unless you can safely get by without having to stop.

For driving Division 1.1, 1.2, or 1.3 explosives, you are required to travel according to a pre-planned route as determined by your carrier. If these materials are collected somewhere aside from your employer's loading and unloading terminal, you are then permitted to plan your route before departing. The plan needs to be formulated ahead of your trip and you need to keep a copy with you while transporting the explosives. When you hand over a shipment of explosives, make sure the person accepting it is authorized or the items are delivered to locked rooms specifically designated for explosives storage.

It is up to the carrier to decide the safest route for transporting placarded radioactive materials. After the route is chosen, the carrier must share details of the radioactive cargo and route plan.

No Smoking

Make sure you do not smoke within 25 feet of a placarded cargo tank carrying Class 3 (flammable liquids) or Division 2.1 (gases). All smoking products should not come within 25 feet of any vehicle containing:

- Class 1 (Explosives)
- Class 3 (Flammable Liquids)
- Class 4 (Flammable Solids)
- Class 4.2 (Spontaneously Combustible)

Refuel with Engine Off

Always turn your engine off before adding fuel to a CMV carrying hazardous materials and make sure someone is standing near the nozzle controlling the flow of fuel.

10 B:C Fire Extinguisher

A fire extinguisher with a UL rating equal to or more than 10 B:C is required to be attached to the power unit of a vehicle with warning labels.

Check Tires

Your vehicle's tires must be properly inflated and not flat or leaking in any way. Check each tire prior to every trip and each time you stop to park using a tire pressure gauge. If a tire is leaking or flat, do not drive unless it is necessary to get to a safe place to get it repaired.

If a tire is overheated, remove it and stow it a safe distance from your vehicle. Don't start up again until the cause of the overheating is determined. The regulations regarding parking and attending placarded vehicles are applicable even when checking, repairing, or replacing tires—make sure to obey them.

Where to Keep Shipping Papers and Emergency Response Information

Never consent to a hazardous material shipment that does not have a correctly prepared, easily recognizable shipping paper. When you are transporting hazardous materials, it is important for others to be able to quickly locate the shipping paper following a crash. In order to make them easily identifiable from other papers, attach tabs or some other feature or store them on top of the other papers.

Store the shipping papers within reach or in a pouch on the driver's side door while you are driving so they can be located quickly and easily.

When you are not driving, stow shipping papers in the driver's door pouch or on the seat. Make sure emergency response information is stored with the shipping paper.

Papers for Division 1.1, 1.2 or, 1.3 Explosives

Each driver transporting Division 1.1, 1.2, or 1.3 explosives must obtain the following from their carrier: (1) a copy of Federal Motor Carrier Safety Regulations (FMCSR), Part 397, and (2) written directions about what to do if they are delayed or in an accident. The written instructions should include:

- A contact list of names and phone numbers (including carrier agents or shippers).
- The type of explosives being transported.
- Emergency instructions in case of fires, accidents, or leaks.

Drivers need to sign a receipt for these documents and make sure they have the proper:

- Shipping papers.
- Emergency instructions.
- A written route plan.
- A copy of FMCSR, Part 397

Equipment for Chlorine

If you are carrying chlorine, the vehicle must have an approved gas mask and an emergency kit on the cargo tank designed to control any leaks in dome cover plate fittings.

Stop Before Railroad Crossings

You are required to stop at a railroad-crossing if your vehicle:

- Is placarded.
- Is transporting any amount of chlorine.
- Has hazardous material cargo tanks, either loaded or empty.

Make sure you stop 15 to 50 feet prior to the nearest rail. Drive forward only when you are positive a train is not coming and you can cross the tracks without stopping. Do not shift gears while driving across the tracks.

Hazardous Materials: Emergencies

Emergency Response Guidebook (ERG)

It is imperative that your shipping papers contain the proper shipping name, identification number, label, and placards of the material(s) you are transporting.

Firefighters, police, and industry personnel use a reference book published by The Department of Transportation that outlines how to use protective measures for hazardous materials. In case of an accident, emergency workers will check the item(s) on the shipping paper against those listed in this guidebook, which is indexed by shipping name and hazardous material identification number.

Crashes/Incidents

If there's an issue or accident involving your vehicle, your job as a professional driver is to:

- Direct people away from the scene.
- Control the hazardous material if you can do so safely.
- Make first responders aware of the risks of the hazardous cargo.
- Share the shipping papers and emergency response information with emergency personnel.

Follow this checklist:

- Make sure your driving partner is not injured.
- Have the shipping papers with you.
- Make sure people stay away and upwind from the accident.
- Alert others of the cargo's danger.
- Telephone for help.
- Heed the directions of your employer.

Fires

Although you might have experience dealing with minor truck fires, do not attempt to put out a fire involving hazardous materials unless you have the skill and correct equipment. Specialized training and protective gear are required to fight a hazardous materials fire.

As soon as you notice a fire, telephone for assistance. If it is a minor truck fire, use the fire extinguisher to keep the fire from spreading to the cargo area before firefighters arrive. Before attempting to open the trailer doors, feel the outside to check if it is hot. If so, do not open the doors, as there could be a fire in the cargo area. Opening the door could allow the air to feed the fire. Less damage will occur if you keep the doors shut and allow the fire to smolder until firefighters arrive. If the hazardous material is already on fire, you should not attempt to fight it. Keep the shipping papers with you and show them to first responders as soon as they arrive. Make sure to direct others away from the fire and warn them of the risky material.

If you notice a leak in your cargo, use the shipping papers, labels, or package location to help determine the hazardous materials. Use caution when attempting to identify the hazardous material. Don't touch any item that is leaking or try to pinpoint the material or source of the leak by its scent. Hazardous materials are dangerous and could cause injury or cause you to lose your sense of smell even if you can't detect any aroma. Make sure you do not eat, drink, or smoke around a hazardous material leak or spill.

If hazardous materials are leaking out of your vehicle, do not attempt to drive it any further than required. Move the vehicle away from the road and any crowded locations. Try to get help or locate a phone booth or truck stop. Not only is the spillage of hazardous material dangerous to the environment and other people, but it is also costly to clean up. If you notice hazardous materials leaking from your vehicle:

- Park it immediately.
- Secure the area around the vehicle.
- Remain nearby.
- Ask someone else to get help.

When sending someone for help, give that person:

- A description of the incident.
- Your precise location and direction you are travelling.
- Your name, the name of the carrier, and the name of your terminal's location.
- The correct shipping name, hazard class, and identification number of the hazardous materials you are transporting, if you know what they are.

Since this is a good deal of information for someone to relay, it is best to put all the necessary points in writing when you send them to get help. This will help emergency personnel optimally address the situation since they may be a distance away. If they are aware of hazards they are facing, they can then bring the appropriate equipment.

Do not attempt to repack a package that is leaking, unless you have the training and equipment to safely repair leaks. Instead, contact your dispatcher or supervisor for directions and any emergency personnel if necessary.

Responses to Specific Hazards

Class 1 (Explosives)

If you are transporting explosive materials and your vehicle breaks down or gets into an accident, make sure to warn others nearby and keep people out of the way. Do not let anyone smoke or have any kind

of fire near the vehicle. If the material is on fire, warn others of the risk of explosion. If your vehicle has collided with other vehicles, make sure to separate all explosives and place them at least 200 feet from the vehicles and occupied buildings. Make sure you stay a safe distance away from them.

Class 2 (Compressed Gases)
If you discover compressed gas leaking from your vehicle, make sure to warn others of the danger and only allow authorized emergency personnel to remove the hazard or debris. Any time an incident involves compressed gas, you must let the shipper know.

If you are on a public road, do not transfer flammable compressed gas unless you are filling machinery designed for road construction or maintenance.

Class 3 (Flammable Liquids)
If you have an accident or vehicle breakdown while carrying a flammable liquid, warn others of the dangerous material, make sure they refrain from smoking, and stay away from the scene. Exit the road if you can safely do so. Never drive a cargo tank that is leaking further than necessary in order to find a safe spot. Except in the case of an emergency, don't transfer flammable liquid between vehicles while on a public road.

Class 4 (Flammable Solids) and Class 5 (Oxidizing Materials)
If you are transporting a flammable solid or oxidizing material that leaks, make sure to warn others of the chance of fire. Do not open any packages of flammable solids that are smoldering or smoking. If you can do so safely, take them out of the vehicle, as well as any that are intact, if it will help lessen the fire hazard.

Class 6 (Poisonous Materials and Infectious Substances)
It is your responsibility to keep yourself and other people and property around you safe. Keep in mind that many items classified as poisonous are also flammable. If you are transporting any Division 2.3 (Poison Gases) or Division 6.1 (Poison Materials) that you think could be flammable, make sure to take the extra safety precautions that are required for flammable liquids or gases. Warn others of the potential hazards that could result by getting too close to the material, including the chance of fire or inhaling vapors, and make sure nobody smokes, has an open flame, or does any welding nearby.

If a vehicle leaks a Division 2.3 (Poison Gases) or Division 6.1 (Poisons) material, it needs to be checked for any traces of poison before being cleared for use.

Get in touch with your supervisor immediately if you see a Division 6.2 (Infectious Substances) package that shows signs of damage or leaking. You should not accept these.

Class 7 (Radioactive Materials)
Notify your dispatcher or supervisor immediately if you notice any radioactive material that is leaking or damaged. Stay a distance away. Refrain from touching or breathing in the material, and do not operate the vehicle until it can be thoroughly cleaned and scanned by a radiation detection meter.

Class 8 (Corrosive Materials)
If you notice a leak or spill involving corrosive materials during transport, use extra caution when moving the containers in order to prevent further damage or incident. If any sections of the vehicle have come

in contact with a corrosive liquid, they must be completely flushed with water. After you remove all the items, make sure to clean out the inside right away prior to reloading.

Since driving a vehicle with a leaking tank is unsafe, make sure to exit the road as soon as possible and try to prevent any additional leaks if you can do so safely. Stop others from coming near the material and fumes and make sure you do all you can to avoid getting hurt.

Required Notification

The National Response Center is in charge of coordinating emergency response to chemical hazards, including notifying the proper police and firefighter personnel to help. Either you or your employer are required to call their 24-hour toll-free line (listed below) in the event any of the following occurs as a direct result of a hazardous materials incident:

- A death.
- An injured person needs to go to the hospital.
- Property damage estimates are greater than $50,000.
- The general public needs to evacuate an area for more than one hour.
- A major transportation artery or facility is closed for at least an hour.
- There is an incident involving fire, damage, spillage, or suspected radioactive contamination.
- There is an incident involving fire, damage, spillage or suspected contamination of etiologic agents (bacteria or toxins).
- A hazardous material causes an incident that the carrier feels should be reported (e.g., continuing danger to life)

National Response Center (800) 424-8802
When you or someone else needs to contact the National Response Center, be prepared to disclose:

- Your name.
- The name and address of the carrier.
- The phone number where you or the person calling can be reached.
- The date, time, and location of the incident.
- Any injuries and the severity.
- The class, name, and quantity of hazardous materials involved, if you have access to this information.
- The nature of the incident and hazardous materials involved and whether or not danger to life continues to exist at the scene.

If the hazardous substance is enough to be reportable, the caller must relay the shipper's name and the amount of the hazardous substance that was involved. Your employer will also need this information since carriers are required to file comprehensive written reports within 30 days of an incident.

CHEMTREC (800) 424-9300
A 24-hour toll-free line is also available via the **Chemical Transportation Emergency Center (CHEMTREC)** in Washington D.C.. CHEMTREC is an agency established to supply technical information about the physical properties of hazardous materials to emergency personnel. CHEMTEC and The National

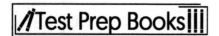

Response Center are in close contact with each other. If you get in touch with one, they will communication the issue to the other agency when necessary.

Do not keep packages labeled radioactive yellow-II or yellow-III around people, animals, or film longer than shown in the following diagram:

Radioactive Separation Table A						
Total Index/Transport	Minimum distance in feet to nearest undeveloped film					To People or Cargo Compartment Partitions
	0–2 hours	2–4 hours	4–8 hours	8–12 hours	Over 12 hours	
None	0	0	0	0	0	0
0.1 to 1.0	1	2	3	4	5	1
1.1 to 5.0	3	4	6	8	11	2
5.1 to 10.0	4	6	9	11	15	3
10.1 to 20.0	5	8	12	16	22	4
20.1 to 30.0	7	10	15	20	29	5
30.1 to 40.0	8	11	17	22	33	6
40.1 to 50.0	9	12	19	24	36	

Classes of Hazardous Materials

Hazardous materials are divided into 9 main hazard classifications, as well as 2 additional categories for consumer commodities and combustible liquids. These are listed in the table below:

Hazard Class Definitions		
Class	Class Name	Example
1	Explosives	Ammunition, dynamite, fireworks
2	Gases	Propane, oxygen, helium
3	Flammable	Gasoline, fuel, acetone
4	Flammable solids	Matches, fuses
5	Oxidizers	Ammonium nitrate, hydrogen peroxide
6	Poisons	Pesticides, arsenic
7	Radioactive	Uranium, plutonium
8	Corrosives	Hydrochloric acid, battery acid
9	Miscellaneous Hazardous Materials	Formaldehyde, asbestos
None	ORM-D (other regulated material-domestic)	Hairspray or charcoal
None	Combustible liquids	Fuel oils, lighter fluid

Hazardous Materials Glossary

This glossary serves as a reference for the various definitions of terms used in this section. Please note that a comprehensive glossary is featured in the federal Hazardous Materials Rules (49 CFR 171.8). Make sure you have a current copy of this guide.

Note: This glossary is for reference purposes only; you will not be tested on it.

Sec. 171.8 Definitions and Abbreviations

Bulk Packaging
Packaging (except a vessel or barge) including a transport vehicle or freight container that contains hazardous materials not contained by any other means and also has:

- A maximum capacity greater than 450 L (119 gallons) to hold a liquid;

- A maximum net mass greater than 400 kg (882 pounds) or a maximum capacity greater than 450 L (119 gallons) to hold a solid; or

- A water capacity greater than 454 kg (1000 pounds) to hold a gas as defined in Sec. 173.115.

Cargo Tank: Bulk packaging that is:

- A tank meant to transport liquids or gases and includes accessories, reinforcements, fittings, and closures (for "tank", see 49 CFR 178.345-1(c), 178.337-1, or 178.338-1, as applicable);

- Permanently affixed to or part of a motor vehicle, or is loaded or unloaded without being detached from the vehicle due to its size, structure, or the way it is attached and;

- Not manufactured using the specs for cylinders, portable tanks, tank cars, or multi-unit tank car tanks.

Carrier: A person who transports passengers or products by:

- Land or water as a common, contract, or private carrier, or
- Civil aircraft

Consignee: The entity that receives the shipment (can be a business or individual)

Division: A hazard classification subdivision

EPA: U.S. Environmental Protection Agency

FMCSR: The Federal Motor Carrier Safety Regulations

Freight Container: A reusable vessel with a capacity of at least 64 cubic feet that can be shipped with its contents intact and is mainly designed to contain packages (in unit form) during transport.

159

Fuel Tank: A tank, (except a cargo tank), used to ship flammable or combustible liquid or compressed gas in order to provide fuel for the transport vehicle it is loaded on, or to operate other components of the vehicle

Gross Weight or Gross Mass: The weight of the packaging combined with the weight of the material inside

Hazard Class: The hazard category allocated to a hazardous material as per the Part 173 descriptive standards and the specifications outlined in the Sec. 172.101 Table. Even though an item may fall under more than one hazard category, it is only assigned to one hazard classification.

Hazardous Materials: A substance or material that the Secretary of Transportation has classified as an extreme risk to health, safety, and property when shipped for business purposes. This includes hazardous substances, wastes, marine pollutants, high temperature materials, materials categorized as hazardous under the hazardous materials table of §172.101, and materials that meet the classification for hazard classes and divisions under §173, subchapter c of this section.

Hazardous Substance: A hazardous material, including any corresponding mixtures and solutions, that:

- Is listed in Appendix A to Sec. 172.101;

- Is an amount within one container that is greater than or equal to the reportable quantity (RQ) listed in Appendix A to Sec. 172.101; and

- When as part of a mixture or solution:

- For radionuclides, conforms to paragraph 7 of Appendix A to Sec. 172.101.

- Is in a weight concentration that is equal to or greater than the amount that corresponds to the material's RQ. See chart below for reference.

Hazardous Substance Concentrations		
RQ Pounds (Kilograms)	**Concentration by Weight**	
	Percent	**PPM**
5,000 (2,270)	10	100,000
1,000 (45)	2	20,000
100 (45.4)	.2	2,000
10 (4.54)	.02	200
1 (0.454)	.002	20

This definition is not applicable to petroleum based lubricants or fuels (see 40 CFR 300.6).

Hazardous Waste: In reference to this section, hazardous waste is defined as any material subject to the Hazardous Waste Manifest Requirements of the U.S. Environmental Protection Agency specified in 40 CFR Part 262.

Intermediate Bulk container (IBC): Portable packaging (except a cylinder or portable tank), that is used for mechanical handling. It can be made from either rigid or flexible material. The standards for IBCs manufactured in the United States are listed in subparts N and O §178.

Limited Quantity: The maximum amount of a hazardous material for which there may be a specific exclusion regarding its labeling or packaging.

Marking: The information used on hazardous materials packaging to indicate the danger level of the material. Includes the descriptive name, identification number, instructions, cautions, weight, specification, and/or UN marks.

Mixture: A hazardous material that contains more than one chemical compound or element.

Name of Contents: The material's proper shipping name as outlined in Sec. 172.101.

Non-Bulk Packaging: Packaging with:

- A container for liquids with a maximum capacity of 450 L (119 gallons);

- A container for solids with maximum net mass of less than 400 kg (882 pounds) and a maximum capacity of 450 L (119 gallons) or less; or

- A container for a gas as defined in Sec. 173.115 with a water capacity greater than 454 kg (1,000 pounds) or less.

N.O.S.: Not otherwise specified

Outage or Ullage: The amount (usually expressed in percentage by volume) that a package falls short of being full of liquid

Portable Tank: Bulk packaging (other than a cylinder with a water capacity of 1,000 pounds or less) meant to be loaded onto or temporarily affixed to a vehicle or ship that is equipped with skids, mountings, or accessories in order to mechanically ease the tank handling. This does not include cargo tanks, tank cars, multi-unit tank car tanks, or trailers carrying 3AX, 3AAX, or 3T cylinders.

Proper Shipping Name: The name of the hazardous materials listed with Roman numerals (not italics) in Sec. 172.101

P.s.i. or psi: Pounds per square inch

P.s.i.a. or psia: Pounds per square inch absolute

Reportable Quantity (RQ): The amount listed in Column 2 of the Appendix to Sec. 172.101 for any material specified in Column 1 of the Appendix

RSPA: Now **PHMSA**—The Pipeline and Hazardous Materials Safety Administration, U.S. Department of Transportation, Washington, DC 20590

Shipper's Certification: A statement on the shipping paper signed by the person who shipped the goods, certifying that he or she correctly prepared the shipment as per legal regulations. For example:

- "This is to certify that the materials listed above are classified, described, packaged, marked and labeled correctly, and are suitable for transport as per the pertinent rules or the Department of Transportation." or

- "I hereby declare that the contents of this shipment are completely and properly described according to the accurate shipping name, are classified, packaged, marked and labeled/placarded, and are in proper order for transport by * as per appropriate international and national government law."

* Signifies the type of transport (rail, aircraft, motor vehicle, vessel)

School Buses

Since state and local laws and regulations regulate so many aspects of school transportation and the operation of school bus equipment, much of the information discussed in this section varies from state to state. You will need to be well versed in the specific laws and regulations that pertain to your state and local school district.

Danger Zones and Use of Mirrors

Danger Zones

The area along the sides of the bus that poses the most danger of impact to children (either via another vehicle or their own bus) is called the **danger zone**. These zones may reach as far as 30 feet from the front bumper. The first 10 feet are considered most dangerous; ten feet from each side and ten feet behind the back bumper. The region to the left of the bus is also deemed dangerous due to the possibility of passing cars. These danger zones are referenced in the diagram below.

The Danger Zones

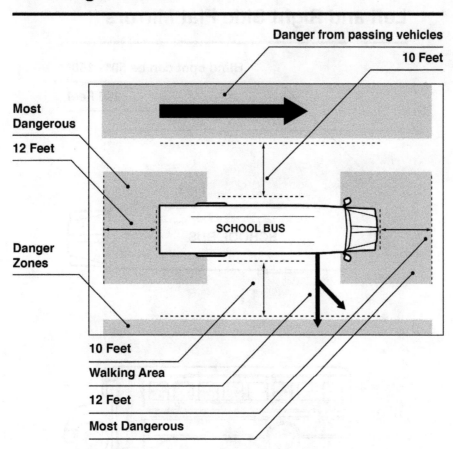

163

Correct Mirror Adjustment

In order to safely operate a school bus, you must be able to identify the danger zone around the bus and check for students, traffic, and other hazards. Adjusting and using mirrors correctly is imperative. Always check and adjust each mirror so you have the best possible view.

Outside Left and Right Side Flat Mirrors

The mirrors located at the left and right front corners of the bus near the side or front of the windshield are used to monitor traffic, check clearances, and watch for students on each side and to the back of the bus. It is important to note that a blind spot is located directly below and in front of each mirror and behind the rear bumper. The blind spot in back of the bus is typically a distance of 50 to 150 feet, but it can extend up to 400 feet depending on the length and width of the bus. Make sure your mirrors are adjusted so you can see:

- 200 feet or 4 bus lengths in back of the bus.
- Along each side.
- Where the rear tires touch the ground.

The diagram below outlines the method for adjusting the outside left and right side flat mirrors.

Left and Right Side Flat Mirrors

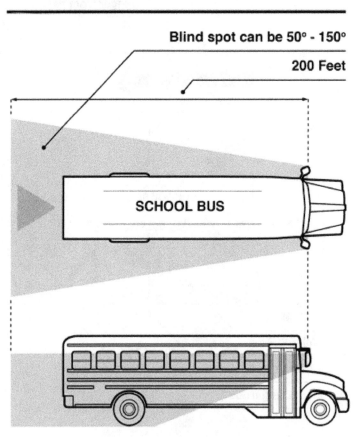

Outside Left and Right Side Convex Mirrors

The **convex mirrors** are situated underneath the outside flat mirrors. Designed to show a wide-angle view, they allow the driver to see traffic, clearances, and students on the sides of the bus. However, keep in mind that the image shown by these mirrors is not an accurate reflection of the size and distance from the bus that people and objects appear.

These mirrors should be adjusted to view:

- The whole side of the bus up to the mirror mounts.
- Where the front of the rear tires touch the ground.
- At least one traffic lane on either side of the bus.

The diagram below shows the proper method for adjusting the outside left and right side convex mirrors.

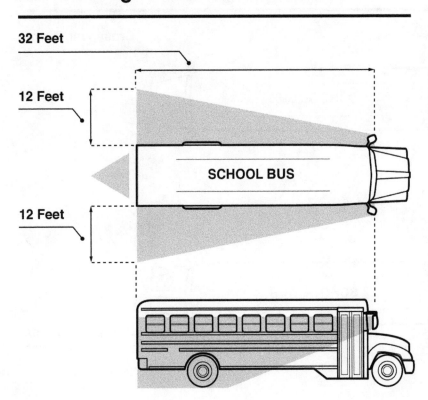

Outside Left and Right Side Crossover Mirrors

Located at the left and right front corners of the bus, these **crossover mirrors** are designed to help the driver see the front bumper "danger zone" immediately in front of the bus that is not in direct view, and to see the "danger zone" area on the sides of the bus, including the service door and front wheel area.

165

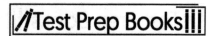

Just as with the convex mirrors, keep in mind that the image shown by the crossover mirrors is not an accurate reflection of the size and distance from the bus that people and objects appear.

Make sure these mirrors are adjusted correctly so you can view:

- The area directly in front of the bus ranging from the bottom front bumper to an area where it is possible to see clearly. There should be an overlap between direct and mirror view vision.

- Where the right and left front tires touch the ground.

- The area from the front of the bus to the service door.

Scan these mirrors, along with the convex and flat mirrors, in order to make sure a child or object is not located in any of the danger zones. The diagram below shows the techniques for adjusting the left and right side crossover mirrors.

Left and Right Side Crossover Mirrors

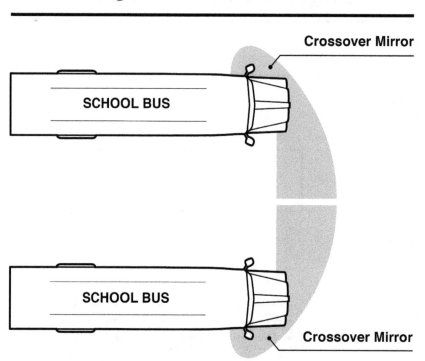

Overhead Inside Rearview Mirror

Located right above the windshield on the driver's side of the bus, the **overhead inside rearview mirror** helps the driver check the movement of passengers inside the bus. If the bus has a glass-bottomed rear emergency door, this mirror may offer a limited view in the back of the bus. In addition, keep in mind that blind spots are located right behind the driver's seat in the region starting with the rear bumper and

up to 400 feet or more in back of the bus. In order to scan traffic in these zones, use the exterior side mirrors.

You should adjust the mirror so you can view:

- The top of the rear window in the area at the top of the mirror.
- All the students, including those sitting in the seats right behind you.

Loading and Unloading

Since more students are killed or injured while entering or exiting a school bus than while riding as passengers, it is imperative to be thoroughly familiar with the procedure for loading and unloading students. The following paragraphs outline the safety processes to prevent injuries and fatalities during and after loading and unloading students.

This material is not meant to be an absolute set of directions, but rather it is designed to offer a broad overview. It is very important to know and follow the state laws and regulations regarding loading/unloading operations in your area.

Approaching the Stop

Official bus routes and school bus stops are determined by each school district and therefore require approval before stopping at any location. Never deviate from the official route or stops without written approval from the sanctioned school district administrator.

The safety of the students is critical—use extreme caution when approaching a school bus stop. It is imperative that you thoroughly know and observe all state and local laws and regulations, including the correct operation of mirrors, alternating flashing lights, and the moveable stop signal and crossing control arm if the bus is so equipped.

When approaching the stop, you should:

- Enter the area slowly and carefully.

- Scan the area for pedestrians, traffic, or other objects before, during, and after stopping.

- Constantly check all mirrors.

- If the bus has them, turn on the alternating flashing amber warning lights at least 200 feet or 5 to 10 seconds before the school bus stop or as per state regulations.

- Activate the right turn signal about 100 to 300 feet or approximately 3 to 5 seconds before pulling over to the stop.

- Scan mirrors regularly in order to check danger zones for students, traffic, and other items.

- Pull the bus over as far to the right as you can away from the traveled portion of the road or street.

When stopping you should:

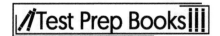

- Make sure the school bus comes to a complete stop, with the front bumper at a distance of at least 10 feet from students waiting at the assigned stop. As a result, the students will need to walk toward the bus to enter, providing a clearer view of their actions.

- At each stop, make sure the transmission is in park. If the bus is not equipped with a park function, put the bus in neutral and engage the parking brake.

- Turn on the alternating red lights when traffic is a safe distance away from the school bus and the stop arm is activated.

- Make a final scan to make sure all traffic has come to a stop before opening the door to signal students to enter.

Loading Procedures

Stop safely as described in the section above, constantly scanning all mirrors. At each stop, you should see the students waiting in the assigned area facing the bus as you approach. Allow them to board once you give the signal. Make sure you do a headcount of the students waiting at the bus stop so you can check that they all get on board.

If you can, memorize the names of the students at each stop. If you notice one is missing, ask the other students if they know where they are. Check all mirrors and make sure you don't see anyone running to try to catch the bus. If you feel one of the students is missing, stop the bus, take the key, and check outside, around, and under the bus.

Ensure that the students get on board slowly in single file and utilize the handrail. If it is dark outside, make sure the dome light is on. Before driving to the next stop, make sure the students have located seats and are sitting in a forward facing position.

When all students are accounted for, get ready to proceed by:

- Shutting the door.
- Engaging the transmission.
- Releasing the parking brake.
- Turning the alternating flashing red lights off.
- Turning on left turn signal.
- Checking all the mirrors one more time.
- Allowing any traffic to clear out of your path.

When it is safe, pull ahead and into the flow of traffic to continue to the next stop. The same basic loading procedures should be followed whenever students are getting on the bus, barring for a few exceptions.

When students are getting on the bus at school, you should:

- Make sure the ignition is off.
- Take the key if you need to exit the bus.
- Oversee the students getting on the bus as per your state or local regulations or recommendations.

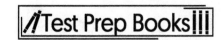

Unloading Procedures on the Route

Stop safely as described in the section above, constantly scanning all mirrors. Make sure the students stay in their seats until you give the signal to exit. Do a headcount of the students getting off to make sure it matches up with the location of the stop before proceeding to the next one. When exiting, instruct students to move at least 10 feet away from the side of the bus so you can clearly see all of them.

Do another mirror check, making sure all students are a safe distance away from the bus. If you do not see one of the students who got off at the stop, make sure the bus is stopped and parked and check all around the sides and under the bus.

When all students are accounted for, prepare to leave by:

- Shutting the door.
- Engaging the transmission.
- Releasing the parking brake.
- Turning the alternating flashing red lights off.
- Turning on left turn signal.
- Checking all the mirrors one more time.
- Allowing any traffic to clear out of your path.

When it is safe, pull ahead and into the flow of traffic to continue to the next stop.

Note: Do not back up if you drive past a student's stop. Instead, make sure to follow local procedures.

Additional Procedures for Students That Must Cross the Roadway

You will need to know the proper procedures students should follow when getting off the school bus and crossing in front of it, bearing in mind they may not always heed the directions correctly.

When crossing the road, a student or group of students should do the following:

- Walk about 10 feet away from the side of the school bus to a location where you can spot them.
- Walk at least 10 feet in front of the right corner of the bus's bumper, still keeping a distance away from the front of the school bus.
- Stop at the right edge of the road or street. Their feet should be in full view.

When students reach the edge of the road, they should:

- Stop and look both ways, ensuring the path is clear and safe to proceed.
- Check whether or not the red flashing lights on the bus are still flashing.
- Wait to get a signal from you before crossing the road.

After receiving your signal, the students should:

- Keep far enough in front of the school bus when crossing so you can fully see them.
- Pause at the left edge of the bus and once again wait for your signal to continue to cross.
- Scan up and down the road for traffic, making sure it is safe to proceed.
- Cross the road, continuing to check in all directions.

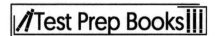

Note: As the school bus driver, you should impose any state or local regulations or recommendations regarding student actions outside the school bus.

Unloading Procedures at School

When dropping off students at school, keep in mind that state and local laws and regulations often vary from those along the regular school bus route, especially when unloading occurs in the school parking lot or some other place that is not on the travelled road. You will need to fully comprehend and heed these state and local laws and regulations. The procedures listed below are designed to serve as general guidelines to follow.

When unloading students at school, you should:

- Come to a safe stop at the assigned unloading area as described in the above section on "Approaching the Stop."
- Make sure the bus is secure by:
- Turning the ignition switch off.
- Taking the key if you need to exit the driver's seat.
- Direct the students the stay in their seats until it is safe to exit.
- Supervise the students exiting the bus as per state or local requirements or recommendations.
- Make sure students get off the bus in a safe, organized way.
- Check that the students walk away from the unloading region.
- Walk up and down the aisle of the bus to check for hiding/sleeping students and any items left behind.
- Scan all mirrors to make sure there are no students coming back toward the bus.
- If the bus is secure and you cannot account for a student, do a check around and under the bus.

When all students have exited and are accounted for, prepare to drive away by:

- Shutting the door.
- Fastening your safety belt.
- Starting the engine.
- Engaging the transmission.
- Releasing the parking brake.
- Turning the alternating flashing red lights off.
- Turning the left turn signal on.
- Rechecking all the mirrors.
- Waiting until traffic has cleared.

When it is safe to proceed, drive away from the unloading area.

Special Dangers of Loading and Unloading

Dropped or Forgotten Objects

Pay attention to students as they near the bus and check for any who suddenly vanish from your view. A student could drop something near the bus during loading or unloading, posing a potential danger if they bend down or go back to pick it up, causing them to disappear from your view.

Students should be instructed not to attempt to pick up a dropped object. Instead, they should move to a safe spot and ask the driver to get the item for them.

Handrail Hang-Ups
Handrails can pose a serious and sometimes fatal hazard to students with loose clothing while entering or exiting the bus. Always carefully account for all students leaving the bus to make sure that they are away from the bus prior to driving away.

Post-Trip Inspection

You will need to perform a post-trip bus inspection once your route or school activity trip has ended. Walk down the aisle and scan each seat for the following:

- Items left behind by students
- Sleeping students
- Open windows or doors
- Obvious mechanical malfunctions with safety mechanisms
- Any sort of damage to the vehicle

All hazardous or out-of-the-ordinary findings must be reported to a supervisor as soon as the problem is noted.

Emergency Exit and Evacuation

A school bus emergency can occur at any time. This includes an accident, stalling on a railroad-highway crossing or a high-traffic intersection, an electrical fire in the engine area, or a medical emergency involving a student, among other things. Being aware of how to handle an emergency—before, during and after evacuating the bus—can make all the difference.

Planning for Emergencies

Determining Need to Evacuate Bus
Pinpointing the hazard is first and foremost in an emergency situation. If you have enough time, call your dispatcher to relay the issue before deciding to evacuate the school bus. Most of the time, the safety and management of the students is best upheld by retaining them on the bus during an emergency and/or potential danger situation, as long as it does not subject them to any needless hazard(s). Keep in mind that the choice to have the students exit the bus must be done quickly.

When deciding whether or not to evacuate the bus, consider the following circumstances:

- Is there a fire or the potential of fire?
- Do you smell or see leaking fuel?
- Is the bus in the way of other vehicles, increasing the possibility of getting struck?
- Do you see a tornado or rising floodwater?
- Do you see power lines down?
- Would evacuating students put them in harm's way of speeding traffic, extreme weather, or a hazardous environment such as downed power lines?

- If in an accident, would evacuating students intensify fractures and neck and back injuries?
- Is there a hazardous spill in the vicinity? It may be safer for students to stay on the bus and out of the way of this dangerous substance.

Mandatory Evacuations

The driver must evacuate the bus when:

- The bus is on fire or there is the risk of a fire.
- The bus has stalled or broken down on or near a railroad crossing.
- There is the potential for the bus to shift position, increasing the risk of an accident.
- There is an impending risk of impact.
- There is a hazardous materials spill that requires quick evacuation.

Evacuation Procedures

Be Prepared and Plan Ahead

If feasible, ask 2 responsible, older students to supervise each emergency exit, explaining how to help other students safely exit the bus. Designate another student to take the students to a "safe place" after they have exited the bus. In the event there are no older, responsible students present during an emergency situation, you will need to explain these procedures to all the students, including proper operation of the various emergency exits and the significance of listening to and following directions.

Use these guidelines to help find a safe location:

- It should be at least 100 feet away from the road facing oncoming traffic to help prevent students from being hit by wreckage if another vehicle crashes into the bus.

- If there is a fire on or near the bus, direct students to a place upwind.

- Direct students to a location as far away from railroad tracks as possible and facing the direction of an oncoming train.

- Direct students at least 300 feet upwind of the bus if there is the danger of a hazardous materials spill.

- If you see a tornado directly in the path of the bus and are directed to evacuate, lead students to a nearby ditch or culvert if there is no safe spot in a building. Have them lie face down, with their hands over their head, at enough distance away from the bus so that it can't tip over on top of them. Make sure to keep away from any areas susceptible to flash flooding.

General Procedures

First decide whether evacuating students is the safest course of action, and if so, the best method to exit the bus:

- Leaving via the front, rear or side doors, or a combination of the three.
- Exiting through the roof or window(s).

Secure the bus by:

- Putting the transmission in park, or neutral if there is no shift point.
- Engaging the parking brakes.
- Turning the engine off.
- Taking the ignition key.
- Turning on the hazard-warning lights.

If you have the time to do so, alert the dispatch office of your location, circumstances, and the kind of help that is required. Place your telephone or radio (if working) outside the driver's side window so you can use it later. If the radio is not operational, flag down a passing motorist or ask someone nearby to call for assistance. If none of these options are viable, instruct two older, responsible students to go for assistance.

Direct the students to evacuate, assisting where necessary. Make sure you do not attempt to move any student(s) who have a potential neck or spinal injury unless their life is in immediate danger; neck and spinal injuries require special evacuation methods to avoid further harm.

Ask a mature student to direct students to a safe location nearby, and then walk up and down the aisle to make sure all students have exited the bus. Leave the bus to join the students, taking any emergency equipment with you. Once off the bus, do a student headcount and check that they are safe.

Protect the area by placing emergency warning devices around the perimeter where essential and have information ready for emergency personnel.

Railroad-Highway Crossings

Pavement Markings

Pavement markings have the same meaning as the advance warning sign. They are found on two-lane roads and are marked with an "X," the letters "RR" and a no passing indicator. Two-lane roads will also have a no passing zone sign. At some crossings, a white stop line may be painted on the pavement in front of the railroad tracks. While stopped at the crossing, make sure the school bus stays behind this line. See diagram below for reference.

Pavement Markings

173

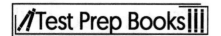

Recommended Procedures

The laws and regulations regarding the required procedures for school buses at railroad-highway crossings vary by location. You will need to recognize and follow the laws and regulations in your region. In most cases, school buses need to stop at all crossings, making sure it is absolutely safe before crossing the tracks.

Even though a school bus is one of the safest vehicles on the highway, it is imperative to obey all safety procedures at all train crossings. Due to its larger size and weight, it takes longer for a train to stop. Trains do not have an emergency escape plan. The steps listed below will help you avoid school bus/train accidents:

> Approaching the Crossing:
> - o Slow down. If the bus has a manual transmission, shift down into a lower gear. Test your brakes.
> - o When you are about 200 feet from the crossing, turn on the hazard lights to alert others of your objectives.
> - o Look all around the bus perimeter and check to see if there are any vehicles in back of you.
> - o If possible, keep to the right.
> - o Think of an escape route in case your brakes fail or there are issues in back of you.
> At the Crossing:
> - o To ensure that you have the best view of the tracks, make sure when you stop that the bus is not nearer than 15 feet and no more than 50 feet from the closest rail.
> - o Put the transmission in park. If the bus does not have a park feature, put the bus in neutral and engage the service or parking brakes.
> - o Turn off the radio and any other noisy equipment, and make sure the students are quiet.
> - o Open the service door and driver's window so you can look and listen for an oncoming train.
> Crossing the Track:
> - o Prior to going forward, scan the crossing signals one more time.
> - o If it is a multiple-track crossing, make sure you come to a stop in front of the first set of tracks only.
> - o Once you are positive that there are no trains coming, drive across the tracks until you have totally cleared them.
> - o When you are driving across the tracks, stay in a low gear and do not try to change gears while crossing.
> - o If the gate swings down after you have started driving through the crossing, keep going, even if it means breaking through the gate.

Special Situations

Bus Stalls or Trapped on Tracks
If your bus happens to stall or gets stuck on the tracks, evacuate all the students to a spot far away from the tracks at an angle facing the train.

Police Officer at the Crossing

If a police officer is present at the crossing, follow all instructions. If you think the signal is not working correctly, but there is no police officer at the crossing, call your dispatcher to relay the issue and request directions on the best course of action.

Obstructed View of Tracks

When approaching highway-rail grade crossings, make sure you can see enough in the distance down the tracks in both directions to be completely sure no trains are coming. Use extra caution at passive crossings (those lacking any type of traffic control device). You still need to look and listen all around even at active railroad crossings with signals indicating the tracks are clear to cross.

Containment or Storage Areas

Be aware of the size of the bus you are driving and the containment area at highway-rail crossings on your route, in addition to any you come across during a school activity trip. If the bus won't fit, do not proceed. If you encounter a crossing where the signal or stop sign is on the opposite side, size up the amount of room and make sure the containment or storage area of the bus is large enough to completely cross the railroad tracks on the other side if you need to stop. To help verify whether the containment or storage area will clear the tracks, add 15 feet to the span of the school bus.

Student Management

Don't Deal with On-bus Problems When Loading and Unloading

To make sure students are safely transported to and from school in a timely manner, you need to fully concentrate on your job responsibilities. Keep in mind that you need to focus all your attention during the loading and unloading process, not what is occurring outside the bus. If one or more students are misbehaving, wait until the students getting off the bus have safely exited and walked away, and then pull the bus over to the side of the road if you need to address the issue.

Handling Serious Problems

To help deal with serious issues, follow the guidelines below:

- Understand and obey the procedures for your district regarding discipline or refusal of students to ride the bus.

- Find a safe location away from the road, such as a parking lot or a driveway where you can stop and park the bus.

- Make sure the bus is safe; if you need to leave your seat, take the ignition key with you.

- Turn around and face the students, addressing the student(s) acting up in a respectful, considerate, yet firm tone. Remind them of the behavior required when riding the bus. Do not exhibit anger, but do make sure they know you are serious.

- Ask a student to move to a seat near you if you think this is necessary.

- Never remove a student from the bus unless it is at school or their assigned bus stop. If you feel the behavior is uncontrollable and it is unsafe to drive, call for a school official or the police to come and get the student. When requesting assistance, always make sure to obey the procedures specific to your region.

Antilock Braking Systems

Vehicles Required to Have Antilock Braking Systems

The Department of Transportation requires that the following vehicles have antilock braking systems:

- Air brake vehicles, (trucks, buses, trailers, and converter dollies) manufactured on or after March 1, 1998.

- Hydraulically braked trucks and buses with a gross vehicle weight rating of 10,000 pounds or greater built on or after March 1, 1999.

Note: Many school buses built before these dates have been voluntarily outfitted with ABS. If the bus you are driving is so equipped, it will have a yellow ABS malfunction lamp on the instrument panel.

Braking with ABS

If your vehicle is equipped with ABS, use your brakes as you normally would:

- Use only enough brake pressure as is required to safely stop and retain control.

- Use the brakes in the same manner, regardless of whether the bus is equipped with ABS. However, if you need to brake quickly, make sure you do not pump the brakes if the bus has ABS.

- As you slow your speed, watch your bus and decrease brake pressure (if it is safe to do so) to maintain control.

Special Safety Considerations

Strobe Lights

Some school buses have white strobe lights mounted to the top of the roof. Use the **overhead strobe light** when you do not have a clear view of your surroundings in the front, rear, or next to the school bus. This applies whether your view is only a little diminished or so impaired that you cannot see anything. No matter the circumstance, make sure you comprehend and follow your state or local regulations regarding the use of these lights.

Driving in High Winds

Use extra caution driving a school bus when there are strong winds. Since the height of the bus can mimic the sail on a sailboat, wind gusts can cause the bus to tilt sideways, pushing it off the road or even knocking it over if conditions are intense. If you are caught in strong winds:

- Hold the steering wheel with a strong, steady grip.
- Try to predict strong wind gusts.
- Slow down to buffer the wind's influence, or pull over to the side of the road and wait it out.
- Call your dispatcher to get more information on weather conditions and determine next steps.

Backing

Backing up a school bus is not recommended, as it is risky and increases your chances of an accident. Only attempt to back up the bus when you have no other method to move it, and never do so when students are near the perimeter.

If there's no other way to proceed, and it is absolutely necessary to back the bus, follow these procedures:

- Assign someone to be a lookout in order to alert you to items in your way, persons walking toward the bus, and other vehicles. This person's job does not involve giving instructions on how to back up the bus.

- Silence your passengers.

- Do frequent scans of all mirrors and rear windows.

- Proceed backing slowly and steadily.

- If there is nobody around to serve as a lookout:

    o Engage the parking brake.
    o Turn the motor off and take the keys with you.
    o Walk around the bus to see if you have a clear path.

- If it is necessary to back up at a spot where you pick up students, make sure all the students are on the bus before you start to back up, and keep on the lookout for any late arrivals.

- Make sure all students are safely in their seats before starting to back up.

- If it is necessary to back up at a spot where you drop off students, make sure all the students have exited after you are done backing up.

Tail Swing

Keep in mind that a school bus can have up to a 3-foot **tail swing**. Before and while performing any turning maneuvers, monitor the tail swing of the bus by carefully checking your mirrors.

Pre-Trip Vehicle Inspection Test

Prior to operating your vehicle, you will need to demonstrate that it is safe to drive by participating in a pre-trip inspection. This involves walking around the perimeter of the vehicle, pointing out each item to the examiner, and describing what you are inspecting and for what reason. You will NOT have to crawl under the hood or the vehicle.

All Vehicles

Study the vehicle parts listed below that pertain to the type of vehicle you will be using during the CDL skills tests. You must be able to recognize each component and explain to the examiner what you are seeking or checking.

Engine Compartment (Engine Off)

Check for puddles of liquid on the ground under the engine and any fluid dripping under the engine and transmission. Check the hoses to see if they are in good condition and whether any are leaking.

Oil Level
Point out the location of the dipstick and check to see that it is within the normal range, with the level above the refill marker.

Coolant Level
Check the reservoir sight glass, or (if the engine is not hot), remove the radiator cap and make sure the coolant level is good.

Power Steering Fluid
Point out the location of the power steering fluid dipstick and check to see that it is within the normal range, with the level above the refill marker.

Engine Compartment Belts
Make sure the following belts are snug enough (up to 3/4 inch of play in the center of the belt), and check for any cracks or frays:

- Power steering belt
- Water pump belt
- Alternator belt
- Air compressor belt

Note: If any of the components listed above are not belt driven, you must:

- Explain which part(s) are not belt driven.
- Check that the part(s) are working correctly, are not damaged or leaking, and are firmly mounted.

Safe Start

Push in the clutch, put the gearshift control in neutral (or park, for automatic transmissions). Start up the engine, then slowly release the clutch.

Cab Check/Engine Start

Oil Pressure Gauge

Make sure the oil pressure gauge shows increasing or normal oil pressure or that the warning light goes off. If the vehicle is so equipped, the oil temperature gauge should slowly start to increase to the normal operating range.

Temperature Gauge

Make sure the temperature gauge indicates a rise in temperature to the normal operating range or the temperature light is off.

Air Gauge

Make sure the air gauge is in proper working order and the air pressure builds to governor cut-out, roughly 120 to 140 psi.

Ammeter/Voltmeter

Make sure the gauges indicate that the alternator and/or generator is charging or the warning light is off.

Mirrors and Windshield

Check that the mirrors are clean and correctly positioned from the inside and the windshield is clear with no illegal stickers, damage, or items obstructing your view.

Emergency Equipment

Make sure the following items are present:

- Spare electrical fuses
- 3 red reflective triangles
- 6 fuses or 3 liquid burning flares
- A fire extinguisher that is fully charged and has the correct rating

Note: If the vehicle does not have electrical fuses, make sure to tell the examiner.

Wipers/Washers

Make sure windshield wiper arms and blades are safely in place and in good working order. If the vehicle has windshield washers, they must be operational.

Lights/Reflectors/Reflector Tape Condition (Sides & Rear)

Check that the dash indicators work for the corresponding lights:

- Left turn signal
- Right turn signal
- Four-way emergency flashers
- High beam headlight

179

- Anti-lock Braking System (ABS) indicator

Make sure all external lights and reflective components are clean and working properly. Light and reflector checks incorporate the following:

- Clearance lights (red in the back of the vehicle, amber in other locations)
- Headlights (both high and low beams)
- Taillights
- Back up lights
- Turn signals
- Four-way flashers
- Brake lights
- Red reflectors (in the back of the vehicle) and amber reflectors (in other locations)
- The condition of the reflector tape

Note: Inspection of the brake, turn signal, and four-way flasher lights must be done separately.

Horn
Make sure the air horn and/or electric horn work.

Heater/Defroster
Check that the heater and defroster are in good working condition.

Parking Brake Check
With the parking brake on (trailer brakes released on combination vehicles), test that the parking brake will hold the vehicle by slowly trying to drive forward.

Release the parking brake and engage the trailer parking brake (combination vehicles only). Test the trailer parking brake by slowly trying to drive forward.

Hydraulic Brake Check
Test the hydraulic brakes by pumping the brake pedal 3 times, then pressing on it for 5 seconds. Make sure the brake pedal does not move during these 5 seconds. If the vehicle has a hydraulic brake reserve (backup) system, make sure the key is off, and then press down on the brake pedal and listen for noise coming from the reserve system electric motor. Ensure that the warning buzzer or light is turned off.

Air Brake Check (Air Brake Equipped Vehicles Only)
It is very important to properly inspect all 3 sections of the air brake—if you do not, you will automatically fail the vehicle inspection test. The test is intended to make sure that your vehicle's safety component(s) is in proper working order when air pressure drops from normal to a low air condition. If there is a hill where the vehicle is parked, use wheel chocks during the air brake check for safety. Although air brake safety devices differ, use the following method to perform the air brake check:

- Bring the air pressure up to governor cutoff (120–140 psi), turn off the engine, chock your wheels (if needed), release the parking brake and tractor protection valve (on combination vehicles only), and completely engage the foot brake. Press down on the foot brake for one full minute and make sure the air pressure drops no more than 3 pounds (single vehicle) or 4 pounds (combination vehicle).

- With the engine off, turn the electrical power to the "on" or "battery charge" mark. Release the air pressure by quickly pressing and releasing the foot brake. The low air warning indicators (such as the buzzer, light, flag, etc.) should turn on prior to the air pressure falling under 60 psi or the level designated by the manufacturer.

- Keep releasing air pressure—the tractor protection valve and parking brake valve should shut (pop out) when the level reaches about 40 psi on a tractor-trailer combination vehicle (or level specified by the manufacturer). On combination vehicle types and single vehicle types, just the parking brake valve should close (pop out).

Service Brake Check

The air or hydraulic service brakes need to be inspected to ensure that the brakes are in proper working order and that the vehicle is not pulling to one side or the other. Slowly move forward at 5 mph, engage the service brake and come to a stop. Make sure the vehicle is not pulling to either side and that it comes to a complete stop when the brake is engaged.

Safety Belt

Make sure the seat belt is securely attached, and that it adjusts, latches properly, and there are no rips or frays.

External Inspection (All Vehicles)

Steering

Steering Box/Hoses

The steering box should be firmly attached, and all nuts, bolts, and cotter keys should be in place. Make sure the power steering fluid is not leaking and the power steering hoses do not show any signs of damage.

Steering Linkage

Check for cracks and other wear and tear to the connecting links, arms, and rods that extend from the steering box to the wheel. Make sure the joints and sockets are not damaged or coming loose and all nuts, bolts, and cotter keys are in place.

Suspension

Springs/Air/Torque

Check that all leaf and coil springs are in place and none are loose, cracked, or damaged in any way.

If the vehicle has torsion bars, torque arms, or is equipped with some other kind of suspension, make sure they are in good working order and firmly fastened. Check the air ride suspension for any signs of leaking and wear and tear.

Mounts

Make sure spring hangers do not show signs of cracks or damage, bushings are in place and undamaged, and bolts, U-bolts, and other axle mounting parts are not broken, loose, or missing. Inspect the mounts at each point where they are fastened to the vehicle frame and axle(s).

181

Shock Absorbers

Check that shock absorbers are in proper working order and no leaks are present.

Note: Make sure you inspect the suspension parts on every axle (both the tractor and trailer, if the vehicle is so equipped).

Brakes

Slack Adjustors and Pushrods

Make sure none of the components are broken, loose, or missing. If the vehicle has a manual slack adjustor, the brake pushrod should not budge more than an inch (with the brakes released) when manipulated by hand.

Brake Chambers

Make sure the brake chambers have no leaks, cracks, or dents and are firmly fastened.

Brake Hoses/Lines

Check to see that hoses do not show any signs of cracks, wear and tear, leaking hoses, lines, or couplings.

Drum Brake

Make sure there are no visible cracks, dents, holes, or loose or missing bolts, and the drum brake is not tainted with dirt or oil/grease. Check that the brake linings are not worn dangerously thin.

Brake Linings

Some types of brake drums have openings where the brake linings are visible from outside the drum. If your vehicle is so equipped, make sure that you can see a portion of the brake lining.

Note: Make sure you inspect the brake parts on every axle (both the tractor and trailer, if the vehicle is so equipped).

Wheels

Rims

Make sure rims are not dented or damaged and there are no signs of have welding repairs.

Tires

Check every tire for the following:

- Tread depth: Needs to be at least 4/32 on steering axle tires and 2/32 on all other tires.

- Tire condition: Make sure the tread wear is consistent on each tire, there are no signs of cuts or other damage to the tread or sidewalls, and the valve caps and stems are not missing, broken, or damaged.

- Tire inflation: Use a tire gauge to make sure the tires are inflated to the correct level.

Note: You will not receive positive marks on the CDL exam if you kick the tires to check to see if the tires are inflated properly.

Hub Oil Seals/Axle Seals
Make sure there are no leaks coming from the axle or hub oil/grease seals and that the oil level is in the proper range if the wheel has a sight glass.

Lug Nuts
Make sure none of the lug nuts or boltholes are cracked or distorted, all the lug nuts are in place, and there are no rust trails or shiny threads (an indicator of looseness).

Spacers or Budd Spacing
If the vehicle has spacers, make sure they are squarely positioned and do not show any signs of damage or rust, with the dual wheels and tires evenly separated.

Note: Be ready to do the same type of check on every axle (both the tractor and trailer, if the vehicle is so equipped).

Side of Vehicle

Door(s)/Mirror(s)
Make sure the door(s) and hinges do not show any signs of damage and they open and close correctly from the outside. Make sure the mirror(s) and mirror brackets are clear and without cracks or scratches and are firmly attached with no loose fittings.

Fuel Tank
Make sure the fuel tank(s) are firmly in place, the cap(s) fit snugly, and you do not see any signs of leaking from the tank(s) or lines.

Drive Shaft
Check that the drive shaft is not damaged and the couplings are firmly in place without any obstructions.

Exhaust System
Make sure the exhaust system is undamaged, firmly connected and attached, and free of any signs of leaking, such as rust or carbon soot.

Frame
Check for signs of damage, such as cracks, broken welds, holes, etc., to the longitudinal frame members, cross members, box, and floor.

Rear of Vehicle

Splash Guards
If the vehicle has splashguards or mud flaps, make sure they are undamaged and firmly attached.

Doors/Ties/Lifts
Make sure all doors and hinges do not display any signs of damage and they are in good working order, including outside latches if the vehicle has them.

183

Check that all ties, straps, chains, and binders are firmly in place.

If the vehicle has a cargo lift, make sure it is fully retracted and securely fastened and there are no signs of leaks, damage, or missing parts. You must be able to describe the inspection process to the examiner to determine that it is in good working order.

Tractor/Coupling

Air/Electric Lines
Make sure air hoses and electrical lines do not show any signs of having been cut, scraped, spliced, or worn (you should not see the steel braid underneath), and listen carefully for any leaking air. Make sure the air and electrical lines are not twisted, pinched, or brushing against tractor components.

Catwalk/Steps
Make sure the steps to the cab entrance and catwalk (if the vehicle has one) are in good condition, free of obstructions, and firmly attached to the tractor frame.

Mounting Bolts
Make sure all mounting brackets, clamps, bolts, and nuts are in place and securely attached, including the fifth wheel and slide mounting. If the coupling system is a different type (e.g., ball hitch, pintle hook, etc.), make sure all coupling parts and mounting brackets are in place and undamaged.

Hitch Release Lever
The hitch release lever should be firmly in place.

Locking Jaws
Check the fifth wheel gap and make sure locking jaws are fully surrounding the kingpin. Other types of coupling systems (e.g., ball hitch, pintle hook, etc.) should be checked to make sure the locking mechanism is working and locked correctly and no components are missing or damaged. If so equipped, the safety cables/chains must be firm and without any kinks or excessive slack.

Fifth Wheel Skid Plate
Make sure the fifth wheel skid plate is lubricated correctly, firmly attached to the platform, and all bolts and pins are securely in place.

Platform (Fifth Wheel)
Make sure the platform structure supporting the fifth wheel skid plate does not show any signs of damage such as cracks or fractures.

Release Arm (Fifth Wheel)
If the vehicle has a release arm, make sure it is engaged and the safety latch is secure.

Kingpin/Apron/Gap
Make sure the kingpin and the exposed section of the apron do not show any signs of damage such as bending, cracks, or fractures. Make sure the trailer is flush on the fifth wheel skid plate (you should not see any spaces).

Locking Pins (Fifth Wheel)

If the vehicle has a fifth wheel, make sure none of the pins in the slide mechanism of the sliding fifth wheel are loose or missing. If it is air powered, check for signs of leaking. Check that the locking pins are properly connected and the fifth wheel is properly situated so the tractor frame can clear the landing gear when turning.

Sliding Pintle

Make sure the sliding pintle, nuts, bolts, and cotter pin are firmly in place.

Tongue or Draw-Bar

Make sure that the tongue/draw-bar does not show any signs of damage such as bending, twisting, fractured welds or stress cracks, and extreme wear and tear.

Tongue Storage Area

Make sure the storage area is firm and attached to the tongue, and the cargo in the storage area, such as chains, binders, etc., is securely in place.

School Bus Only

Emergency Equipment

When inspecting a school bus, check for the following:

- Spare electrical fuses (if the bus is so equipped)
- 3 red reflective triangles
- Charged and rated fire extinguisher
- Emergency Kit
- Body Fluid Cleanup Kit

Lighting Indicators

Besides checking the lighting indicators listed in the previous section, when inspecting a school bus, make sure to check the following lighting indicators (internal panel lights):

- Alternately flashing amber lights, (if so equipped).
- Alternately flashing red lights.
- Strobe light (if so equipped).

Lights/Reflectors

Besides checking the lights and reflective devices listed in the previous section, when inspecting a school bus, make sure to check the following (external) lights and reflectors:

- Strobe light (if the bus has one).
- Stop arm light (if the bus has one).
- Alternately flashing amber lights (if the bus has one).
- Alternately flashing red lights.

Student Mirrors

Besides checking the outside mirrors, those driving a school bus also need to inspect the inside and outside mirrors that are used to keep an eye on students. Check for:

- Proper adjustment.
- Any damage to mirrors and mirror brackets. Make sure they are firmly attached and no fittings have come loose.
- Cleanliness. Make sure mirrors are clear so you can see properly.

Stop Arm

If the bus has a stop arm, make sure it is firmly attached to the frame and there is no damage or loose fittings.

Passenger Entry/Lift

Make sure the entrance to the bus is free from damage and that it is in proper working order, including closing securely from the inside. Check that the handrails are firmly attached, the steps are free from any obstructions with no loose or extremely worn treads, and the step light is working, if the bus has one.

If there is a handicap lift, make sure it is fully retracted and firmly locked. Check for any leaks, damage, or missing parts and demonstrate how to inspect the lift to make sure it is working correctly.

Emergency Exit

Check all emergency exits to make sure they do not show any signs of damage and are in good working order, including closing completely from the inside. Make sure emergency exit warning devices are working properly.

Seating

Make sure seat frames are undamaged and securely fastened to the floor, and seat cushions are firmly fastened to the seat frames.

Trailer

Trailer Front

Air/Electrical Connections
Make sure trailer air connectors are firmly closed and undamaged. Check that the glad hands are securely fastened and show no signs of damage or air leaks. Ensure that the trailer electrical plug is secured and tightly locked in place.

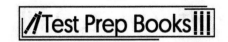

Header Board

If the vehicle has a header board, make sure it is firmly in place, undamaged, and sturdy enough to properly stow cargo. If there is a canvas or tarp carrier, check that it is firmly attached. If the vehicle has an enclosed trailer, inspect the front section for any damage such as cracks, warps, or holes.

Side of Trailer

Landing Gear

Make sure the landing gear is in a completely raised position, the crank handle is firmly in place, the support frame is undamaged, and there are no missing parts. If it is power operated, make sure there are no air or hydraulic leaks.

Doors/Ties/Lifts

If the vehicle has door ties or lifts, make sure the doors show no signs of damage and they open, close, and latch correctly from the outside. Check that the ties, straps, chains, and binders are firmly in place. If the vehicle has a cargo lift, make sure it is fully retracted and firmly latched, with no signs of leaks, damage, or missing components. Be prepared to demonstrate how it should be checked for proper operation.

Frame

Check for damage to the frame, cross members, box, and floor such as cracks, broken welds, fractures or holes.

Tandem Release Arm/Locking Pins

If the vehicle has a tandem release arm/locking pins, make sure the locking pins are firmly fastened and the release arm is locked.

Remainder of Trailer

Please refer to the previous section "External Inspection (All Vehicles)" for detailed inspection methods regarding the following components:

- Wheels
- Suspension system
- Brakes
- Doors/ties/lift
- Splash guards

Coach/Transit Bus

Passenger Items

Passenger Entry/Lift

Make sure the entrance to the bus is free from damage and that it is in proper working order, including closing securely from the inside. Check that the handrails are firmly attached, the steps are free from any obstructions with no loose or extremely worn treads, and the step light is working, if the bus has one.

187

If there is a handicap lift, make sure it is fully retracted and firmly locked. Check for any leaks, damage, or missing parts and demonstrate how to inspect the lift to make sure it is working correctly.

Emergency Exits

Check all emergency exits to make sure they do not show any signs of damage and are in good working order, including closing completely from the inside. Make sure emergency exit warning devices are working properly.

Passenger Seating

Make sure seat frames are undamaged and securely fastened to the floor, and seat cushions are firmly fastened to the seat frames.

Entry/Exit

Doors/Mirrors

Make sure the entrance and exit doors do not show any signs of damage and work properly from the outside. Check that the hinges are firmly in place and the seals are not cracked or broken.

Inspect the passenger exit mirrors and all external mirrors and mirror brackets for signs of damage and to make sure they are undamaged and firmly fastened with no loose fittings.

External Inspection of Coach/Transit Bus

Level/Air Leaks

Confirm that the vehicle is level (both the front and back), and check for any signs of air leaks coming from the suspension system if it is air-equipped.

Fuel Tank(s)

Make sure the fuel tank(s) are firmly in place and no leaks are coming from the tank(s) or lines.

Baggage Compartments

Make sure the baggage and other outside compartment doors are undamaged and in good working order, including locking firmly.

Battery/Box

Make sure battery(s) are properly situated, cell caps are in place and connections are firm, without any signs of extreme corrosion. Make sure the battery box and cover/door is securely attached and there are no signs of damage.

Remainder of Coach/Transit Bus

Please refer to the previous section "External Inspection (All Vehicles)" for detailed inspection methods for the rest of the vehicle's components. Keep in mind that you must pass the pre-trip vehicle inspection prior to taking the basic vehicle control skills test.

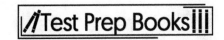

Taking the CDL Pre-Trip Inspection Test

Class A Pre-Trip Inspection Test

If applying for a Class A CDL, you will need to complete one of the four types of pre-trip inspections in the vehicle you have brought to the exam. The tests are similar and you will not know in advance which one you will be taking.

All 4 tests include starting the engine and an inspection of the cab and the coupling system. For the rest of the test, you might need to inspect the entire vehicle or only certain section(s) pointed out by the CDL Examiner.

Class B and C Pre-Trip Inspection Test

If applying for a Class B CDL, you will need to complete one of the 3 types of pre-trip inspection in the vehicle you have brought with you for testing. The tests are similar and you will not know in advance which one you will be taking.

All 3 tests include starting the engine and an inspection of the cab. For the rest of the test, you might need to inspect the entire vehicle or only certain section(s) pointed out by the CDL Examiner. You will also be required to check any features specific to the type of vehicle (e.g, school or transit bus).

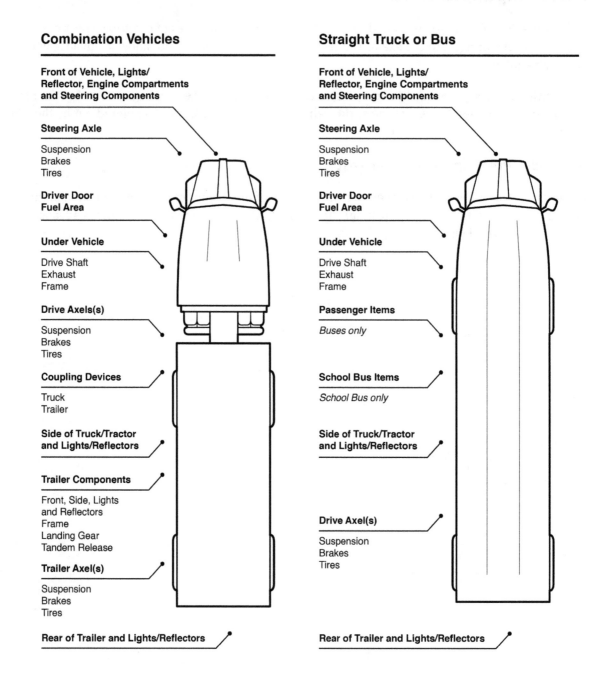

Combination Vehicles

Front of Vehicle, Lights/ Reflector, Engine Compartments and Steering Components

Steering Axle

Suspension
Brakes
Tires

Driver Door
Fuel Area

Under Vehicle

Drive Shaft
Exhaust
Frame

Drive Axels(s)

Suspension
Brakes
Tires

Coupling Devices

Truck
Trailer

Side of Truck/Tractor and Lights/Reflectors

Trailer Components

Front, Side, Lights
and Reflectors
Frame
Landing Gear
Tandem Release

Trailer Axel(s)

Suspension
Brakes
Tires

Rear of Trailer and Lights/Reflectors

Straight Truck or Bus

Front of Vehicle, Lights/ Reflector, Engine Compartments and Steering Components

Steering Axle

Suspension
Brakes
Tires

Driver Door
Fuel Area

Under Vehicle

Drive Shaft
Exhaust
Frame

Passenger Items

Buses only

School Bus Items

School Bus only

Side of Truck/Tractor and Lights/Reflectors

Drive Axel(s)

Suspension
Brakes
Tires

Rear of Trailer and Lights/Reflectors

190

Basic Vehicle Control Skills Test

The basic control skills exam you need to take during the road test could include one or more of the following maneuvers, in a location that is off-road or somewhere along the street:

- Straight line backing
- Offset back/right
- Offset back/left
- Parallel park (driver side)
- Parallel park (conventional)
- Alley dock

These exercises are outlined below.

Scoring

- Crossing Boundaries (encroachments)
- Pull-ups
- Vehicle Exits
- Final Position

Encroachments
You will be marked down for each time you touch or cross a boundary line or cone with any part of your vehicle.

Pull-Ups
If you pull forward to clear an encroachment or to reposition the vehicle, it is scored as a **"pull-up."** Stopping without changing direction does not count as a pull-up. At first you will not receive a negative score for pull-ups; however, if you do this several times, you will get marked down.

Outside Vehicle Observations (Looks)
The examiner may allow you to come to a complete stop and get out of the vehicle in order to check on its position (look). If this is the case, put the vehicle in neutral and set the parking brake(s). When you leave, continuously maintain 3 points of contact with the vehicle. If it is a bus, always keep a firm grip on the handrail. If you neglect to safely stop and leave the vehicle, you may automatically fail the basic control skills test.

You are allowed to check the position of your vehicle twice, except in the case of the Straight Line Backing exercise, which permits one chance only. You will receive one "look" score for each time you open the door and/or give up physical control of the vehicle by moving from a seated position or walk to the back of a bus to get a better view.

Final Position
Keep in mind that you must complete each part of the test precisely as directed by the examiner. If you do not move the vehicle into its final position as instructed by the examiner, you will be marked down and could potentially fail the basic skills test.

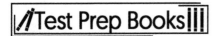

Exercises

Straight Line Backing

The examiner may direct you to back up your vehicle in a straight line between two rows of cones without touching or crossing over the boundaries. (See the diagram below for reference.)

Offset Back/Right

The examiner may direct you to back into a space located on the right rear side of your vehicle after pulling straight ahead to the outer boundary. Starting from that location, you must be able to back the vehicle into the opposite lane until the front of your vehicle has cleared the first set of cones without hitting any cones or border lines. (See the diagram below for reference.)

Offset Back/Left

The examiner may direct you to back into a space located on the left rear side of your vehicle after pulling straight ahead to the outer boundary. Starting from that location, you must be able to back the vehicle into the opposite lane until the front of your vehicle has cleared the first set of cones without hitting any cones or border lines. (See the diagram below for reference.)

Parallel Park (Driver Side)

The examiner may direct you to back into a space located on your left. You must be able to:

- Drive past the designated parking space, pulling your vehicle parallel to the parking area.
- Back into the space without cutting into the front, side or rear boundaries marked by cones.
- Park your whole vehicle entirely into the space. (See the diagram below for reference.)

Parallel Park (Conventional)

The examiner may direct you to back into a space located on your right. You must be able to:

- Drive past the designated parking space, pulling your vehicle parallel to the parking area.
- Back into the space without cutting into the front, side, or rear boundaries marked by cones.
- Park your whole vehicle entirely into the space. (See the diagram below for reference.)

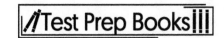
Alley Dock

The examiner may direct you to sight-side back your vehicle into an alley. You must be able to:

- Drive past the alley, pulling your vehicle parallel to the outside boundary.
- Back into the alley, moving the rear of your vehicle within 3 feet of the back of the alley without touching the boundary lines or cones.
- When parked, your vehicle must be straight within the alley/lane. (See the diagram below for reference.)

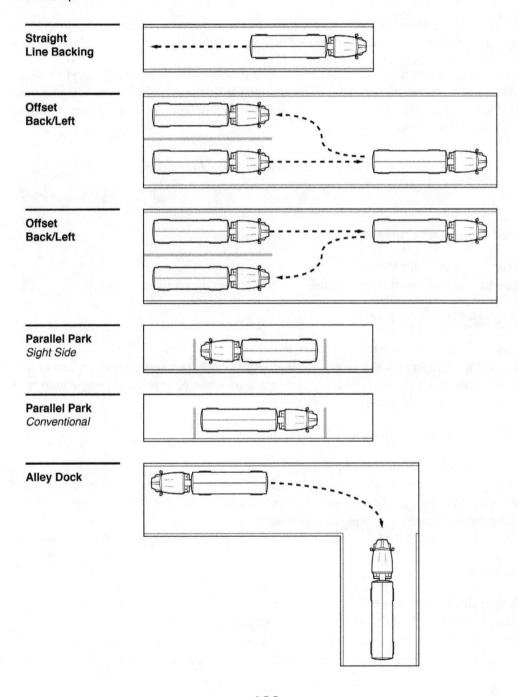

On-Road Driving

This section covers how you will be tested. Your exam route will cover a wide range of traffic situations. Throughout the duration of the test, you must drive safely and responsibly; and

- Keep your safety belt fastened.
- Yield to all traffic signs, signals, and regulations.
- Finish the exam without an accident or moving violation.

During the driving portion of the exam, follow the tester's instructions. He or she will be grading you on specific driving exercises as well as your general driving performance.

The examiner will give you the instructions in advance so you will have plenty of time to execute the various maneuvers. You will not be asked to do anything considered unsafe. If the test route lacks a specific traffic condition, the examiner may ask you to do a simulation, which will require explaining how you would handle that particular situation.

How You Will Be Tested

Turns

When asked to turn, make sure to:

- Scan traffic in all directions.
- Use turn signals and safely maneuver into the required lane to make the turn.

As you approach the turn, be sure to:

- Use turn signals to warn others around you that you are turning.
- Smoothly begin to slow the vehicle, changing gears as necessary to maintain power, but do not coast in an unsafe manner. Unsafe coasting occurs when your vehicle is not in gear for longer than the distance of your vehicle.

If you need to stop before making the turn, make sure to:

- Stop smoothly without skidding.
- Stop completely behind the stop line, crosswalk, or stop sign. If you are stopping behind another vehicle, make sure to allow enough distance so you can see the other vehicle's back tires.
- Keep the front wheels pointing straight ahead.
- Prevent your vehicle from rolling.

When ready to turn:

- Scan traffic in all directions.
- Keep both hands firmly on the steering wheel during the turn.
- Check your mirror frequently to make sure you do not scrape anything on the inside of the turn.
- Make sure you do not drive into oncoming traffic, and you finish the turn in the proper lane.

194

After turn:

- Check that the turn signal is off.
- Increase speed, turn on your turn signal, and slowly merge into the right-hand lane when you can safely do so (if not there already).
- Check mirrors and traffic.

Intersections

As you approach an intersection:

- Thoroughly scan traffic in all directions.
- Gradually start slowing down.
- Put gentle pressure on the brakes and change gears if needed.
- Completely stop (without coasting) at any stop signs, signals, sidewalks, or stop lines, making sure to keep a safe distance behind any vehicle in front of you.
- Make sure you do not roll forward or backward.

When driving through an intersection:

- Thoroughly scan traffic in all directions.
- Gradually start slowing down and give the right of way to any pedestrians and/or traffic in the intersection.
- Do not make any lane changes.
- Keep both hands firmly on the steering wheel.

Once through the intersection:

- Continue scanning mirrors and traffic.
- Slowly and smoothly speed up and make gear changes as needed.

Urban Business

For this section of the exam, you will be required to check traffic frequently and keep a safe following distance between your vehicle and those in front of you. You should stay in the middle of the right-hand lane and drive with the traffic flow (but not above the posted speed limit).

Lane Changes

For this section of the exam, you will be required to change lanes to the left, and then back to the right. Make sure you first do any essential traffic checks, then use the correct signals and change lanes smoothly when you can safely do so.

Expressway/Rural/Limited Access Highway

Before entering the expressway:

- Scan traffic.
- Use correct signals.

195

- Smoothly merge into the correct traffic lane.

Once on the expressway:

- Stay in the correct lane and maintain speed and enough space around your vehicle.
- Continue to systematically scan traffic in all directions.

When exiting the expressway:

- Check traffic as needed.
- Use correct signals.
- Slow down smoothly while in the exit lane.
- Once on the exit ramp, continue to slow down while staying within the lane margins, and keep enough distance between your vehicle and others around you.

Stop/Start

For this part of the test, you will need to pull your vehicle over to the side of the road and stop as if you were going to exit the vehicle to check something.

Make sure to completely scan traffic in all directions and then carefully guide the vehicle to the right-hand lane or shoulder.

As you prepare for the stop:

- Check traffic.
- Turn your right turn signal on.
- Slow down and brake smoothly and steadily, changing gears as needed.
- Bring your vehicle to a complete stop without coasting.

Once stopped:

- Make sure your vehicle is parallel to the curb or shoulder and out of the way of the traffic flow. It should not be obstructing driveways, fire hydrants, intersections, signs, etc.
- Make sure your turn signal is off.
- Turn on your four-way emergency flashers.
- Engage the parking brake.
- Put the gearshift into neutral or park.
- Take your feet off of the brake and clutch pedals.

When instructed to resume:

- Scan traffic and check all mirrors completely in all directions.
- Switch your four-way flashers off.
- Turn on your left turn signal.
- When it is safe to enter traffic, release the parking brake and slowly pull straight ahead.
- Do not turn the steering wheel before starting to drive.
- Scan traffic in every direction, especially on your left side.

- Guide the vehicle slowly into the correct lane when you can safely do so.
- Once you have entered the traffic flow, turn your left turn signal off.

Curve

When approaching a curve:

- Thoroughly scan traffic in all directions.
- Slow down prior to taking the curve so you will not need to brake or shift down while in the curve.
- Keep the vehicle within the lane boundaries.
- Keep scanning traffic in all directions.

Railroad Crossing

Prior to reaching a railroad crossing, you should:

- Slow down, brake steadily and shift gears as needed.
- Look and listen for trains.
- Scan traffic in every direction.
- Do not stop, change gears, switch lanes, or attempt to pass another vehicle while in the crossing.

If you are taking the test in a bus, a school bus, or a vehicle displaying placards, you must be ready to obey the following procedures at every railroad crossing (unless the crossing is exempt):

- Turn on the four-way flashers as you approach the crossing.
- Come to a stop within 50 feet but not less than 15 feet from the nearest track.
- Look and listen in both directions up and down the track for any trains and signals that signify a train is approaching. If you are driving a bus, you may also need to open the window and door before crossing the tracks.
- Keep both hands firmly on the steering wheel as you cross. Do not stop, switch gears, or make any lane changes while any component of your vehicle is passing over the tracks.
- Turn off your four-way flashers once you are across.
- Keep scanning mirrors and traffic.

Note: CDL procedures for scoring railroad crossings may vary from state to state. Make sure to check with your state DMV for specifics.

Keep in mind that some routes will not have railroad crossings. For your test, you may be required to describe and show your examiner the proper railroad crossing procedures at a simulated location.

Bridge/Overpass/Sign

After driving under an overpass or over a bridge, the examiner may ask you to recite the figure for posted clearance, height, or weight. If there are no bridges or overpasses on your test route, he or she may ask you for information about some other traffic sign. Be ready to recognize and describe any traffic sign that could appear along the route.

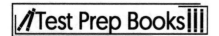

Student Discharge (School Bus)

If you are applying for a School Bus endorsement, you will need to show the proper method for loading and unloading students. Please refer to the "School Bus" section of this guide for specifics.

General Driving Behaviors

You will receive a score regarding your overall performance in the following general driving behavior categories:

Clutch Usage (for Manual Transmission)

- Always push in the clutch when you need to shift.
- Double-clutch while shifting. Make sure you do not rev or lug the engine.
- Make sure you do ride the clutch to control your speed, coast with the clutch pushed in, or "pop" the clutch.

Gear Usage (for Manual Transmission)

- Do not grind or clash the gears.
- Choose the gear that does not rev or lug the engine.
- Do not shift gears while in turns or intersections.

Brake Usage

- Do not ride or pump the brakes.
- Do not slam on the brakes or use a jerky motion. Brake smoothly and steadily.

Lane Usage

- Do not run over or onto curbs, sidewalks, or lane markings.
- Make sure to stop behind stop lines, crosswalks, or stop signs.
- When driving on a multi-lane road, make sure you finish a turn in the correct lane (a left turn should be completed in the lane directly to the right of the center line).
- Right turns should be completed in the right-hand lane.
- Always stay in or switch over the right-hand lane unless it is blocked.

Steering

- Do not steer the vehicle too much or too little.
- Make sure both hands are always firmly gripping the steering wheel (except while shifting). As soon as you are done shifting, bring both hands back to the wheel.

Regular Traffic Checks

- Check traffic and mirrors frequently, especially when entering, in the middle of, and exiting an intersection.
- Continuously scan traffic in high volume and pedestrian-heavy areas.

Use of Turn Signals

- Use our turn signals correctly.
- Switch on turn signals when required and applicable.
- Switch off turn signals when you finish turning or make a lane change.

199

CDL Practice Test #1

Section: Driving Safely

1. Which of the following is NOT a critical item to check during a mid-trip vehicle inspection?
   a. Brakes
   b. Engine oil
   c. Cargo securement devices
   d. Lights and reflectors

2. Accelerating too roughly can cause what to happen?
   a. Engine overheating
   b. Tires blowing out
   c. Braking system failure
   d. Trailer coupling damage

3. Before starting to drive down a hill, a driver should slow the vehicle and do what?
   a. Downshift to a gear that allows the driver to control the vehicle without slamming on the brakes.
   b. Place the vehicle in neutral and brake as needed down the hill.
   c. Upshift to a gear that will allow the vehicle to maintain low RPMs down the hill.
   d. Maintain a lower speed in the same gear that was used before the hill.

4. Failure to do which of the following might create the need for a driver to brake or change lanes quickly?
   a. Anticipating about twelve to fifteen seconds ahead
   b. Checking mirrors
   c. Upshifting while driving uphill
   d. Using a turn signal

5. If a driver needs to park on the side of the road, he or she should activate emergency flashers and set up emergency warning devices within how many minutes of stopping?
   a. Two minutes
   b. Ten minutes
   c. Thirty minutes
   d. Sixty minutes

6. If a road is wet from rain, a driver should reduce their speed by how much compared to dry road speeds?
   a. 20 mph slower
   b. 40 mph slower
   c. One-third slower
   d. One-fourth slower

7. What actions should a driver take if he or she starts hydroplaning?
   a. Pump the brakes gently.
   b. Push in the accelerator and the clutch.
   c. Release the accelerator and push in the clutch.
   d. Push in the brakes and the clutch.

8. If a driver is traveling 40 mph in a 40-foot vehicle, they should follow at least how many seconds behind the vehicle in front of them?
   a. Four seconds
   b. Six seconds
   c. Eight seconds
   d. Ten seconds

9. Which of the following has a potential physical impact on the height of a Commercial Motor Vehicle (CMV)?
   a. Brand of tires used
   b. Total weight of the cargo
   c. State regulations
   d. Manual vs. automatic transmission

10. What is the specific reason that driving near motorists operating rental trucks could be hazardous?
    a. Rental operators have little regard for the vehicle they are driving.
    b. Rental trucks are not subject to inspections, per federal regulations.
    c. Rental operators may not be aware that their views are restricted.
    d. Rental operators are not licensed to operate commercial vehicles.

11. Which of the following is NOT an example of texting?
    a. Reading an email
    b. Typing a destination into a GPS application
    c. Answering a hands-free phone call
    d. Sending a short three-word phrase to a friend

12. What should someone do if they are confronted by an aggressive driver?
    a. Respond to their aggressive actions with hand gestures.
    b. Make eye contact with them to encourage them to back down.
    c. Increase driving speed to demonstrate courage.
    d. Try to stay out of their way.

13. To prevent becoming drowsy during a trip, what should a driver do?
    a. Bring a passenger along for the trip.
    b. Eliminate exercise, as it makes the body more tired.
    c. Take sleeping pills at night to ensure enough sleep.
    d. Keep a steady flow of caffeine in the body.

201

14. Which of the following should a driver do in foggy conditions?
   a. Pull over to the shoulder and stop.
   b. Turn on four-way flashers.
   c. Turn on high-beam headlights.
   d. Increase speed to get through the fog faster.

15. What is the danger of not clearing ice away from the radiator shutter in the winter?
   a. The vehicle will not pass inspection.
   b. The windshield washer fluid will freeze.
   c. The engine could overheat.
   d. The ignition will misfire.

16. In extremely hot temperatures, a driver should inspect their tires every two hours or 100 miles for what?
   a. Elevated air pressure
   b. Excessive tread wear
   c. Punctures from sharp objects
   d. Thin spots in the tire wall

17. Passive and active railroad crossings are separated by what key difference?
   a. Active railroad crossings currently have a moving train on them.
   b. Active railroad crossings do not have warning signs within 100 feet of them.
   c. Active railroad crossings are still in operation.
   d. Active railroad crossings have traffic control mechanisms, such as flashing lights or gates.

18. Which of the following is NOT a factor to consider in determining a safe speed when traveling downhill?
   a. Slope of the hill
   b. Weight of the vehicle and cargo
   c. Height of the vehicle and cargo
   d. Road conditions

19. In the event of a loss of hydraulic pressure in the braking system, a driver should attempt to pump the brakes. Why?
   a. To indicate through the brake lights that other drivers should keep their distance
   b. To generate enough hydraulic pressure to make the vehicle stop
   c. To make the brakes lock, which will stop the vehicle
   d. To activate the emergency brake

20. What is the benefit of an antilock braking system (ABS)?
   a. An ABS allows a driver to stop more quickly.
   b. An ABS prevents the brakes from wearing down over time.
   c. An ABS prevents skidding from pressing the brakes too hard.
   d. An ABS allows a driver to stop the vehicle from any gear.

21. Oversteering can cause a vehicle to skid. What is oversteering?
    a. Using an overhanded grip on the steering wheel
    b. Making a sharper turn than the vehicle can handle
    c. Weaving in and out of traffic lanes
    d. Making more than four turns over a distance of three miles

22. Identify the correct order of procedures following an accident in which the driver is not critically injured.
    a. Protect the area, notify authorities, care for the injured
    b. Notify authorities, protect the area, care for the injured
    c. Care for the injured, protect the area, notify authorities
    d. Notify authorities, care for the injured, protect the area

23. Which of the following classes of fire is an electrical equipment fire?
    a. Class A
    b. Class B
    c. Class C
    d. Class D

24. Legal drugs prescribed by a doctor can be used by a driver under what condition?
    a. If they are used as prescribed
    b. If they are on record with the driver's company
    c. If they are controlled substances
    d. If the doctor has confirmed that they will not affect driving ability

25. Cargo loads that include items such as gasoline, pesticides, and plutonium are regarded as what type of goods?
    a. Poisonous materials
    b. Flammable goods
    c. Combustible goods
    d. Hazardous materials

Section: Transporting Cargo Safely

26. Within how many miles of the start of a trip should you stop to make sure that the cargo is secure?
    a. 50 miles
    b. 100 miles
    c. 200 miles
    d. 500 miles

27. Which of the following statements is true regarding cargo weight limits?
    a. The weight of the cargo must be higher than the minimum GVWR.
    b. The weight of the cargo must be less than the maximum GVWR, GCWR, and axle weight.
    c. The weight of the cargo must be less than the maximum GCWR and axle weight, but higher than the minimum GVWR.
    d. The weight of the cargo must be less than the maximum GVWR and GCWR, but higher than the minimum axle weight.

203

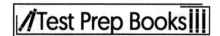

28. Cargo on flat bed trailers needs to be secured using tiedowns. Regardless of the size of the cargo, there needs to be a minimum of how many tiedowns to hold the cargo?
   a. One
   b. Two
   c. Three
   d. Four

29. If a cargo cover appears to be flapping while you are driving, what could that indicate?
   a. The wind speed is higher than usual.
   b. The cover is not large enough for the cargo.
   c. The cargo has shifted and possibly spilled.
   d. The cover might tear away if not secured.

30. When hauling livestock, it is possible for the animals to lean during turns. What can happen as a result?
   a. Nothing—this is normal animal behavior and can be disregarded.
   b. The livestock may fall and become injured.
   c. A rollover could become more likely.
   d. The livestock could fall out of the enclosure.

Section: Transporting Passengers

31. A driver will most likely need a CDL and a passenger endorsement in order to drive what type of vehicle?
   a. A dump truck
   b. A tractor trailer
   c. A taxicab
   d. A bus

32. Which of the following is true about emergency roof hatches on a bus?
   a. They must be closed at all times.
   b. Opening them gives the bus a higher clearance.
   c. They must be completely removed when opened.
   d. Buses do not have emergency roof hatches.

33. All standing bus passengers must stand behind what?
   a. The driver's seat
   b. The emergency exit windows
   c. The first row of seated passengers
   d. The front axle of the bus

34. Why should a bus driver open the front door of their bus at a railroad crossing?
   a. To allow fresh air to enter the bus
   b. To pick up or drop off passengers
   c. To increase their ability to see or hear a train
   d. To ensure that the door still operates properly

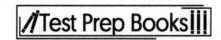

35. Under what circumstances should a disabled bus be towed while carrying passengers?
    a. If it is dangerous for the passengers to exit
    b. If one or more passengers are in wheelchairs
    c. If the nearest service station is within 5 miles
    d. A bus should never be towed while carrying passengers

Section: Air Brakes

36. Which of the following is NOT a type of braking system that comprises air brakes?
    a. Service brake
    b. Parking brake
    c. Emergency brake
    d. Compression brake

37. What is the purpose of an alcohol evaporator in an air brake system?
    a. To remove toxic fumes from the engine
    b. To prevent ice buildup in the radiator
    c. To prevent ice buildup in the air brake valves
    d. To prevent the braking system from becoming too pressurized

38. Why should the brake pedal never be pressed when the spring brakes are engaged?
    a. The spring brakes only work if the brake pedal is fully elevated.
    b. The combination of the springs and air pressure can damage the brakes.
    c. The combination of the springs and air pressure cancel each other and the vehicle will not stop.
    d. The spring brakes cause the air pressure in the pedal to drop and become ineffective.

39. By turning on the electrical power only and pressing up and down on the brake pedal, a driver would be able to test which aspect of an air brake system?
    a. The low-pressure warning signal
    b. The air leakage rate
    c. The parking brake
    d. The brake fluid level

40. Which of the following is a factor in total stopping distance that is exclusive to vehicles with air brakes?
    a. Perception distance
    b. Reaction distance
    c. Brake lag distance
    d. Braking distance

Section: Combination Vehicles

41. Quick, sudden movements of the steering wheel in a tractor trailer creates rearward amplification, which can cause what?
    a. The trailer to sway and/or tip over
    b. The tractor trailer to jackknife
    c. The rear tires to skid
    d. Cargo to eject from the back of the trailer

205

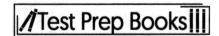

42. When backing up a tractor trailer, turning the steering wheel to the right (clockwise) will cause what to happen?
    a. The back of the vehicle to shift left and the back of the trailer to shift right
    b. The back of the vehicle to shift left and the back of the trailer to also shift left
    c. The back of the vehicle to shift right and the back of the trailer to shift left
    d. The back of the vehicle to shift right and the back of the trailer to also shift right

43. Why should a driver not use the trailer hand valve when parking?
    a. It will release the trailer from the vehicle.
    b. Air might leak and cause the brakes to unlock.
    c. It can drain the life of the battery.
    d. It will unlock the doors of the trailer, increasing the likelihood of theft.

44. Which of the following is NOT a purpose of hose couplers (a.k.a. glad hands)?
    a. To prevent air from escaping
    b. To prevent water from entering the brake lines
    c. To connect the service air line from the truck to the trailer
    d. To connect the emergency air line from the truck to the trailer

45. What can be the result of crossed air lines?
    a. Air will get into the fuel line.
    b. The brake pedal will cause the vehicle to accelerate.
    c. The engine will over-combust, causing a fire.
    d. The trailer spring brakes won't release.

46. How can a driver determine if a vehicle has an antilock brake system?
    a. Check under the vehicle for an electronic control unit and wheel speed sensor wires.
    b. Check to see if the air lines are blue and red, rather than black.
    c. Check the vehicle's registration papers.
    d. Repeatedly pump the brake pedal with only the electrical system on.

47. Which of the following is the first step in coupling a tractor and a trailer?
    a. Chocking the trailer wheels
    b. Inspecting the fifth wheel
    c. Checking the trailer height
    d. Connecting the air lines

48. Which of the following is the correct order of the first three steps of safely uncoupling vehicle units?
    a. Chock the trailer wheels, position the rig, ease pressure on the locking jaws
    b. Chock the trailer wheels, position the rig, lower the landing gear
    c. Position the rig, ease pressure on the locking jaws, chock the trailer wheels
    d. Position the rig, lower the landing gear, ease pressure on the locking jaws

49. When checking a power operated landing gear during a walk-around inspection, what must be ensured?
    a. That the landing gear is in the down position
    b. That the fifth wheel is positioned properly
    c. That the trailer is empty
    d. That there are no air or hydraulic leaks

50. When testing a trailer's service brakes, the brakes should be engaged by using what?
    a. The parking brakes
    b. The foot pedal
    c. The hand-control valve
    d. The air supply knob

Section: Doubles and Triples

51. There are several areas that require extra attention when pulling double and triple trailers. Which of these is NOT a precaution that should be taken?
    a. Looking farther ahead than would normally be required because a double or triple rig cannot maneuver as quickly as a single rig
    b. Allowing extra space between the rig and other vehicles on the road
    c. Driving slightly faster than normal to allow for the extra weight of the extended rig
    d. Making more careful adjustments to steering maneuvers to avoid the crack-the-whip effect

52. Which of the following is NOT an additional check that is required for pulling doubles and triples?
    a. Checking the lower and upper fifth wheels
    b. Opening each of the shut-off valves at the back of each trailer
    c. Making sure the landing gear is in the up position
    d. Inspecting the air and electric lines for damage

53. What will pressing the "trailer air supply" knob do when the air pressure is at a normal level?
    a. Supply air to the emergency supply lines
    b. Release air from the emergency supply lines
    c. Supply air to the service line
    d. Release air from the service line

54. Converter dollies that have antilock brakes (those built after March 1, 1998) will have what color light on the side of the dolly?
    a. Blue
    b. Red
    c. Yellow
    d. Green

55. On a triple trailer rig, where should the trailer with the heaviest cargo be placed?
    a. As the last trailer in the rig
    b. As the middle trailer in the rig
    c. It doesn't matter, as long as the whole rig is within weight guidelines.
    d. Right behind the tractor

Section: Tank Vehicles

56. Do Class A or B CDL licenses require an additional endorsement for carrying liquids or gases?
    a. No, Class A and B CDL licenses can drive any type of tractor-trailer rig without additional endorsements.
    b. No, only Class C CLD licenses require additional endorsements to pull tanker trailers.
    c. Yes, if the material has an individual rated capacity of more than 219 gallons and an aggregate rated capacity of at least 1500 gallons.
    d. Yes, if the material has an individual rated capacity of more than 119 gallons and an aggregate rated capacity of at least 1000 gallons.

57. What is NOT a likely consequence of transporting a tanker that has a leak?
    a. Being given a citation
    b. Being required to attend CDL safe driving courses
    c. Being banned from driving
    d. Being responsible for cleaning up any spills

58. What is a result of a tanker trailer having a high center of gravity compared to regular trailers?
    a. Higher speeds are needed to pull a top-heavy tanker trailer.
    b. The tanker trailer is top-heavy and can become unstable on bends and curves in the road.
    c. Tanker trailers cannot drive on curvy roads or take 90-degree turns due to being top-heavy.
    d. There is minimal difference because tanker trailers are not as tall as regular trailers.

59. Surge (the movement of the liquid inside the tanker) is a unique concern when pulling a tanker trailer. What are some features of the tanker that help to control surge?
    a. Bulkheads and baffled tanks
    b. Un-baffled tanks and outage
    c. Outage and bulkheads
    d. Bulkheads and smooth bore tanks

60. What are some considerations for determining how much liquid can be loaded into a tanker trailer?
    a. How much the liquid will condense during the transport
    b. The weight of the liquid
    c. Whether the tanker has baffled tanks
    d. Whether the liquid is consumable or not

Section: Hazardous Materials

61. Which of the following is NOT considered a hazardous material?
    a. A combustible liquid
    b. Formaldehyde
    c. Non-potable water
    d. A flammable solid

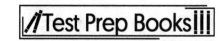

62. What shape is the placard required for vehicles carrying hazardous materials?
    a. A diamond
    b. An octagon
    c. A triangle
    d. A circle

63. What is required in order to obtain a hazardous materials endorsement on a CDL license?
    a. Passing a written test about the regulations and requirements for hauling hazardous materials
    b. Passing a driving test while hauling a hazardous material load
    c. Passing an interview in front of a panel of hazardous materials experts
    d. There are no additional requirements for hauling hazardous materials.

64. Who is responsible for packaging, marking, and labeling the hazardous materials prior to shipment?
    a. The manufacturer
    b. The driver
    c. The carrier
    d. The shipper

65. How many classes of hazardous materials are listed in the Hazardous Materials Table?
    a. 7
    b. 8
    c. 9
    d. 10

66. What materials are indicated as Class 1 hazardous materials, according to the Hazardous Materials Table?
    a. Propane, compressed fluorine, helium
    b. Fireworks, explosive devices, flares, dynamite
    c. Ammonium nitrate, peroxide, methyl ethyl ketone
    d. Ammonium picrate, wetted white, phosphorus sodium

67. On the Hazardous Materials Table, what does the symbol (D) in Column 1 indicate?
    a. That the material is dangerous and should be declined
    b. That the material is packaged to haul internationally but not domestically
    c. That the material is packaged to haul domestically but not internationally
    d. That the material packaging is damaged and cannot be hauled

68. What information must be included in the item description on the shipping paper for hazardous materials?
    a. The number of pages, the certification signature, and the emergency response phone number for the shipper's responsible party
    b. The immediate health hazards, fire or explosive dangers, instructions for cleaning up spills, and first aid procedures
    c. The name and identification number of the material, the name and address of the shipper, and the destination address labels
    d. The identification number, the proper shipping name, the hazard class or division, and the amount and unit of measure of the cargo

209

69. There are two placard tables that help drivers determine when placards must be used when hauling hazardous materials. Table 1 refers to items that must have placards if they are carried in any amount. Table 2 refers to hazardous items over what amount?
   a. 1,001 pounds or more
   b. 501 pounds or more
   c. 1,501 pounds or more
   d. 2,001 pounds or more

70. When the shipping papers include the words "inhalation hazard," what additional placard wording is required to transport the hazardous material?
   a. Beware: Poison Gas
   b. Dangerous Poison Gas
   c. Caution: Poison Inhalation
   d. Poison Gas or Poison Inhalation

71. Smoking is strictly prohibited around which classes of hazardous materials?
   a. Class 1 only
   b. Classes 1 and 2
   c. Classes 1, 2, and 5
   d. Classes 1, 2, 3, 4, and 5

72. What does the abbreviation N.O.S. stand for with regards to hazardous materials transportation?
   a. Noxious odors on surfaces
   b. Non-organic supplies
   c. Not otherwise specified
   d. No other services

Section: School Buses

73. What region(s) around the school bus is/are considered the most dangerous to children?
   a. The first ten feet on each side of the bus and the first ten feet from the back of the bus
   b. Thirty feet from the front bumper of the bus
   c. Thirty feet from all sides of the bus
   d. The first ten feet in front of the bus and thirty feet on the sides and back of the bus

74. The left and right side flat mirrors allow for blind spots around the bus. Where are these blind spots located when driving a school bus?
   a. Below and in front of each mirror
   b. Below and in front of each mirror and behind the rear bumper
   c. Behind the rear bumper
   d. In front of the front bumper

75. When properly adjusted, mirrors on the school bus should allow the driver to see:
   a. Where the front tires touch the ground
   b. 200 feet behind the bus and along each side
   c. 100 feet behind the bus and along each side
   d. 100 feet behind the bus and where the front tires touch the ground

210

76. What is the flaw with the convex mirrors that are located beneath the outside flat mirrors?
    a. They do not show an accurate size or distance from the bus of people or objects.
    b. They do not show traffic, clearances, or students on the sides of the bus.
    c. They are too small and do not show enough detail.
    d. They are poorly positioned on some buses and should not be relied upon for safety.

77. What steps should a school bus driver take when at a railroad crossing?
    a. Stop 200 feet from the crossing guard rail, put the transmission in neutral, and put down the driver's window to listen for an oncoming train.
    b. Stop no more than 15 feet from the nearest crossing guard rail, open the door and driver's window, and listen for an oncoming train while rolling slowly over the tracks.
    c. Stop between 15 and 50 feet from the nearest crossing guard rail, put the transmission in park, and open the door and driver's window to listen for an oncoming train.
    d. Stop between 15 and 50 feet from the crossing guard rail, put the transmission in neutral, and open the door to listen for an oncoming train.

78. Which situation results in a mandatory evacuation of the school bus?
    a. The students are becoming rowdy and unmanageable when staying on the bus.
    b. The weather is wet and rainy, making it more difficult for approaching drivers to see the bus.
    c. The students should only be evacuated if a police officer is present and requires it.
    d. There is the potential for the bus to shift position, which would increase the risk of an accident.

79. When evacuating students from the bus in an emergency, it can be helpful to ask whom to assist with the evacuation?
    a. Two local business owners
    b. Any passersby
    c. A local neighbor or two
    d. Two older, responsible students

80. In addition to following the procedures listed in the study guide, the school bus driver should also always follow:
    a. All state and local laws and regulations
    b. The procedures designated by the parents' organization at the school
    c. The guidelines established by each neighborhood homeowner's association
    d. Any notes or signs that are posted inside the school bus

81. When students must cross a road after exiting the bus, where should they cross?
    a. About ten feet behind the bus
    b. About ten feet in front of the bus
    c. About twenty feet in front of the bus
    d. About twenty feet behind the bus

82. When students are getting off of the bus at the school, the driver should:
    a. Put the transmission in neutral
    b. Release the parking brake
    c. Turn on emergency lights
    d. Turn off the ignition

211

Section: Pre-Trip Inspection

83. Which areas of the engine compartment should be inspected during the pre-trip vehicle inspection?
   a. Power steering fluid, temperature gauge, wipers/washers, horn
   b. Power steering fluid, air gauge, hydraulic brake check, safety belt
   c. Oil pressure gauge, ammeter/voltmeter, parking brake, safe start
   d. Oil and coolant levels, power steering and alternator belts, safe start

84. What is the correct range for the air brake pressure governor cutoff?
   a. 100-120 psi
   b. 120-140 psi
   c. 140-160 psi
   d. 160-180 psi

85. When checking the tires during the pre-trip vehicle inspection, what is the required tread depth on all tires?
   a. At least 2/32 on all tires
   b. At least 2/32 on the steering wheel tires and 4/32 on all other tires
   c. At least 4/32 on the steering axle tires and 2/32 on all other tires
   d. At least 4/32 on all tires

86. What emergency equipment should be inspected during the pre-trip vehicle inspection of a school bus?
   a. First aid kit, strobe lights, spare electrical fuses
   b. Alternately flashing red and amber lights, emergency exit warning devices
   c. Reflective triangles, fire extinguisher, body fluid cleanup kit
   d. Tire jack, tire iron, and lug nut wrench

87. When conducting a pre-trip inspection test for a Class A CDL, how many of the four types of pre-trip inspections will be required?
   a. One
   b. Two
   c. Three
   d. Four

88. When conducting a pre-trip inspection of a trailer, in what position should the landing gear be?
   a. A completely raised position
   b. A completely lowered position
   c. A neutral position
   d. No inspection of the landing gear is necessary.

89. A pre-trip inspection of a coach or transit bus includes which of the following?
   a. Air and electrical connections and header boards
   b. Lights, reflectors, and the stop arm
   c. Mounting bolts, locking jaws, and the kingpin
   d. Emergency exits, battery box, and fuel tanks

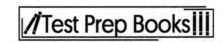

90. How many types of pre-trip inspections are there for a Class B CDL?
   a. One
   b. Two
   c. Three
   d. Four

Section: Basic Control Skills test

91. Which of the following maneuvers is NOT part of the basic vehicle control skills test?
   a. Parallel parking
   b. Freeway driving
   c. Alley docking
   d. Straight line backing

92. How are "pull-ups" counted when scoring the basic vehicle control skills test?
   a. The first pull-up is not counted, but multiple instances will be marked down.
   b. Pull-ups are marked down no matter how often they are done.
   c. Pull-ups are permitted during the test and are not marked down.
   d. Three pull-ups are permitted during the test without losing points.

93. How many times are you permitted to conduct an outside vehicle observation during the basic vehicle control skills test?
   a. None; checking outside the vehicle will result in failure of the test
   b. Once during the straight line backing exercise; twice during the other skills
   c. Twice during any portion of the test
   d. Twice during the straight line backing exercise; once during the other skills

94. What does offset backing, right and left, involve during the basic vehicle control skills test?
   a. Turning right or left with the vehicle in reverse
   b. Changing lanes to the right or left while being able to see behind the vehicle
   c. Backing the vehicle into a parking space to the rear left or rear right
   d. Backing the vehicle into a parking space while allowing appropriate offset space on both the left and the right

95. What does "alley dock" refer to on the basic vehicle control skills test?
   a. Backing the vehicle up to a warehouse dock for loading and unloading
   b. Backing the vehicle into a parallel parking space alongside an alley
   c. Backing the vehicle out of an alleyway
   d. Backing the vehicle into an alley that is perpendicular to the direction the vehicle is moving

Section: On-Road Driving

96. What may happen if the on-road driving test lacks a particular traffic condition?
   a. Not all traffic conditions are expected during the test; nothing will happen if any particular situation is missing.
   b. The examiner may ask you to verbally explain how you would handle the situation.
   c. You will be asked to come back and re-take the test on a more suitable day.
   d. The missing traffic condition will be re-created at the training facility.

213

97. During the on-road driving test, the examiner will check that what additional procedures are taken when crossing railroad tracks in a school bus?
   a. Turning on four-way flashers
   b. Slowing down and braking steadily
   c. Looking and listening for trains
   d. Checking traffic in all directions

98. What special consideration may the examiner ask a driver about when driving under an overpass during the on-road driving test?
   a. Estimating the width of the overpass
   b. Noting how many other vehicles are passing under the overpass
   c. Reciting the posted clearance information
   d. Reporting the speed while passing under the overpass

99. General driving behaviors that will be scored during the on-road driving test include which of the following?
   a. Use of the radios and communication devices inside the vehicle
   b. Use of window mechanisms and adjustments to the mirrors
   c. Lane usage, steering, and regular traffic checks
   d. Appropriate inspections of the vehicle during the test

100. When stopping behind another vehicle before making a turn during the on-road driving test, what part of the vehicle in front of you should be visible?
   a. The vehicle's back window
   b. The vehicle's back tires
   c. The roof of the vehicle
   d. The cargo area of the vehicle

Answer Explanations #1

Section: Driving Safely

1. B: Engine oil should be checked as part of a pre-trip inspection. Choices A, C, and D are incorrect because brakes, cargo securement, and lights and reflectors should all be checked during stops.

2. D: Rough or jerky acceleration can cause damage to the coupling if a driver is hauling a trailer. Choices A and B are incorrect because engine overheating and tire blowouts generally take more time than rough acceleration would provide. Choice C is incorrect because the braking system functions independently of acceleration.

3. A: When driving down a hill, the driver should slow down and downshift to a gear that maintains the lower speed without relying too heavily on the brakes, which could cause them to overheat. Choices B, C, and D are incorrect because they rely too much on braking to maintain control of the vehicle.

4. A: A driver should anticipate about twelve to fifteen seconds ahead to better judge potential upcoming traffic problems. While Choices B, C, and D are all good pieces of advice in general, they would have no bearing on the need to brake or change lanes quickly.

5. B: Emergency warning devices should be setup within ten minutes of stopping if a driver needs to park on the side of the road. Choice A is incorrect because two minutes might not realistically be enough time to set up. Choices C and D are incorrect because they allow too much time to pass, during which an accident could occur as a result of the absence of emergency warning devices.

6. C: A driver should reduce their speed by one-third in wet conditions. For example, if a driver is safely traveling a dry road at 60 mph, he or she should reduce their speed by 20 mph when that road is wet, resulting in a driving speed of 40 mph. Choices A and B are incorrect because they would not necessarily be applicable. For example, reducing from 70 mph to 50 mph (Choice A) might not be an adequate reduction. Meanwhile, reducing from 45 mph to 5 mph (Choice B) is unnecessary and results in lost time. Choice D is incorrect because it might not be enough of a speed reduction to maintain safety in wet conditions.

7. C: Releasing the accelerator and pushing in the clutch allows the vehicle to slow down and the wheels to turn more easily. Choices A and D are incorrect because the brakes should never be used during hydroplaning. Choice B is incorrect because accelerating will make the vehicle even more difficult to control.

8. A: As a rule of thumb, a driver should follow at least one second behind another vehicle for every 10 feet of vehicle that they are driving, assuming a speed of 40 mph. Therefore, the driver of a 30-foot truck should allow at least three seconds, while the driver of a 60-foot truck should allow at least six seconds. Allow more time for higher speeds. Choices B, C, and D are incorrect because, while they allow more time for reaction, they are more difficult to judge and are unnecessary under normal driving conditions.

9. B: A heavy cargo will lower the height of a CMV; an empty trailer will sit up higher. While some aspects of a tire, such as its profile, could impact a CMV's height, the brand of tire would not, so Choice A is incorrect. Choice C is incorrect because a state's regulations cannot physically change the height of a

215

vehicle. Choice *D* is incorrect because there isn't enough of a weight difference between the types of transmission to affect the height of the entire CMV.

10. C: Rental trucks have restricted side and rear views that drivers are typically unaware of. Choice *A* is incorrect because, aside from the typical risks of driving recklessly, rental drivers can be held liable for damage done to a rental vehicle. Choice *B* is incorrect because rental trucks are also subject to regular inspection. Choice *D*, while often true (rental trucks are not considered to be commercial vehicles), is incorrect because rental operators are required to have a standard operator's license, so they are not inherently dangerous.

11. C: Answering a phone call and remaining hands-free does not meet the definition of texting. Texting is defined as typing or reading text from an electronic device. Due to this definition, Choices *A*, *B*, and *D* are all incorrect.

12. D: Staying clear of an aggressive driver is less likely to increase their aggression. It also minimizes danger to self. Choices *A* and *B* are both likely to increase the driver's aggression, creating a more volatile situation. Choice *C* is not only likely to increase the driver's aggression, but driving faster also increases the risk of danger to self.

13. A: Bringing a passenger along during a trip can help provide enough stimulation to keep a driver alert on the road. Choice *B* is incorrect because a small to moderate amount of exercise actually increases energy levels. Choice *C* is incorrect because sleeping pills can cause grogginess upon waking, less restful sleep, and possible dependence. Choice *D* is incorrect because caffeine—and other stimulants—can cause initial alertness, followed by drowsiness as the caffeine wears off.

14. B: Using four-way flashers makes the vehicle more visible in foggy conditions. Choice *A* is incorrect because foggy conditions can distort a driver's view; other drivers may not be able to correctly perceive your location. Choice *C* is incorrect because high-beams in fog can actually lower a driver's range of vision. Choice *D* is incorrect because increased speed in low-visibility conditions, such as fog, increases the odds of a collision.

15. C: The engine could overheat and stop working if the radiator shutter freezes shut. Ice on the vehicle has no bearing on its ability to pass inspection, so Choice *A* is incorrect. While windshield washer fluid can freeze during the winter, this isn't due to ice on the radiator, so Choice *B* is incorrect. Choice *D* is incorrect because the ignition system of a vehicle is completely separate from the cooling system, so a frozen radiator will not impact ignition.

16. A: Air pressure in tires will rise along with the temperature, so it is important to check tire pressure frequently in extremely hot weather to prevent a blowout. If the tires are too hot to touch, allow them to cool down before driving again. Choices *B*, *C*, and *D* are incorrect because the likelihood of these events is not necessarily increased in hot temperatures.

17. D: Active crossings are marked with traffic control mechanisms to regulate traffic that passive crossings do not have. Choices *A* and *C* are incorrect because passive railroad crossing can also be in operation and have moving trains on them. Choice *B* is incorrect because active crossings frequently have warning signs at their location, as well as within 100 feet.

18. C: The height of a vehicle and its cargo have very little impact on its safe speed while traveling downhill. Choices *A* and *B* are incorrect because slope and weight are factors in how fast the vehicle will

216

travel downhill without braking. Choice *D* is incorrect because road conditions play a major role in how effectively braking slows a vehicle.

19. B: Pumping the brakes can sometimes create enough pressure in the braking system to bring the vehicle to a stop. Choice *A* is incorrect because not only is there no guarantee that other drivers would understand the situation, but the activation of brake lights also does nothing physically to slow or stop the vehicle. Choice *C* is incorrect because a loss of hydraulic pressure would make locking the brakes nearly impossible. Additionally, locking the brakes would make the vehicle skid further out of control. Choice *D* is incorrect because the emergency brake is not connected to the hydraulic brake system.

20. C: An ABS prevents the braking system from locking up and making the vehicle skid by reducing pressure in the braking system when the brakes are pressed too hard. Choice *A* is incorrect because an ABS doesn't cause the brakes to work more effectively, it keeps the brakes from failing due to locking up. Choice *B* is incorrect because nothing (other than not using the brakes) can prevent the wearing down of brakes over time. Choice *D* is incorrect because a driver can stop a vehicle from any gear, regardless of the presence of an ABS.

21. B: Making a turn that is too sharp for the vehicle to handle is called oversteering. It can cause a vehicle to skid, or even overturn if the vehicle is top-heavy. Choice *A* is incorrect because using an overhanded grip has no bearing on whether or not the vehicle will skid. Choice *C* is incorrect because, while potentially dangerous, weaving in and out of traffic lanes would not cause the vehicle to skid unless the driver made turns that were too sharp (i.e., oversteering). Choice *D* is incorrect because making more than four turns in three miles is commonplace and completely safe if done properly.

22. A: Protecting the area should be done first to prevent another accident happening in the same location. Next, notify authorities to assist at the scene. Finally, help others who are injured if you are able to, unless someone else at the scene has emergency experience and is dealing with injuries. Choices *B*, *C*, and *D* are all incorrect because the first thing a driver should do in this situation is protect the area to prevent additional accidents at the scene.

23. C: Class C fires involve electrical equipment. These should be extinguished with non-conducting agents like dry chemicals instead of water, which is extremely dangerous because it conducts electricity. Choice *A* is incorrect because Class A fires involve simple ordinary combustibles, such as wood. Choice *B* is incorrect because Class B fires involve flammable liquids or gases, including gasoline and oil. Choice *D* is incorrect because Class D fires involve combustible metals such as magnesium.

24. D: Drivers can safely take prescribed medications as directed only if the doctor has stated that the medication will not impact driving. Choice *A* is incorrect because even when taken as directed, some medications will impair driving ability. Choice *B* is incorrect because having the medication on record does not change the impact that it may have on the driver after it is taken. Choice *C* is incorrect because controlled substances are classes of drugs that are most likely to impair driving. As a result, they are generally illegal to have while on the road.

25. D: Gasoline, pesticides, and plutonium are all considered hazardous materials, or goods that are risky to transport. Hazardous materials include a number of classes of materials, including poisons, flammable goods, and combustibles. Choice *A* is incorrect because gasoline and plutonium are considered flammable and radioactive, respectively. Choices *B* and *C* are incorrect because pesticides and plutonium are not necessarily considered flammable or combustible.

217

Section: Transporting Cargo Safely

26. A: You should stop to check that your cargo is secure within the first 50 miles of a trip. At that time, make adjustments as needed to secure the cargo. Choices *B*, *C*, and *D* are incorrect because they allow too much travel time for the cargo to be damaged or lost if it is not properly secured.

27. B: The cargo you haul must weigh less than the maximum GVWR, GCWR, and axle weight. There are no minimum values for these weights, so Choices *A*, *C*, and *D* are all incorrect.

28. B: There should be a minimum of two tiedowns securing your cargo, regardless of its size. Also, there should be an additional tiedown for every 10 feet of cargo. Choice *A* is incorrect because only one tiedown will not keep a cargo secure. Choices *C* and *D* are incorrect because having three or more tiedowns for a small (less than 10 feet) cargo load is unnecessary and an inefficient use of time and effort.

29. D: If a cargo cover appears to be flapping, it might blow or tear away if not secured. This could expose the cargo to weather conditions or endanger other drivers. Choices *A* and *B* are incorrect because neither high winds nor a cargo cover that is too small should cause the cargo cover to flap if it is tied down securely. Choice *C* is incorrect because it is possible for cargo to shift under a secured cover if the tiedowns are improperly placed. Likewise, it is possible for the cover not to be tightly secured while the cargo itself has been.

30. C: If the livestock lean during turns, they can shift the center of gravity, increasing the likelihood of rollover. Choice *A* is incorrect because, while leaning through turns might be normal behavior, the effect of numerous large animals on the center of gravity cannot be disregarded. Choices *B* and *D* are incorrect because these problems would be more indicative of improperly secured livestock. Even properly secured livestock could lean and create a center of gravity shift.

Section: Transporting Passengers

31. D: Driving a bus typically requires a CDL and passenger endorsement, although the number of passengers making the CDL a requirement varies by state. Choices *A* and *B* are incorrect because neither driving a dump truck nor driving a tractor trailer requires a passenger endorsement, as these vehicles generally do not carry passengers. Choice *C* is incorrect because driving a taxi sometimes requires a chauffeur's license, but not a CDL.

32. B: Partially opening an emergency roof hatch will increase the clearance, or total height of the bus. Choices *A* and *C* are incorrect because these hatches can be opened partially to allow fresh air flow as needed. Choice *D* is incorrect because many buses have emergency roof hatches. These hatches allow easier exiting of the bus if it is overturned on its side.

33. A: Bus passengers that are standing must remain behind the driver's seat, as well as the standee line on the floor, while the bus is in motion. Choices *B* and *C* are incorrect because they are unnecessarily far back and may be impractical. Choice *D* is incorrect because the front axle of the bus may or may not be behind the driver's seat, and most passengers would have no way of knowing its location.

34. C: Opening the door at a railroad crossing can sometimes increase a driver's ability to see or hear a train approaching. Choice *A* is incorrect because fresh air can be obtained through windows or emergency roof hatches. Choice *B* is incorrect because passengers should be picked up or dropped off at

designated stops and never at railroad crossings, which is unsafe. Choice *D* is incorrect because door operation should be inspected between trips.

35. A: The safety of the passengers is most important; if exiting the buss is too dangerous, the passengers can remain inside while the bus is towed. Choice *B* is incorrect because being in a wheelchair does not increase a passenger's safety while the bus is towed. Choice *C* is incorrect because a bus carrying passengers should only be towed to the nearest safe place for passengers to exit, which is not dependent on the location of a service station. Choice *D* is incorrect because a bus can be towed while carrying passengers if it is too dangerous for them to exit.

Section: Air Brakes

36. D: While compression plays a vital role in the use of air brakes, a compression brake is not a component of the air brake system. Choices *A*, *B*, and *C* are all incorrect because service brakes, parking brakes, and emergency brakes are the three braking systems that comprise air brakes.

37. C: The alcohol evaporator works by depositing alcohol into the air brake system and preventing ice buildup. Choice *A* is incorrect because removal of toxic fumes is not the purpose of a braking system. Choice *B* is incorrect because preventing ice buildup in the radiator is the purpose of antifreeze. Choice *D* is incorrect because removing pressure from the braking system is the purpose of the safety valve.

38. B: The combined forces of the springs and the air pressure from the brake pedal can damage the brake system. Choice *A* is incorrect because spring brakes become activated when the air pressure drops, regardless of the height of the brake pedal. Choice *C* is incorrect because the force of the two brakes will combine rather than cancel each other out. Choice *D* is incorrect because spring brakes are activated after the air pressure has already dropped; the spring brakes do not cause the drop to occur.

39. A: Pressing up and down on the brake pedal to decrease pressure in the air tanks while the electrical power is on should activate the low-pressure warning signal. If the signal doesn't activate, the driver could lose air pressure unknowingly. Choice *B* is incorrect because the air leakage rate is tested by pressing the brake pedal fully and holding it for one minute. Choice *C* is incorrect because the parking brake should be tested while the vehicle is running in a low gear. Choice *D* is incorrect because air brake systems use compressed air instead of brake fluid to generate the pressure needed to operate the brakes.

40. C: Brake lag is a property exclusive to air brakes, which need at least one-half of a second for the air to reach the brakes. Choices *A*, *B*, and *D* are incorrect because they are also factors in total stopping distance for hydraulic braking systems.

Section: Combination Vehicles

41. A: The swaying motion of a trailer is caused by rearward amplification. The effect increases if more trailers are attached (e.g., triples). Choices *B* and *C* are incorrect because jackknifes and skids are more likely to happen as a result of over-braking (braking too hard) or oversteering (turning more sharply than the vehicle can handle). Choice *D* is incorrect because rearward amplification affects the left-to-right motion of the trailer, not the front-to-back motion that would cause the cargo to eject from the back.

42. C: When backing up with a trailer, turning the steering wheel will cause the back of the vehicle to move in the same direction, just like backing up in a car. The back of the trailer, however, will shift in the

219

opposite direction, due to the hinge created where the vehicle and trailer connect. This is what allows the tractor trailer to jackknife, but is also the reason that Choice C is correct. Choice A is incorrect because the back of the vehicle will move in the same direction as the steering wheel. Choices B and D are incorrect because the back of the vehicle and the back of the trailer will move in opposite directions.

43. B: Using the trailer hand valve (which controls the trailer brakes) when you park can cause air to leak, which can cause the brake to unlock. Choices A, C, and D are incorrect because the trailer brakes and the trailer hand valve that controls them are not connected to these systems.

44. B: While glad hands would keep water out of the service and emergency air lines, this is not their primary purpose. The purposes of glad hands are to connect the service and emergency air lines from the truck to the trailer, and to prevent air from escaping the system. Therefore, Choices A, C, and D are incorrect.

45. D: If the air lines are crossed, supply air will go through the service line, rather than the emergency line, so the spring brakes won't be able to release. Choice A is incorrect because the air brake system is not connected to the fuel lines. Choices B and C are incorrect because the braking system is not connected to the engine system.

46. A: The electronic control unit and wheel speed sensor wires are components of an antilock brake system. Choice B is incorrect because the blue and red colors of the air lines are intended to allow someone to differentiate between the service and emergency air lines. Choice C is incorrect because the presence of an ABS is not indicated on a vehicle's registration papers. Choice D is incorrect because this procedure is used to test the low pressure warning signal.

47. B: Checking the fifth wheel coupling mechanism for damage, lubrication, and positioning is the first step in the coupling process. Chocking the trailer wheels (Choice A) is part of the next step. Checking the trailer height (Choice C) and connecting the air lines (Choice D) are closer to the middle of the process, after positioning, backing up, and securing the tractor.

48. C: The first three steps of safely uncoupling vehicle units are to position the rig, ease pressure on the locking jaws, and chock the trailer wheels. Choices A and B are incorrect because it would be impossible to position the rig if the trailer wheels were chocked. Choice D is incorrect because lowering the landing gear is the fourth step of uncoupling and occurs after easing pressure on the locking jaws.

49. D: Ensure that there are no air or hydraulic leaks in the landing gear system to allow for proper functioning. Choice A is incorrect because the landing gear should be in the up position during a walk-around inspection. Choice B is incorrect because the fifth wheel is part of the coupling system and not part of the landing gear system. Choice C is incorrect because a walk-around inspection can occur regardless of whether a trailer has cargo in it.

50. C: The trailer's service brakes should be tested using the hand-control valve. Choice A is incorrect because the parking brakes should be released when testing the service brakes. Choice B is incorrect because the foot pedal should be used to operate the service brakes during normal operation, not during testing. Choice D is incorrect because the air supply knob is used for testing the trailer's emergency brakes, not service brakes.

220

Section: Doubles and Triples

51. C: Pulling two or three trailers requires more attention and careful maneuvers to avoid losing control of the rig. These include Choices *A*, *B*, and *D*, looking farther ahead in order to prepare for necessary adjustments in advance, allowing extra space between the rig and other vehicles, and making more careful maneuvers to avoid the crack-the-whip effect, respectively. Choice *C* is the correct answer because an increased speed could cause a loss of control and an inability to break or steer the rig in the event of an incident and is therefore not an extra precaution that should be taken.

52. B: The shut-off valve at the rear of the front trailer should be open. The valve at the rear of the last trailer and the air tank drain valve on the converter dolly should be closed, making Choice *B* the correct answer. Choices *A*, *C*, and *D* are all part of the additional inspections for doubles and triples.

53. A: Pressing the "trailer air supply" knob when the pressure is at a normal level will supply air to the emergency supply lines. Choice *B*, then, is incorrect, as it does not release air from the lines. Choices *C* and *D* are also incorrect, as the knob does not affect the service line.

54. C: Converter dollies that have antilock brakes will have a yellow light on the left side of the dolly, making Choices *A*, *B*, and *D* incorrect.

55. D: On a triple trailer rig, the trailer with the heaviest cargo should be placed immediately behind the trailer. The lightest trailer should be placed at the end of the rig. Placing the heaviest trailer farther back will affect the balance and maneuverability of the rig, potentially causing it to become unstable, making Choices *A*, *B*, and *C* incorrect.

Section: Tank Vehicles

56. D: Additional endorsements for Class A or B CDL licenses are required if the transported material has an individual rated capacity of more than 119 gallons and an aggregate rated capacity of at least 1000 gallons. Choices *A* and *B* are incorrect because additional endorsements are required in the given situations. Choice *C* is incorrect because the numbers of gallons permitted are incorrect.

57. B: While attending additional training is never a bad idea, it is not a specific consequence of transporting a leaking tanker. However, Choices *A*, *C*, and *D* are likely to be imposed on an offending driver.

58. B: A tanker trailer sits higher off the ground than a regular trailer, which makes the trailer top-heavy. A top-heavy trailer can tip over more easily, particularly on bends, curves, and turns. Thus, Choice *D* is incorrect. Driving faster, especially on curves and turns, is likely to create problems, making Choice *A* incorrect. Choice *C* is incorrect because tankers can be pulled on curvy roads as well as make 90-degree turns. However, extra care is needed.

59. A: Bulkheads break the tank into smaller sections, which helps control the movement of the liquid. Baffled tanks have bulkheads with holes in them to allow the liquid to flow in a more controlled manner. Both of these help control the surge in the tank. Choices *B* and *D* are incorrect because they include un-baffled tanks, also called smooth bore tanks, which have nothing inside them to slow the movement of the liquid. Choices *B* and *C* are incorrect because outage refers to the extra room that is required in a tanker to account for the heat expansion of the liquid being transported. This does not help control surge.

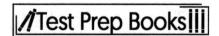

60. B: The weight of the liquid must be considered when determining how much to fill the tanker. Some liquids are more dense and thus heavier than others, and a full tanker can easily exceed the legal weight limits. Choice *A* is incorrect because liquids can expand (not condense) during transport, so room must be left in the tanker to account for this. The presence or absence of baffled tanks does not affect how much liquid goes into the tank, making Choice *C* incorrect, and smooth bore tanks are usually only required for liquids that have sanitation requirements and also do not affect the amount of liquid in the tanker, making Choice *D* incorrect.

Section: Hazardous Materials

61. C: Hazardous materials include all types of explosives and flammable or combustible materials, as well as acidic and corrosive materials, making Choices *A, B,* and *D* incorrect. The only non-hazardous material listed is non-potable (undrinkable) water.

62. A: Vehicles carrying hazardous materials must display a diamond-shaped warning placard, making Choices *B, C,* and *D* incorrect.

63. A: In order to haul hazardous materials, a driver must have a hazardous materials endorsement added to the CDL, which requires passing a written test about the regulations and requirements for hauling hazardous materials. Choices *B* and *C* are incorrect, as the only requirement is passing the written test, though passing the test may require taking additional classes or attending additional training programs. Choice *D* is incorrect, as there is an additional requirement beyond simply having a CDL.

64. D: It is the shipper's responsibility to properly package, mark, and label hazardous materials for shipping. The manufacturer, Choice *A*, is not responsible for shipping requirements. While Choices *B* and *C* are incorrect, the carrier and driver should also be checking that the shipper's labels are accurate and complete.

65. C: There are nine classes of hazardous materials listed on the Hazardous Materials Table, making Choices *A, B,* and *D* incorrect.

66. B: Class 1 includes fireworks, explosive devices, flares, and dynamite. The items in Choice *A* are included in Class 2. The items listed in Choices *C* and *D* are in classes 5 and 4, respectively.

67. C: The symbol (D) indicates that the material is packaged for domestic shipping but may not be appropriate for international shipping. Choice *B*, then, is incorrect. While all hazardous material should be considered dangerous, it can be safely shipped, meaning that Choice *A* is incorrect. Damaged packaging can certainly be problematic and may not be able to be safely transported; however, this is not indicated by this symbol on the table, making Choice *D* incorrect.

68. D: The item description must include the identification number, the proper shipping name, the hazard class or division, and the amount and unit of measure of the cargo. While the items listed in Choice *A* are to be included with the shipping papers, they are not part of the item description. The information in Choice *B* must be included with the emergency response information in the shipping papers, but is not part of the item description. Choice *C* lists the information that may be included in the package markings and labels, but this is not part of the item description.

69. A: Placard Table 2 indicates that placard requirements are in place when the total amount of these items is 1,001 pounds or more. Choices *B*, *C*, and *D* are incorrect amounts.

70. D: When transporting hazardous materials labeled as "inhalation hazard," additional placards with the words Poison Gas or Poison Inhalation are required. Choices *A*, *B*, and *C* include extra words, such as "beware," "dangerous," and "caution" that should not be included.

71. D: Smoking is prohibited around the first five classes of hazardous materials. While Choices *A*, *B*, and *C* do include some of the correct classes, Choice *D* is the correct answer because it includes all of the first five classes.

72. C: The abbreviation N.O.S. stands for "not otherwise specified." The phrases given in Choices *A*, *B*, and *D* are made-up phrases that have no relation to transporting hazardous materials.

Section: School Buses

73. A: The most dangerous areas for children are the first ten feet on each side of the bus and the first ten feet behind the bus. Choice *B* is incorrect because the entire danger zone can be as far as 30 feet from the back bumper, but that is not the most dangerous zone. Choices *C* and *D* represent a combination of the whole danger zone and the most dangerous region.

74. B: The blind spots are located below and in front of each mirror and directly behind the rear bumper of the bus. Choices *A* and *C*, then, are each only partially correct. Choice *D* is incorrect. The driver should be able to see directly in front of the bus.

75. B: When the mirrors are properly adjusted, the school bus driver should be able to see 200 feet behind the bus and along each side. In addition, the driver should be able to see where the rear tires touch the ground, not the front tires, making Choice *A* incorrect. Choices *C* and *D* represent an incorrect distance behind the bus as well as a reference to front tires rather than rear tires.

76. A: The convex mirrors do not show an accurate size of people or objects, and they do not show how far they are from the bus. Choice *B* is incorrect because the mirrors do show traffic, clearances, and students at the sides of the bus. Choice *C* is incorrect because, while the mirrors are small, they do show enough detail to be helpful to the driver in making sure the areas around the bus are clear. Choice *D* is incorrect because the mirrors are correctly placed in the described situation and can be helpful for safety.

77. C: When the school bus is at the crossing (not approaching it), the driver should stop the bus between 15 and 50 feet from the nearest crossing guard rail, put the bus in park, and open the door and driver's window to listen for an oncoming train. The 200 feet mentioned in Choice *A* is where the driver should turn on the bus's hazard lights as the driver approaches the tracks, and the bus should be put in park at the crossing, not neutral. Choice *B* is incorrect because the driver should not stop closer than 15 feet and should listen for an oncoming trail before crossing the tracks. Choice *D* is incorrect because the bus should be in park, not neutral.

78. D: There are several circumstances in which it is mandatory to evacuate the school bus, including when the bus has a potential to shift position, which would increase the risk of an accident. Choice *A* is incorrect because students are generally safer on the bus rather than off of it, even if they are getting rowdy and impatient. Choice *B* is incorrect because wet, rainy weather makes evacuating the bus even

223

more dangerous for students, as they would be more difficult for drivers to see than the large school bus. Choice *C* is incorrect because, while it is important for the bus driver to obey any instructions by police officers who are on the scene, this is not the only situation in which students should be evacuated.

79. D: When evacuating students from the bus in an emergency situation, it can be helpful to ask two older, responsible students to help at the emergency exit and assist students in exiting the bus. While there may be other people in the area, as in Choices *A, B,* and *C,* the driver cannot leave the students on the bus to seek their assistance, and other people would not be aboard the bus and able to assist from inside.

80. A: While each school and school district may have their own procedures, it is important that the school bus driver always follow all state and local laws and regulations. The school may take into consideration the requests of parents or specific neighborhoods and may post signage inside the school bus as in Choices *B, C,* and *D,* but these will not always be the case.

81. B: When crossing the road after leaving the bus, student should cross about ten feet in front of the bus, where the driver can clearly see them, including their feet. Choice *C* is incorrect because twenty feet in front of the bus is too far away for the driver to be able to watch students clearly. Choices *A* and *D* are incorrect because students should never cross the street behind the bus.

82. D: When students are unloading from the bus at the school, the driver should turn off the ignition. Putting the bus in neutral, as in Choice *A,* would allow the bus to roll, as would releasing the parking brake, as in Choice *B.* Choice *C* is incorrect because the emergency lights can be distracting both to students and to other drivers.

Section: Pre-Trip Inspection

83. D: The engine compartment check during the pre-trip vehicle inspection includes checking the oil and coolant levels, power steering fluid, various engine compartment belts (including the power steering and alternator belts), and conducting a safe start. Choices *A, B,* and *C* include items from the cab check rather than just those from the engine compartment check.

84. B: The correct range for the air brake pressure governor cutoff is 120-140 psi. Choices *A, C,* and *D* are all either too low or too high.

85. C: During the pre-trip vehicle inspection, the tread depth must be at least 4/32 on the steering axle tires and at least 2/32 on all other tires. Choice *B* has the correct numbers reversed, and Choices *A* and *D* do not account for the different requirements for the steering axle tires versus the rest of the tires.

86. C: During the pre-trip vehicle inspection of a school bus, it is necessary to make sure that the bus is properly equipped with reflective triangles, a fire extinguisher, and a body fluid cleanup kit. While Choice *A* includes some emergency equipment (the spare electrical fuses, if the bus is equipped with them, and the first aid kit), the items listed are not part of the standard equipment. Choice *B* includes lighting and emergency exit items rather than emergency equipment, and Choice *D* is standard tire-changing equipment rather than emergency equipment.

87. A: For a Class A CDL, you will be required to complete only one of the four types of pre-trip inspections. Choices *B, C,* and *D* are incorrect, though you should know all of the different kinds of inspections, as you will not know ahead of time which one you will need to conduct for the test.

88. A: When inspecting the landing gear of a trailer during the pre-trip inspection, the landing gear should be in a completely raised position. Choices *B* and *C,* then, are incorrect. In addition, the landing gear must be inspected, making Choice *D* incorrect.

89. D: A pre-trip inspection of a coach or transit bus should include the emergency exits, the battery box, and the fuel tanks. Choices *A* and *C* both refer to equipment on trailers, and Choice *B* refers to school bus inspections.

90. C: There are three types of pre-trip inspections for a Class B CDL. While you will only be required to complete one inspection during the test, Choices *A, B,* and *D* are incorrect because there are three types.

Section: Basic Control Skills test

91. B: Freeway driving is not part of the basic vehicle control skills test. The test includes straight line backing, offset back right and left, parallel parking on both the driver's side and conventional, and alley docking. Choices *A, C,* and *D,* then, are incorrect, as they are all included in the test.

92. A: Pulling forward to reposition the vehicle during the test is called a "pull-up." The first instance of using a pull-up is not counted negatively, but multiple instances will be marked down. Choices *B, C,* and *D,* then, are incorrect.

93. B: During the basic vehicle control skills test, the driver may conduct an outside vehicle observation once during the straight-line backing exercise and twice during each of the other skills. Choice *A* is incorrect, though conducting an outside vehicle observation incorrectly could be grounds for failing the test. Choice *C* is incorrect because it does not include the check during the straight-line backing exercise, and *D* is incorrect because it reverses the correct number of checks allowed.

94. C: Offset backing, both right and left, refers to backing the vehicle into a parking space that is behind the vehicle and offset to either the right or the left. Turning the vehicle while backing up, as indicated in Choice *A,* is part of alley docking the vehicle. Changing lanes is not part of the basic control test, making Choice *B* incorrect. While the driver should attempt to center the vehicle in a parking space, Choice *D* is not the correct answer here.

95. D: "Alley dock" refers to backing the vehicle into an alley that is perpendicular to the direction the vehicle is traveling. It is one of the parking requirements in the basic vehicle control skills test. Choices *A, B,* and *C* are incorrect descriptions of "alley dock" on the basic vehicle control skills test.

Section: On-Road Driving

96. B: If a particular traffic situation does not occur during the on-road driving test, the examiner may ask you to verbally explain how that potential situation should be handled. While it is true that not all possible conditions are guaranteed to occur during the test, Choices *A, B,* and *C* are incorrect.

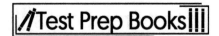

97. A: School buses must have their four-way flashers on when crossing railroad tracks. Choices *B, C,* and *D* are applicable to all vehicles when it comes to railroad crossings. Only Choice *A* is specifically applicable to school buses.

98. C: When driving under an overpass, the examiner may ask you to recite the posted clearance information, including the noted height or weight limits. While it is important to be aware of other vehicles on the road as well as your speed during the on-road test, Choices *B* and *D* are incorrect. The width of the overpass is not usually a consideration as it will be at least the width of the roadway, making Choice *A* incorrect as well.

99. C: The on-road driving test will include assessment of your lane usage, steering, and regular traffic checks. While knowledge of the radios and communication devices and use of the window mechanism and mirrors are important to know, they should not be done while driving, making Choices *A* and *B* incorrect. Choice *D* is incorrect because inspections should be conducted before the on-road driving test, not during it.

100. B: If you have to stop behind another vehicle before making a turn, make sure you are far enough back that you can see the vehicle's back tires. While you will likely be able to see the vehicle's roof, back window, and cargo area, as listed in Choices *A, C,* and *D*, being able to see those parts of the vehicle does not indicate that you are far enough behind the vehicle, making these answers incorrect.

CDL Practice Test #2

Section: Driving Safely

1. When should you first check for proper air pressure in your vehicle's tires?
   a. After refilling the fuel tank
   b. During the pre-trip inspection
   c. Before pulling into a rest stop for the night
   d. Before returning from a delivery

2. When should you check the stability of cargo securement devices?
   a. Only when you see that cargo has shifted
   b. Before you head into an inspection station
   c. Every time that you stop driving, including fuel and rest stops
   d. Whenever you cross state lines

3. Which of the following is an indication of a faulty suspension system?
   a. A hairline crack in the brake drum
   b. A rusted hole in the muffler
   c. Difficulty turning the steering wheel
   d. Fluid leaking out of a shock absorber

4. How can you avoid rollback when stopped on an incline in a manual transmission vehicle?
   a. Shift into first gear and partially engage the clutch before releasing the brake pedal.
   b. Engage the parking brake and release the brake pedal.
   c. Rev up the engine to high speed and dump the clutch pedal.
   d. Rollback is inevitable; make sure you leave enough clearance behind you before stopping.

5. Since a bridge can have air flowing above and beneath its surface, it will freeze _____ the road surface on either side of the bridge freezes.
   a. At the same time as
   b. After
   c. Before
   d. Only if

6. How should you adjust the distance between your vehicle and the one in front of you if it begins raining?
   a. Shorten the distance so that you can see what's in front of you more clearly.
   b. Don't adjust your distance; the traffic around you will get confused.
   c. Stop and wait on the side of the road for the rain to end.
   d. Increase the distance so that you have more room to slow down and adjust if necessary.

7. If you are prescribed corrective lenses, how often should you wear them while driving?
   a. Only at night
   b. Only during inclement weather
   c. Whenever your supervisor instructs you to do so
   d. Every time that you drive

227

8. If you find yourself nodding off or feeling sleepy, what should you do to stay safe while driving?
   a. Stop for some coffee or an energy drink before continuing your drive.
   b. Open the windows to get fresh air circulating through the cabin.
   c. Stop as soon as it is safe to do so and sleep until you feel rested, typically eight to nine hours.
   d. Play loud music or talk radio to keep your attention while you drive.

9. How much time does it typically take for a tractor-trailer to cross a double set of train tracks?
   a. About five seconds
   b. A minute or more
   c. Five to ten seconds
   d. At least fifteen seconds

10. What should you do before starting down a long/steep downhill grade?
    a. Check your headlights to make sure they function properly.
    b. Double-check that your CB radio is on the right frequency.
    c. Shift into a lower gear to take advantage of engine braking.
    d. Press lightly on the brakes and hold them until you reach the bottom.

11. What type of fire can be put out using water?
    a. Electrical
    b. Gasoline
    c. Wood, paper, or cloth
    d. Combustible metal

12. How can you lower your blood alcohol concentration (BAC) after consuming alcoholic drink(s)?
    a. Drink a cup of coffee or two.
    b. Wait for your body to process the alcohol, which can take hours.
    c. Flush out your system with a detox remedy.
    d. Take a quick twenty-minute nap to refresh yourself.

13. Due to alcohol's effects on the body's muscle control, vision, and coordination, drivers with a high BAC are _____ to cause an accident.
    a. Less Likely
    b. Just as likely
    c. More likely
    d. Guaranteed

14. Which of these is an example of a Class 5 Oxidizer?
    a. Propane
    b. Arsenic
    c. Dynamite
    d. Hydrogen peroxide

15. Which of the following is NOT a safety rule regarding hauling hazardous materials?
    a. Contain the product.
    b. Expedite delivery.
    c. Communicate risk.
    d. Ensure that drivers and equipment remain safe.

228

16. What type of brake would you use to secure the vehicle in place while you are outside the cab?
    a. Service brake
    b. Parking brake
    c. Emergency brake
    d. Drag chute

17. How often should air tanks with manual drains be emptied?
    a. Only when pressure is lower than normal
    b. Before driving and after every day of driving
    c. Before driving into an inspection station
    d. Every time you fill the fuel tank

18. What should be done first before adding coolant to an overheating engine?
    a. Shut off the engine and wait until the radiator cap is cool to the touch.
    b. Use the drain valve to empty the radiator of coolant.
    c. Slowly turn the cap until you hear a hissing sound.
    d. Turn on a fan and point it at the engine.

19. What should you do if you approach a railroad safety gate and the lights are flashing, but no train is visible?
    a. Drive around the gate; it must have been activated by accident.
    b. Get out of the vehicle and stand on the tracks to get a better view.
    c. Wait for the gate to rise and call road maintenance if you worry that the system is malfunctioning.
    d. Call the fire department; there must have been an accident further up the tracks.

20. Which of these is a benefit of having an anti-lock braking system(ABS)?
    a. You are able to drive faster without needing to worry about stopping distance.
    b. Your maximum stopping power is increased.
    c. Your brakes will never fail on steep downhill grades.
    d. Your wheels are prevented from locking up while braking.

21. What should you do if your vehicle enters into a skid?
    a. Press on the brake pedal as hard as you can.
    b. Release the brake and acceleration pedals and countersteer to regain control.
    c. Honk the horn and attempt to steer off the right side of the road.
    d. Downshift and press the accelerator pedal to power through the skid.

22. Where should you keep documentation for hazardous materials?
    a. Packed away with the material itself
    b. At the home office for future reference
    c. At the point of delivery for proper unloading
    d. Inside the cab for easy access during transport

23. How should cargo weight be balanced inside an enclosed trailer?
    a. On the right side to counteract the driver's weight
    b. Pushed toward the front of the trailer
    c. Secured in the center of the trailer
    d. Held in the rear of the trailer for easy door access

24. When securing cargo to a flatbed trailer, you should use a minimum of _____ tiedown(s) placed _____ feet apart.
    a. Five, five
    b. Two, ten
    c. Three, twenty
    d. Ten, two

25. A placarded vehicle must have placards on the _____ of the vehicle at all times.
    a. Front
    b. Front and rear
    c. Rear
    d. Front, rear, and both sides

Section: Transporting Cargo Safely

26. Which of the following is the loaded weight of a single vehicle as stipulated by its manufacturer?
    a. The tire load
    b. The axle weight
    c. The Gross Vehicle Weight Rating (GVWR)
    d. The Gross Combination Weight Rating (GCWR)

27. How should cargo be loaded to reduce the risk of rollovers?
    a. With heavy items on top of light items
    b. With heavy items beneath light items
    c. With heavy items to the right of light items
    d. With heavy items to the left of light items

28. The collective limit of any securement system must be at least _____ times the weight of the cargo.
    a. 1/10
    b. Two
    c. 1/2
    d. Ten

29. Driving in an overloaded vehicle _____ the distance required to come to a complete stop.
    a. Increases, depending on various factors,
    b. Does not affect
    c. Triples
    d. Doubles

30. How can you prevent cargo weight from shifting while transporting livestock?
    a. Use tranquilizers to keep the livestock asleep on the floor of the container/trailer.
    b. Completely fill the container/trailer with livestock to prevent them from moving around.
    c. Only transport livestock cargo that includes multiple types of animals.
    d. Use false bulkheads to corral the livestock into the center of the container/trailer.

Section: Transporting Passengers

31. When should you refuel your vehicle while traveling with passengers?
    a. Whenever the fuel tank is 50 percent empty
    b. Only while passengers are outside the vehicle, such as during a restroom break
    c. Never; make sure you have enough fuel for the entire journey before departing.
    d. Whenever the fuel tank is less than 10 percent full

32. When approaching an ungated railroad crossing, you should stop _____ the tracks.
    a. Between fifteen and fifty feet before
    b. Right up against
    c. At least one hundred feet before
    d. Only if there is a train on

33. Which of the following is prohibited on a bus that carries passengers?
    a. Small arms ammunition
    b. Disposable cigarette lighters
    c. Car batteries
    d. Pharmaceuticals

34. Passengers on a bus with standing room are permitted to stand _____.
    a. Behind the standee line next to the driver's seat
    b. In the back of the bus near the emergency exit
    c. Wherever there is room to stand
    d. In front of the door to facilitate a speedy exit

35. The _____ of a bus can be left partially open to allow fresh air to circulate.
    a. Back door
    b. Front door
    c. Emergency roof hatches
    d. Luggage compartment(s)

Section: Air Brakes

36. What type of brake uses components of multiple brake systems to stop the vehicle?
    a. Engine brake
    b. Service brake
    c. Emergency brake
    d. Parking brake

37. Where would you find the air compressor on a vehicle with air brakes?
    a. Attached to the engine through gears or a v-belt
    b. Behind the vehicle's transmission
    c. Attached directly to the front passenger brake
    d. Underneath the steering wheel

38. An air brake system is considered to be leaking if it loses more than _____ during an air leakage test for a single vehicle.
    a. 10 psi in ten minutes
    b. 3 psi in one minute
    c. 1 psi in thirty seconds
    d. 5 psi in five minutes

39. What should you do if the low-air pressure light/alarm activates while driving?
    a. Slow down to about 25 mph until the tanks refill.
    b. Increase engine speed to make the compressor work faster.
    c. Engage the parking brake.
    d. Immediately find a safe place to stop and inspect the system for leaks.

40. Air brakes _____ than hydraulic brakes.
    a. Engage more quickly
    b. Engage less quickly
    c. Have less stopping distance
    d. Have more stopping distance

Section: Combination Vehicles

41. A vehicle with a rearward amplification of 2.0 is _____ as likely to have its trailer tip over as its tractor.
    a. Half
    b. Twice
    c. Twenty times
    d. Equally

42. When navigating around a bend in a combination vehicle, the vehicle will offtrack, which is what happens when:
    a. The rear wheels are out of line with the front wheels
    b. The tractor begins to skid slightly
    c. The blind spot expands to obscure all traffic behind the vehicle
    d. The differential struggles to compensate for different wheel speeds

43. When backing up with a trailer, you should turn the steering wheel _____ to go _____.
    a. Right, right
    b. Until it locks, in reverse
    c. Back and forth, in reverse
    d. Right, left

232

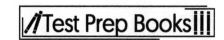

44. If you notice while backing up that the vehicle has deviated from its intended path, you should _____ to make necessary re-alignments.
    a. Turn off the air compressor
    b. Pull forward
    c. Turn the steering wheel the opposite direction
    d. Call for a backup driver

45. The trailer service air line transports air that is regulated by the _____.
    a. Emergency braking system
    b. Foot brake or trailer hand brake
    c. Main air compressor
    d. Trailer protection valve

46. A hose coupler, or glad hand, is used to:
    a. Connect the air lines between vehicle components
    b. Connect the fuel nozzle to the fuel tank
    c. Recharge the vehicle's air conditioning system
    d. Refill the hydraulic brake fluid reservoir

47. How can you check to see if a trailer is equipped with ABS?
    a. Look for red and blue couplers located on the front of the trailer.
    b. Inspect the tire valve stems to see if there is a metal sensor.
    c. Look for a green electrical connector near the trailer coupler.
    d. Look behind the wheels for ECU and wheel speed sensor wires in the brakes.

48. What should you do before lowering the landing gear while decoupling a trailer?
    a. Disconnect the air lines.
    b. Unlock the fifth wheel.
    c. Chock the wheels to prevent trailer movement.
    d. Pull the tractor forward clear of the trailer.

49. What happens to a trailer's braking capability when the ABS fails?
    a. The brakes will still operate normally but will be unable to prevent themselves from locking up.
    b. The brakes will no longer function, creating a dangerous situation.
    c. The brakes will be stuck in the down or on position, potentially causing the trailer to skid.
    d. The brakes will be unaffected and will operate the same as if ABS were operational.

50. What should you do if your trailer gets hung up on the tracks at a rail crossing?
    a. Back up and try again with greater speed.
    b. Downshift and power through; both the trailer and the tracks can handle brief contact.
    c. Call a tow truck and wait in the vehicle for it to arrive.
    d. Immediately exit the vehicle, walk away from the tracks, and call 911 and/or the posted emergency number beside the tracks.

233

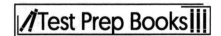

Section: Doubles and Triples

51. The crack-the-whip effect, which is magnified in doubles and triples, refers to what phenomenon?
    a. The sound that air brakes make
    b. The likelihood that a trailer will flip over due to rearward amplification
    c. The difficulty in judging whether it is safe to change lanes
    d. The difficulty in controlling speed while driving downhill

52. When uncoupling the rear trailer from a twin trailer setup, why should the landing gear of the rear trailer be lowered?
    a. To ensure the trailer's stability
    b. To check for damage prior to uncoupling
    c. To reduce the weight load from the dolly
    d. To activate the spring brakes

53. Which of the following is true regarding coupling and uncoupling triple trailers?
    a. The procedure is very similar to that of coupling and uncoupling doubles.
    b. All of the trailers need to be coupled before attaching the tractor.
    c. The procedure is very different from that of coupling and uncoupling doubles.
    d. Coupling and uncoupling triples do not make use of a converter dolly.

54. During a walk-around inspection, what position should the shut-off valves be in for the rear of the front trailers and for the rear of the last trailer?
    a. Front trailer open, last trailer closed
    b. Front trailer open, last trailer open
    c. Front trailer closed, last trailer closed
    d. Front trailer closed, last trailer open

55. To ensure that air in a braking system is flowing to all of the trailers in a double or triple, a driver should go to the back of the last trailer and do what?
    a. Make sure that the shut-off valves are closed.
    b. Press the red trailer air-supply knob.
    c. Open the cargo doors and listen for air flow.
    d. Open the emergency shut-off valve and listen for air flow.

Section: Tank Vehicles

56. For which of the following vehicles might a tank endorsement be required?
    a. A vehicle requiring a Class A CDL, hauling ten 150-gallon containers of liquid material
    b. A vehicle requiring a Class A CDL, hauling fifteen 100-gallon containers of liquid material
    c. A vehicle requiring a Class A CDL, hauling 500 gallons of gaseous material
    d. A Class C vehicle carrying non-hazardous material and three passengers

57. Which of the following is NOT a likely penalty for hauling a tank with a leak?
    a. A police citation
    b. Being banned from driving
    c. Responsibility for spill cleanup
    d. Class-action lawsuit

58. What is the purpose of bulkheads in tanks carrying liquid?
    a. To prevent the tank from tipping on its side
    b. To reduce the effect of liquid sloshing in the tank
    c. To reduce pressure within the tank
    d. To minimize damage caused by spills

59. What does "outage" refer to?
    a. The amount of cargo that spills from a leaking tank
    b. The density of the liquid that is being hauled in a tank
    c. The increase of pressure in the tank on cold days
    d. The expansion of liquids in tanks due to heat

60. Which of these statements is true regarding braking with tankers?
    a. Tankers have more complex braking systems than other tractor trailers.
    b. Liquid surges do not occur while braking with tankers, only while accelerating.
    c. Empty tankers may take longer to stop than full tankers.
    d. Full tankers take longer to stop than empty tankers.

Section: Hazardous Materials

61. What section of the Code of Federal Regulation (CFR) regulates hazardous materials transportation?
    a. 29 CFR 100-185
    b. 39 CFR 100-185
    c. 49 CFR 100-185
    d. 59 CFR 100-185

62. Who is responsible for marking hazardous materials cargo with hazard warning labels?
    a. The shipper
    b. The driver
    c. The receiver
    d. The federal government

63. Which of the following tasks regarding hazardous materials is the responsibility of the driver?
    a. Preparing the shipping papers
    b. Supplying emergency response information
    c. Providing placards
    d. Placarding the vehicle

64. Why is it important to keep shipping papers easily accessible while transporting hazardous materials?
    a. So the driver can read more about the cargo
    b. So first responders can know the driver is hauling hazardous materials
    c. So they can be referred to for proper placarding
    d. So the papers are not separated prior to delivery

235

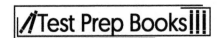
65. Spills of a reportable quantity of hazardous materials must be reported to which two federal governing bodies?
   a. Department of Transportation and Environmental Protection Agency
   b. Department of Transportation and Department of Labor
   c. Department of Transportation and Department of Energy
   d. Department of Transportation and Department of Health and Human Services

66. Hazardous material placards must be placed where on the vehicle?
   a. On the driver's door only
   b. On the driver's side of the tank only
   c. On the rear of the tank only
   d. On both sides and ends of the vehicle

67. A driver must use a closed cargo space for which of the following hazardous materials?
   a. Flammable gases
   b. Flammable liquids
   c. Oxidizers
   d. Poisons

68. Driving a hazardous materials cargo tank with open valves or covers is illegal unless what condition is met?
   a. The vehicle maintains a speed under 15 mph.
   b. The vehicle is properly placarded.
   c. The cargo tank is empty.
   d. The distance driven is less than 5 miles.

69. If a driver is hauling Division 1.1, 1.2, or 1.3 explosives, he or she must park at least how many feet from an open fire?
   a. 100 feet
   b. 300 feet
   c. 500 feet
   d. 1,000 feet

70. Which of the following is NOT required to stop at a railroad crossing?
   a. A placarded vehicle
   b. A vehicle transporting chlorine
   c. A vehicle with an empty hazardous material cargo tank
   d. A vehicle with three passengers that is hauling a water tank

71. Which of the following should be contacted to coordinate an emergency response to chemical hazards, particularly if a death results from a hazardous materials incident?
   a. The National Response Center
   b. The Federal Bureau of Investigation
   c. The Centers for Disease Control
   d. The National Institutes of Health

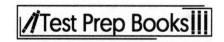

72. How is the Emergency Response Guidebook used?
    a. Drivers use it to determine whom to contact in case of an emergency.
    b. Emergency workers use it to match the materials on shipping papers to the appropriate protective measures.
    c. Emergency Medical Technicians (EMTs) use it to reference first aid techniques.
    d. Drivers use it to determine the proper name of the materials they are transporting.

Section: School Buses

73. Why is the region to the left of a school bus considered a danger zone?
    a. Because children exit a school bus from its left side.
    b. Because of the possibility of passing cars.
    c. Because of the presence of drunk drivers.
    d. Because a bus is more likely to impact a child on the left.

74. The blind spot at the back of a bus can extend how far?
    a. 50 feet
    b. 100 feet
    c. 200 feet
    d. 400 feet

75. When approaching a school bus stop, the driver should activate the alternating flashing amber warning lights at least how many feet prior to the stop?
    a. 50 feet
    b. 200 feet
    c. 500 feet
    d. 1000 feet

76. When loading students on a school bus from a bus stop on their route, what should a driver do if a student appears to be missing from the stop?
    a. Ask other students if they know the missing student's whereabouts.
    b. Call the student's parents in case the student is skipping.
    c. Contact the student's school.
    d. Proceed along the route as they normally would.

77. When unloading students at school, why is it important for a driver to scan the mirrors?
    a. To ensure that they are oriented properly
    b. To check for passing cars
    c. To see if students are coming back toward the bus
    d. To inspect them for dirt or mud

78. If there is a fire on a school bus, what should be done regarding the students?
    a. Evacuate the bus and direct the students to a place upwind of the fire.
    b. Evacuate the bus and direct the students to a place downwind of the fire.
    c. Evacuate the bus and ask the students to help put out the fire.
    d. Evacuate the bus and inspect the students for injuries.

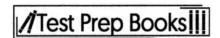

79. When stopping a bus at a railroad crossing, how far should the bus be from the closest rail?
    a. 5 to 10 feet
    b. 10 to 25 feet
    c. 15 to 50 feet
    d. 20 to 60 feet

80. If a student is causing serious problems on a school bus and making it unsafe to drive, which course of action is appropriate?
    a. Restrain the student and call their parents.
    b. Expel the student from the bus.
    c. Ignore the issue and take the student to their designated stop.
    d. Call for a school official or the police to come and get the student.

81. Which of the following is true about antilock braking systems (ABS) on school buses?
    a. Modern school buses are not required to have ABS.
    b. Many older school buses have been voluntarily equipped with ABS.
    c. Buses with ABS do not have malfunction lamps on the instrument panel.
    d. Buses with ABS require different braking techniques than other vehicles with ABS.

82. What should a school bus driver do in heavy wind conditions?
    a. Slow down to lower the wind's influence.
    b. Accelerate to get through the windy area.
    c. Use a higher gear to improve stability.
    d. Turn on the emergency flashers.

Section: Pre-Trip Inspection

83. When checking engine compartment belts (e.g., the alternator belt), how much play should there be in the center of the belt to ensure a snug fit?
    a. up to $\frac{3}{4}$ inch
    b. up to $\frac{7}{8}$ inch
    c. up to 1 inch
    d. up to 2 inches

84. What two things does checking the service brakes ensure?
    a. That the brakes have enough fluid and a proper amount of air pressure
    b. That the brakes are working properly and the vehicle is not pulling to either side
    c. That the parking brake is functioning and that there is sufficient air pressure
    d. That the parking brake is functioning and that there is enough brake fluid

85. How much tread depth does there need to be on the steering axle tires?
    a. $\frac{1}{32}$ inches
    b. $\frac{2}{32}$ inches
    c. $\frac{3}{32}$ inches
    d. $\frac{4}{32}$ inches

238

86. If a driver has an air-powered fifth wheel, what additional check should take place?
    a. That the locking pins are not loose or missing
    b. That the fifth wheel is properly lubricated
    c. That air is not leaking from the system
    d. That the kingpin is not damaged

87. Which of the following is NOT a necessary check to make regarding school bus seating?
    a. Seat frames are undamaged.
    b. Seats are securely fastened to the floor.
    c. Seat cushions are fastened to the seat frames.
    d. Seat cushions are not torn or split.

88. What should be the status of a cargo lift during a pre-trip inspection?
    a. Fully retracted, firmly latched, no signs of leaks
    b. Fully extended, firmly latched, no signs of leaks
    c. Fully retracted, firmly latched, glad hands fastened
    d. Fully extended. Firmly latched, glad hands fastened

89. Which of the following is NOT part of the external inspection of a coach or transit bus?
    a. Fuel tank
    b. Baggage compartment
    c. Emergency exits
    d. Battery box

90. Which of these statements is true regarding the Class A pre-trip inspection test?
    a. The test-taker must complete all four types of pre-trip inspections in the vehicle brought to the exam.
    b. The test-taker must complete one of the four types and will not know which one will be conducted.
    c. The test-taker must complete one of the four types and will be told which one will be conducted.
    d. The test-taker must complete three of the four types and gets to choose which will be conducted.

Section: Basic Control Skills test

91. The basic control skills exam may include which set of maneuvers?
    a. Forward driving, perpendicular parking, and offset backing
    b. Parallel parking, straight-line backing, and perpendicular parking
    c. Offset backing, parallel parking, and straight-line backing
    d. Alley docking, forward driving, and parallel parking

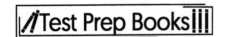

92. What should a driver's procedure be for an outside vehicle observation during the basic control skills exam?
   a. Put the vehicle in neutral, set the parking brake, and exit while maintaining three points of contact.
   b. Put the vehicle in park, set the parking brake, and exit while maintaining three points of contact.
   c. Put the vehicle in neutral, set the parking brake, and exit while maintaining two points of contact.
   d. Put the vehicle in park, set the parking brake, and exit while maintaining three points of contact.

93. What is offset backing?
   a. Backing up a vehicle that has no trailer attached
   b. Backing up a vehicle that has a trailer attached
   c. Backing into a space on the left or right side of the vehicle
   d. Backing into a space directly behind the vehicle

94. Which of the following are NOT considered as part of the basic control skills exam scoring process?
   a. Encroachments
   b. Steering hand positions
   c. Pull-ups
   d. Vehicle exits

95. If an examiner requires a driver to back into a space on the right side of the vehicle that has cones in the front and back of the space, what is the examiner asking the driver to do?
   a. Offset back (left)
   b. Offset back (right)
   c. Parallel park (driver's side)
   d. Parallel park (conventional)

Section: On-Road Driving

96. If a driver is stopping behind another vehicle in traffic, how much distance should he or she put between them and the vehicle in front?
   a. 3 feet
   b. Enough space to see the front vehicle's license plate
   c. Enough space to see the front vehicle's rear tires
   d. 50 feet

97. Which statement is true regarding driving back into traffic after pulling over and stopping at the side of the road?
   a. Do not turn the steering wheel before starting to drive.
   b. Keep the four-way flashers on until the vehicle is back on the road.
   c. Travel for at least 200 feet before moving back onto the road.
   d. Signal with the horn while moving back onto the road.

98. During the on-road test, the examiner may ask a driver to recite which piece of information?
    a. The steps in navigating a four-way stop
    b. Information about observed traffic signs
    c. The different classes of hazardous materials
    d. The name and address of the current destination

99. When making a left-hand turn on multi-lane roads, where should a driver finish the turn?
    a. In the rightmost lane
    b. In the center turning lane
    c. In the lane directly to the left of the center line
    d. In the lane directly to the right of the center line

100. In which situation is it acceptable to drive while using the steering wheel with one hand only?
    a. While shifting gears
    b. While calling police
    c. While using the turn signal
    d. While backing up

Answer Explanations #2

Section: Driving Safely

1. B: Having too much or too little air in your tires can lead to dangerous or fatal results. As such, Choice *B* is correct you should check your vehicle's tire pressure before it starts moving, during the pre-trip inspection. Choices *A, C,* and *D* are incorrect because waiting until after you've begun driving to check air pressure could cause tire failure, leading to damage, injury, or death.

2. C: Choice *C* is correct because cargo security is an imperative component of safety and should be checked every time the vehicle is parked, even if it is only parked for a few minutes. Choices *A, B,* and *D* are incorrect because lack of regular cargo inspections could lead to an unsafe shift of weight or loss of cargo while driving.

3. D: While all of these options describe safety concerns, Choice *D* is correct because the shock absorber is the only component listed that is part of a vehicle's suspension system. Choice *A* is a brake component, Choice *B* is an exhaust component, and Choice *C* is a steering component.

4. A: Choice *A* is correct because partially engaging the clutch will hold the vehicle in position while you quickly move from the brake to the acceleration pedal. Choices *B, C,* and *D* are incorrect because those actions would not prevent the vehicle from rolling back on a hill.

5. C: Choice *C* is correct; since the space beneath a bridge is empty, it lacks the insulation that a road built on the ground has. This allows the temperature of the bridge's surface to drop much faster than the surrounding road, meaning it will freeze before the rest of the road. Choices *A, B,* and *D* are incorrect because they do not reflect the effects of temperature fluctuations on a bridge.

6. D: When it is raining, the road surface may become slippery, which decreases the effectiveness of your vehicle's brakes. Your vehicle will require more distance to stop, so increasing your follow distance is the best way to drive safely. This makes Choice *D* the correct answer. Choices *A, B,* and *C* are incorrect because they would cause an unsafe condition while driving.

7. D: If you need corrective lenses to read text or see details at various distances, you should wear them every time you drive. It is illegal to drive without lenses if your driver's license indicates a need for them. Choices *A, B,* and *C* are incorrect because they describe unsafe and illegal conditions.

8. C: Drowsiness is a killer of many drivers who don't realize how sleepy they are. Choice *C* is correct because if you are tired, stopping and letting yourself sleep is the only way to regain your energy. Choices *A, B,* and *D* are incorrect because those actions will not make you less fatigued.

9. D: A tractor-trailer is significantly longer than a typical passenger vehicle, so extra time is needed to get across a double set of tracks. Choice *D* is correct because you should give yourself at least fifteen seconds make the crossing and look both ways before crossing each track. Choices *A, B,* and *C* are incorrect because they describe too short or too long of a time period.

10. C: Relying only on the brakes while going downhill can cause them to overheat and/or fail, leading to disastrous consequences. Choice *C* is correct because shifting into lower gear allows the engine to assist in slowing down or maintaining speed while driving downhill. Choices *A* and *B* are incorrect because

242

neither the headlights nor the CB radio will not assist with a downhill grade, and Choice *D* is incorrect because holding down your brakes for too long can cause them to overheat and fail.

11. C: Choice *C* is correct because you should only use water to put out fires fueled by wood, paper, cloth, or other organic combustibles. Choices *A*, *B*, and *D* are incorrect because attempting to put out an electrical, gasoline, or combustible metal fire with water could cause a shock or explosive hazard.

12. B: Your BAC is dependent on many variables, including your weight, the amount of alcohol you've consumed, and how quickly you consumed it. As a result, some people can become inebriated after just one drink. Your liver can only process about 1/8th ounce of alcohol per hour, so the only way to reduce your BAC is time, which means Choice *B* is the correct answer. Choices *A*, *C*, and *D* are incorrect because those actions will not do anything to reduce your BAC.

13. C: Drivers with a high BAC may feel confident driving on familiar roads, but the effects of alcohol can be subtle or unnoticed until it is too late. Choice *C* is correct; due to a loss of awareness and reaction time, drunk drivers are more likely to and indeed cause more accidents than average. Choices *A*, *B*, and *D* are incorrect because they do not reflect the likelihood of an accident while inebriated.

14. D: Choice *D* is correct because hydrogen peroxide is the only listed oxidizer. Choices *A*, *B*, and *C* are incorrect because propane is a Class 2 Gas, arsenic is a Class 6 Poison, and dynamite is a Class 1 Explosive.

15. B: Choice *B* is correct because, while timely delivery of hazardous materials is important, it comes second to safety. Choices *A*, *C*, and *D* are incorrect because you should ensure safe travel of hazmat deliveries by communicating risk, containing material, and prioritizing safety.

16. B: When unoccupied, the vehicle needs to be secured in place. This is best done with the parking brake, which will prevent the wheels from moving until released, making Choice *B* the correct answer. Choices *A*, *C*, and *D* are incorrect because they are not designed to hold the vehicle in place while unoccupied.

17. B: Water can condense inside of the air tanks, which can freeze and cause the brakes to fail. Daily emptying of the air tanks will allow this water to drain, ensuring safe conditions for the brakes and making Choice *B* the correct answer. Choices *A*, *C*, and *D* are incorrect because infrequent draining of the tanks can lead to unsafe conditions.

18. A: Serious injury or damage can occur if you attempt to add coolant while the engine is still hot. Choice *A* is correct because you should wait for the engine and coolant to cool down before attempting any repair or addition of fluid. Choices *B*, *C*, and *D* are incorrect because they can lead to damage or injury if the engine or coolant are still hot.

19. C: You should never attempt to pass through railroad safety gates; there may be a train approaching that you do not see or hear. It is also unsafe to walk on active train tracks and unwise to call an emergency line for a non-emergency, so Choice *C*, waiting and contacting road maintenance is the best option. Choices *A*, *B*, and *D* are incorrect because they describe actions that could lead to damage, injury, or an unnecessary use of emergency services.

20. D: Choice *D* is correct because the ABS uses sensors to detect wheel lock-up and adjust braking accordingly to maximize braking potential. Choices *A, B,* and *C* are incorrect because all other facets of the braking system remain the same.

21. B: Attempting to speed up or slow down during a skid can result in a sudden change of direction, and there may not be room for you to exit the road. Choice *B* is correct because counter steering and releasing the pedals will use inertia to straighten out your vehicle. Choices *A, C,* and *D* are incorrect because those actions will not assist in safely getting through a skid.

22. D: Choice *D* is correct, because when carrying hazardous materials, you want to be able to immediately access the documentation at any point during your trip. This is easier when it is carried with you in the cab. Choices *A, B,* and *C* are incorrect because those locations would make accessing documentation inconvenient or risk the loss of documentation.

23. C: Improper weight distribution can cause loss of traction or rollovers when rounding curves. Choice *C* is correct because securing the load to the center of the trailer allows for equal weight distribution. Choices *A, B,* and *D* are incorrect because they would cause cargo weight to be dangerously unbalanced.

24. B: Every load on a flatbed should have multiple tiedowns spaced close together to maximize security. Typically, this is achieved with a minimum of two tiedowns placed every ten feet down the trailer, making Choice *B* the correct answer. Choices *A, C,* and *D* are incorrect because they describe either too few or too many tiedowns as compared to what is necessary for cargo security.

25. D: Placards should be visible on the vehicle when viewing it from any angle. Choice *D* is correct because the only way to accomplish this is to have a placard on all four sides of the vehicle. Choices *A, B,* and *C* are incorrect because having too few placards results in the hazard being unknown when viewed from certain angles.

Section: Transporting Cargo Safely

26. C: Choice *C* is correct because the GVWR describes the loaded weight of a single vehicle. Choice *A* is incorrect because it describes the maximum weight a tire can safely bear. Choice *B* is incorrect because it describes the weight transferred to the ground by one or more sets of axles. Choice *D* is incorrect because it describes the combined weight of the vehicle, trailer, and cargo being carried.

27. B: Rollovers are best avoided with a low center of gravity, so heavy items should be on the bottom, making Choice *B* the correct answer. Choices *A, C,* and *D* are incorrect because they would increase the risk of rollover when the vehicle rounds a bend or makes a turn.

28. C: Choice *C* is correct because it reflects federal regulations requiring securement system limits to be at least 50 percent of the weight of the cargo. Choices *A, B,* and *D* are incorrect because they describe either too low or too high of a limit compared to what is necessary.

29. A: Typically, the heavier the vehicle, the more distance is needed to brake to a stop. When a vehicle is overloaded beyond the manufacturer's limits, it will increase the stopping distance. The precise amount of increased distance is dependent on multiple factors beyond the weight of the vehicle, such as brake type, road condition and grade, and so on, making Choice *A* the correct answer. Choice *B* is incorrect because a heavier vehicle does need more space to stop. Choices *C* and *D* are incorrect because there is no precise formula to determine how much stopping distance is needed; instead, a

driver must use their judgment to determine the necessary stopping distance based on the road conditions and the vehicle itself.

30. D: Livestock will typically move around within an unsecured container/trailer and will lean into turns to keep themselves upright. Choice *D* is correct because corralling livestock to the center of the container/trailer will minimize weight shift. Choices *A, B,* and *C* are incorrect because they would not prevent weight shift and would potentially cause injury to the livestock.

Section: Transporting Passengers

31. B: Passengers should not be on board during refueling due to the inherent safety risks involved in handling combustible liquids, making Choice *B* the correct answer. Choices *A* and *D* are incorrect because they do not take passenger safety into consideration. Choice *C* is incorrect because any vehicle will need to refuel if it is traveling beyond the range of the fuel tank's capacity.

32. A: You should stop close enough to the tracks to see oncoming trains, but far enough away to remain safe in the event of a train crossing, making Choice *A* the correct answer. Choices *B* and *D* are incorrect because they would create the potential for collision with the train, and Choice *C* is incorrect because the increased distance may not allow you proper visibility to look both ways before crossing.

33. C: Unsecured and large amounts of hazardous materials are not allowed on passenger vehicles, even if the materials themselves are usually permitted. Choice *C* is correct because car batteries have the potential to leak large amounts of acid if punctured or tipped over. Choices *A, B,* and *D* are incorrect because they describe small amounts of sealed hazardous materials that are typically permitted on passenger vehicles.

34. A: Federal regulations dictate that the driver of a bus must be undistracted and unobstructed while the vehicle is in motion. Choice *A* ensures that everyone is safe and the driver is able to drive without obstacles or distractions, making it the correct answer. Choices *B, C,* and *D* are incorrect because they describe potentially dangerous situations.

35. C: Choice *C* is correct because the roof hatches will circulate air while maintaining the security of passengers and luggage. Choices *A* and *B* are incorrect because leaving the doors open could lead to unsafe conditions while driving, and Choice *D* is incorrect because leaving the luggage compartments open won't circulate air and will create a hazard.

Section: Air Brakes

36. C: The only situation in which you would need to employ components of multiple braking systems is in an emergency, making Choice *C* the correct answer. Choices *A, B,* and *D* are incorrect because they each describe individual brake systems that work independently of each other.

37. A: The air compressor needs to be powered to function correctly, so it must be connected in some fashion to the engine, making Choice *A* the correct answer. Choices *B, C,* and *D* are incorrect because those positions would result in the compressor being unpowered.

38. B: Due to the effects of temperature and container expansion/contraction on an air supply, it is normal to see slight fluctuations in pressure readings during testing. Choice *B* is correct because it

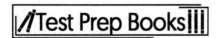

suggests a rapid loss of air pressure, signaling the need for adjustments or repairs. Choices A, C, and D are incorrect because they describe a much slower loss of air pressure.

39. D: If the low-pressure alarm activates while driving, it means that you lack the air pressure needed for effective braking. This could lead to dangerous conditions, so you should stop as soon as safely possible, making Choice D the correct answer. Choices A, B, and C are incorrect because they do not mitigate the dangers of low air pressure.

40. B: Air and other gases are compressible fluids, while water and other hydraulic fluids are incompressible. This means that hydraulic brakes apply stopping power almost instantaneously, while air brakes will need a small amount of time to apply pressure and stopping power, making Choice B the correct answer. Choice A is incorrect because hydraulic brakes engage more quickly, and Choices C and D are incorrect because stopping distance depends on multiple variables beyond the type of fluid used in the braking system.

Section: Combination Vehicles

41. B: A combination vehicle's rearward amplification describes the comparative likelihood of the trailer tipping over to that of the tractor. This is expressed as a multiple, so a rearward amplification of 2.0 describes a trailer that is twice as likely to tip over as its tractor, making Choice B the correct answer. Choices A, C, and D are incorrect because they describe likelihoods that do not reflect the given rearward amplification.

42. A: When a combination vehicle enters a bend or turn, the tractor wheels will be pointed in a different direction than the offtracking trailer wheels, making Choice A the correct answer. Choices B, C, and D are incorrect because they describe conditions irrelevant to the vehicle's offtrack status.

43. D: When backing up a vehicle with a trailer, the trailer will travel in the opposite direction of the vehicle, so the steering wheel needs to be turned in the opposite direction of the intended path, making Choice D the correct answer. Choices A, B, and D are incorrect because they do not describe the behavior of trailered vehicles in reverse.

44. B: If a vehicle it begins to deviate from the intended path while backing up, the only way to make corrections is to pull forward and readjust, making Choice B the correct answer. Choices A, C, and D are incorrect because they will not result in needed adjustments to the path of reverse travel.

45. B: The service air line is the air line that is used whenever the trailer is connected for travel. It supplies air to the trailer brakes whenever the foot brake or hand lever is activated, making Choice B the correct answer. Choices A, C, and D are incorrect because they describe components that do not regulate the air in the service line.

46. A: Hose couplers, or glad hands, are primarily used to connect the service and emergency air lines between a tractor and trailer, making Choice A the correct answer. Choices B, C, and D are incorrect because they describe procedures that would not make use of hose couplers.

47. D: A vehicle's anti-lock braking system connects the vehicle computer or ECU with the braking system, using speed sensors and signal wires connected to the brakes to function, making Choice D the correct answer. Choices A, B, and C are incorrect because they describe components that are not part of the ABS

48. C: When a trailer's landing gear contacts the ground and begins lifting the front of the trailer, this can cause shifts in weight balance and center of gravity, possibly resulting in trailer or tractor movement. Choice *C* is correct because chocking the wheels will prevent the trailer from moving while using the landing gear. Choices *A, B,* and *D* are incorrect because those actions would create a dangerous situation if completed before the landing gear is securely deployed.

49. A: A vehicle's anti-lock braking system is a supplemental component that prevents the wheels from locking up while braking. In the event of failure, the brake system itself still functions but is susceptible to locking during heavy braking, making Choice *A* the correct answer. Choices *B, C,* and *D* are incorrect because they describe conditions that would not result from ABS failure.

50. D: A trailer becoming hung up on train tracks is a dangerous and potentially life-threatening situation requiring the assistance of emergency services to prevent collision with a train, making Choice *D* the correct answer. Choices *A, B,* and *C* are incorrect because they describe actions that would result in vehicle damage or risk the injury or death of the driver and/or passengers.

Section: Doubles and Triples

51. B: Crack-the-whip refers to the effect of rearward amplification, in which the last trailer of a double or triple is impacted most by side-to-side movement. Quick side-to-side movements, such as changing lanes rapidly, can cause a trailer to flip on its side as a result. Choice *A* is incorrect because the sound of air brakes is not magnified in doubles and triples. Although changing lanes can cause the crack-the-whip effect, Choice *C* is incorrect because the effect is unrelated to judging whether changing lanes is safe. Choice *D* is incorrect because controlling speed affects the front-to-back movement of a vehicle, rather than the side-to-side movement involved in the crack-the-whip effect.

52. C: Lowering the landing gear of the trailer will reduce the weight load on the dolly, which makes uncoupling easier. Choice *A* is incorrect because the trailer should be stabilized either through spring brakes or by chocking the wheels. Choice *B* is incorrect because a check for damage should occur during a previous walk-around inspection. Choice *D* is incorrect because the spring brakes are not connected to the landing gear.

53. A: Most of the procedure used for coupling and uncoupling doubles can be used for triples as well. As a result, Choice *C* is incorrect by default. Choice *B* is incorrect because the tractor should be coupled to the first trailer before additional trailers are coupled. Choice *D* is incorrect because converter dollies are used to connect trailers to each other, including triples.

54. A: The shut-off valves at the back of the front trailers should be open during a walk-around inspection, while the shut-off valves at the back of the last trailer should be closed. Choice *B* is incorrect because leaving the valves on the last trailer open would let air leave the system, causing the brakes to fail. Choices *C* and *D* are incorrect because closing the valves of the front trailer would not allow air to travel through the lines to the last trailer.

55. D: By briefly opening the emergency shut-off valve and listening for air flow, a driver can determine whether air is reaching all of the trailers. Choice *A* is incorrect because closed valves will not make a sound that indicates air flow. Choice *B* is incorrect because the trailer air-supply knob is located in the tractor. Choice *C* is incorrect because opening the cargo doors will not allow a driver to hear air flow in the braking system.

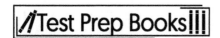

Section: Tank Vehicles

56. A: Tank endorsement is required for Class A and Class B vehicles hauling a total cargo (liquid or gas) of at least 1,000 gallons in containers that are at least 119 gallons, or for Class C vehicles hauling hazardous materials or sixteen or more passengers. Choice *B* is incorrect because the individual containers are less than 119 gallons each. Choice *C* is incorrect because the total cargo is less than 1,000 gallons. Choice *D* is incorrect because the vehicle is not hauling hazardous materials or sixteen passengers.

57. D: A class-action lawsuit is not a likely penalty for hauling a tank with a leak. Such a lawsuit occurs when many individuals are damaged by an action, usually one by a large company rather than an individual driver. Choices *A*, *B*, and *C* are all incorrect because they are possible penalties for driving with a leaking tank.

58. B: A bulkhead splits a tank up into smaller sections, which reduces the effect of back-to-front sloshing. Choice *A* is incorrect because bulkheads don't minimize the side-to-side momentum that might cause a tank to tip on its side. Choice *C* is incorrect because bulkheads have no means to reduce pressure within a tank; they are simply solid barriers that divide the tank. Choice *D* is incorrect because the bulkheads are inside the tank and have no effect on the damage from a spill.

59. D: Outage refers to the expansion of liquid in a tank due to heat. As a result, a little room in the tank should be left to accommodate the expansion. Choice *A* is incorrect because the cargo that spills from a leak would be referred to as spillage. Choice *B* is incorrect, although it relates to outage because the density of a liquid increases as it expands. Choice *C* is incorrect because cold temperatures cause decreases in pressure.

60. C: An empty tanker may take longer to stop than a full tanker. This is because the full weight of the cargo keeps the tires down, providing more traction. This means that Choice *D* is incorrect. Choice *A* is incorrect because tankers use the same kinds of braking systems that other tractor trailers use. Choice *B* is incorrect because liquid surges commonly occur while braking with tankers. Having bulkheads in the tank can minimize this.

Section: Hazardous Materials

61. C: The regulations found in 49 CFR 100-185 concern the transportation of hazardous materials. Title 49 of the CFR regulates the Department of Transportation in general. Choice *A* is incorrect because Title 29 of the CFR regulates the Department of Labor. Choice *B* is incorrect because Title 39 regulates the Postal Service. Choice *D* is incorrect because Title 59 of the CFR does not exist. The Code is divided into 50 titles.

62. A: The shipper is responsible for marking cargo as hazardous, as well as for providing the required paperwork, emergency information, and placards. Choice *B* is incorrect because the driver doesn't necessarily know what they are transporting without the shipper's information. Choices *C* and *D* are incorrect because neither the receiver nor the federal government would have access to the materials before they are shipped.

63. D: The driver is responsible for placarding the vehicle with the materials that the shipper provides. Choices *A*, *B*, and *C* are incorrect because these are all duties that the shipper is responsible for.

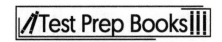

64. B: If an accident occurs, the driver may be unable to provide the papers showing the hazardous cargo. If the papers are easily accessible, first responders still may be able to find them and determine the most appropriate course of action. Choice *A* is incorrect because reading while transporting the cargo (i.e., driving) is very dangerous. Choice *C* is incorrect because placarding should have occurred prior to transporting the cargo. Choice *D* is incorrect because keeping papers together is not related to making them easily accessible.

65. A: Hazardous material spills of a reportable quantity must be reported, either by the driver or the driver's employer, to the federal Department of Transportation and the Environmental Protection Agency. Appendix A to 49 CFR 172.101 lists the reportable quantities for different hazardous materials. Choices *B*, *C*, and *D* are incorrect because hazardous material spills do not need to be reported to the Departments of Labor, Energy, or Health and Human Services.

66. D: Hazardous material placards must be displayed on both sides and both ends of the vehicle. Choices *A*, *B*, and *C* are incorrect because each of these choices indicate placard placement on only one side or end of the vehicle.

67. C: Class 5 Oxidizers must be transported using closed cargo space. Choices *A*, *B*, and *D* are incorrect because flammable gases, flammable liquids, and poisons can all be transported in open cargo space; they do not have the same closed space restrictions as oxidizers, explosives, or flammable solids.

68. C: Per federal regulations, it is illegal to drive a cargo tank for hazardous materials with open valves or covers unless the tank is empty. Choices *A* and *D* are incorrect because the regulations make no exception due to speed or distance traveled. Choice *B* is incorrect because a vehicle carrying hazardous materials should be placarded properly anyway.

69. B: A vehicle hauling Division 1.1, 1.2, or 1.3 explosives must park at least 300 feet from open fires, bridges, tunnels, buildings, or places where people meet. Choice *A* is incorrect because 100 feet from open fire may be too close and cause an explosion. Choices *B* and *D* are incorrect because, while relatively safe options, parking 500 or 1,000 feet away from an open fire would not be necessary.

70. D: A vehicle hauling a water tank would not be required to stop at a railroad crossing. The vehicles listed in Choices *A*, *B*, and *C* are all required to stop at a railroad crossing. Please note that a vehicle with a hazardous material cargo tank, whether it is loaded or empty (as indicated in Choice *C*), is required to stop at a railroad crossing.

71. A: The National Response Center coordinates emergency response related to chemical hazards and should be contacted by a driver or driver's employer right away if a death results from a hazardous materials incident. Choice *B* is incorrect because the Federal Bureau of Investigation is responsible for enforcing the law and investigating crime. Choice *C* is incorrect because the Centers for Disease Control is responsible for providing information and tools to people to protect their health. Choice *D* is incorrect because the National Institutes of Health is responsible for conducting medical research.

72. B: The Emergency Response Guidebook, published by the Department of Transportation, is used by emergency workers to determine the best course of action in response to hazardous materials emergencies. They often reference a driver's shipping papers to determine the materials in question. Choices *A* and *D* are incorrect because drivers do not use the Emergency Response Guidebook. Additionally, drivers should know to contact their employer, if applicable, and the local authorities. Shipping papers should contain the proper name of the materials being transported. Choice *C* is

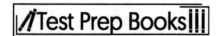

incorrect because, while the Guidebook does contain first aid techniques, they are a minor focus of the book and would not be very useful for EMTs.

Section: School Buses

73. B: The risk of passing cars makes the left side of a school bus a danger zone. Choice *A* is incorrect because children typically exit a school bus from its right side. Choice *C* is incorrect because drunk drivers are not a risk that is specific to the left side of a school bus. Choice *D* is incorrect because a bus is more likely to impact a child that is in front of the bus.

74. D: The blind spot at the back of a bus can extend as far as 400 feet, depending on the length and width of the bus. Choices *A*, *B*, and *C* are incorrect because, while these are typical blind spot distances, blind spots can actually extend much further.

75. B: A driver should activate the alternating flashing amber warning lights at least 200 feet, or 5 to 10 seconds prior to the stop. Choice *A* is incorrect because 50 feet is not enough of a warning distance. Choices *C* and *D* are incorrect because they are excessively long warning distances that could needlessly cause traffic problems among other drivers.

76. A: The first step to take if a student appears to be missing is to ask other students where that student might be. Additionally, check mirrors and surroundings to see if the student is running to catch the bus. Choices *B* and *C* are incorrect because it is not the duty of a bus driver to report absences or truancy to parents or to schools under normal circumstances. Choice *D* is incorrect because steps should first be taken to attempt to account for the missing student before proceeding.

77. C: It is possible for students to try to return to the bus to retrieve an item they left behind. A driver should check their mirrors to see if any students are approaching. Choice *A* is incorrect because mirror orientation should be checked pre-trip, although occasional re-checks are fine. Choice *B* is incorrect because passing cars is generally not a concern when unloading students at school. Choice *D* is incorrect because dirty mirrors should be checked pre-trip.

78. A: The safety of the students is paramount. As such, a bus that is on fire should be evacuated and the students should be directed to a place upwind of the fire. Choice *B* is incorrect because being downwind of a fire could put the students at risk as the fire spreads. Choice *C* is incorrect because fighting the fire puts students at great risk of injury or death. Choice *D* is incorrect because it is more important to get the students away from the fire. The driver can check for injuries after making sure the students are safe from further harm.

79. C: The bus should be no closer than 15 feet and no further than 50 feet from the closest rail when stopping at a railroad crossing. Choices *A* and *B* are incorrect because they would allow the bus to be stopped closer than 15 feet from the closest rail. Choice *D* is incorrect because it would allow the bus to be stopped further than 50 feet from the closest rail.

80. D: If a student's behavior is out of control and is making it unsafe to drive, a driver should stop the bus and call for school officials or the police to get the student. Choice *A* is incorrect because restraining the student should only be done in self-defense or to protect other students, at which point the authorities should be called. Choice *B* is incorrect because it is unsafe for the student to be removed from the bus unless the bus is at school or their designated stop. Choice *C* is incorrect because it may be

hazardous to continue driving in such a situation. Additionally, the issue needs to be dealt with rather than ignored.

81. B: Buses built before 1998 were not required to have ABS, but many of these buses that are still in operation have been voluntarily equipped with these systems. Choice *A* is incorrect because buses with air brakes have been required to have ABS since 1998 (or 1999 for hydraulic brakes). Choice *C* is incorrect because buses equipped with ABS will have a yellow ABS malfunction lamp on the instrumentation panel. Choice *D* is incorrect because all vehicles with ABS can use the same braking techniques.

82. A: In windy conditions, slowing down can reduce the impact of the wind. Choice *B* is incorrect because accelerating or speeding up can increase the influence that the wind has on the bus. Choice *C* is incorrect because shifting to a higher gear does nothing to increase the stability of a vehicle. Choice *D* is incorrect because, aside from alerting other drivers of potential danger (such as the wind blowing the bus into them), turning on emergency flashers does nothing to improve the safety of the bus or its passengers.

Section: Pre-Trip Inspection

83. A: There should be no more than 3/4 inch of play in the center of a belt to ensure a snug fit. Choices *B*, *C*, and *D* are incorrect because they indicate a belt that is too loose and could detach.

84. B: Checking the service brakes is done to ensure that the brakes are working properly and that the vehicle is not pulling to one side. Choice *A* is incorrect because a brake system that uses brake fluid will not also use air pressure to function. Choices *C* and *D* are incorrect because the service brakes are a separate system from the parking brake.

85. D: Tread depth should be at least 4/32 inches on the steering axle tires. Choices *A*, *B*, and *C* are incorrect because they are not enough tread depth for the steering axle tires. Please note that a depth of 2/32 inch is acceptable for tires that are not on the steering axle.

86. C: In a fifth wheel setup that is air-powered, make sure that there are no leaks, because these could cause malfunction. Choices *A*, *B*, and *D* are incorrect because they are all normal parts of a fifth wheel inspection, regardless of whether or not it is air-powered.

87. D: Torn or split seat cushions are not a necessary check for school bus seating. Choices *A*, *B*, and *C* are incorrect because they are all checks that should be conducted, as they are directly related to the safety of the passengers.

88. A: If a driver has a cargo lift, it should be fully retracted, firmly latched, and show no signs of leaks or damage during the pre-trip inspection. Choices *B* and *D* are incorrect because the cargo lift should not be extended during the inspection. Choice *C*, as well as Choice *D*, is incorrect because glad hands are not a part of the cargo lift.

89. C: The emergency exits of a coach or transit bus should be checked during the internal inspection of the bus, including ensuring that they close completely from the inside. Choices *A*, *B*, and *D* are incorrect because they should all be part of the external inspection of the bus.

251

90. B: A driver applying for a Class A CDL must complete only one of the four types of pre-trip inspection but will not be told which one will be conducted. Choices *A*, *C*, and *D* are all incorrect.

Section: Basic Control Skills test

91. C: The basic control skills exam could include offset backing, parallel parking, and straight-line backing (as well as alley docking). Choices *A*, *B*, and *D* are incorrect because neither forward driving nor perpendicular parking would be a maneuver on the exam; forward driving is assumed and perpendicular parking is generally not done by CDL class vehicles.

92. A: If a driver is allowed to do an outside vehicle observation to check its position, he or she should put the vehicle in neutral, set the parking brake, and exit while continuously maintaining three points of contact (e.g., two hands and one foot stay on the vehicle at all times). Choice *B* is incorrect because the driver should put the vehicle in neutral, not in park. Choices *C* and *D* are incorrect because a driver must maintain three points of contact, not two.

93. C: Offset backing involves backing up into a space that is either to the left or right side of the vehicle. Choices *A* and *B* are incorrect because offset backing can occur regardless of whether or not a trailer is attached. Choice *D* is incorrect because backing into a space directly behind the vehicle is called straight-line backing.

94. B: The position of a driver's hands on the steering wheel does not factor into the scoring process (however, improper placement of the driver's hands on the wheel might make the examiner nervous and cause them to grade more strictly). Choices *A*, *C*, and *D* are incorrect because encroachments, excessive pull-ups, and excessive vehicle exits can lower a test-taker's score.

95. D: Backing into a space on the right side with cones in the front and back of the space is conventional parallel parking. Choices *A* and *B* are incorrect because offset backing would not make use of cones in the front of the space. Choice *C* is incorrect because, in the U.S., the driver's side of the vehicle is the left side. Right side parallel parking is more conventional, hence the name.

Section: On-Road Driving

96. C: When stopping in traffic behind another vehicle, there should be enough space between the vehicles for the driver to see the front vehicle's rear tires. Choices *A* and *B* are incorrect because they are too close and not enough buffer to effectively reduce the chance of a rear-end collision if something goes wrong. Conversely, Choice *D* is incorrect because it is an unnecessarily long space between the two vehicles.

97. A: When driving back into traffic after pulling over, start by pulling away straight before steering back onto the road. This allows the driver to enter road at a similar speed to other traffic and gives other drivers more warning of the re-entry. Choice *B* is incorrect because leaving the four-way flashers on makes the left turn signal (or right turn signal, if needed) ineffective; it will not inform other drivers of the intent to re-enter traffic. Choice *C* is incorrect because a driver should re-enter traffic when it is safe to do so, not after a specific length of travel. Choice *D* is incorrect because the turn signal should be used instead of the horn to indicate re-entry.

98. B: The examiner may ask a driver about information about traffic signs during an on-road test, so it is important to be able to recognize and describe any traffic signs along the route. Choices *A* and *C* are

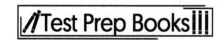

incorrect because these pieces of information would be too frivolous and distracting for a driver to worry about during the on-road test. Choice *D* is incorrect because a destination might not be known or given during testing.

99. D: When making a left-hand turn on multi-lane roads, the driver should finish in the lane that is directly to the right of the center line. Choice *A* is incorrect because it forces the driver across more lanes of traffic than are necessary, which could cause accidents as other drivers also make the turn. Choices *B* and *C* are incorrect because they can lead the driver into oncoming traffic.

100. A: Shifting gears is the only situation in which it is acceptable to drive while using only one hand on the steering wheel. In fact, it would be impossible to shift gears otherwise! Choice *B* is incorrect because drivers should not make phone calls while driving; pull over and stop if an emergency call is needed. Choice *C* is incorrect because the turn signal can be activated while both hands are on the wheel. Choice *D* is incorrect because backing up is potentially more dangerous than driving forward and requires a greater sense of control. Therefore, both hands should be used.

CDL Practice Test #3

To keep the size of this book manageable, save paper, and provide a digital test-taking experience, the 3rd practice test can be found online. Scan the QR code or go to this link to access it:

testprepbooks.com/bonus/cdl

The first time you access the test, you will need to register as a "new user" and verify your email address.

If you have any issues, please email support@testprepbooks.com.

Index

Dear CDL Test Taker,

We would like to start by thanking you for purchasing this study guide for your CDL exam. We hope that we exceeded your expectations.

Our goal in creating this study guide was to cover all of the topics that you will see on the test. We also strove to make our practice questions as similar as possible to what you will encounter on test day. With that being said, if you found something that you feel was not up to your standards, please send us an email and let us know.

We have study guides in a wide variety of fields. If you're interested in one, try searching for it on Amazon or send us an email.

Thanks Again and Happy Testing!
Product Development Team
info@studyguideteam.com

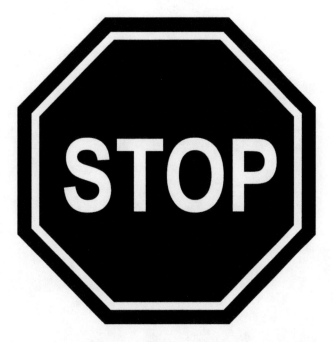

FREE Test Taking Tips Video/DVD Offer

To better serve you, we created videos covering test taking tips that we want to give you for FREE. **These videos cover world-class tips that will help you succeed on your test.**

We just ask that you send us feedback about this product. Please let us know what you thought about it—whether good, bad, or indifferent.

To get your **FREE videos**, you can use the QR code below or email freevideos@studyguideteam.com with "Free Videos" in the subject line and the following information in the body of the email:

   a. The title of your product

   b. Your product rating on a scale of 1-5, with 5 being the highest

   c. Your feedback about the product

If you have any questions or concerns, please don't hesitate to contact us at info@studyguideteam.com.

Thank you!